# Provider-Led Population Health Management:

Key Strategies for Healthcare in the
Cognitive Era, 2$^{nd}$ Edition

**Richard Hodach, MD, MPH, PhD**
**Paul Grundy, MD, MPH**
**Anil Jain, MD, FACP**
**Michael Weiner, DO, MSM, MSIST**

Provider-Led Population Health Management: Key Strategies for Healthcare in the Cognitive Era, 2nd Edition

Published by
John Wiley & Sons, Inc.
10475 Crosspoint Boulevard
Indianapolis, IN 46256
www.wiley.com

Copyright © 2016 by John Wiley & Sons, Inc., Indianapolis, Indiana

Published simultaneously in Canada

ISBN: 9781119277231

ISBN: 9781119277255(ebk)

Manufactured in the United States of America

10 9 8 7 6 5 4 3 2 1

# About the Authors

**Richard Hodach, MD, MPH, PhD,** is Vice President, IBM Watson Health, previously serving as Chief Medical Officer and Vice President of Clinical Product Strategy at Phytel, now part of IBM Watson Health. Dr. Hodach has long been recognized as a leader of population health management strategies. He is responsible for providing strategic direction and clinical expertise for the development of Phytel's solutions. Dr. Hodach is a regular contributor to prestigious peer-review journals such as *The American Journal of Managed Care, The Journal of Population Health Management, hfm* (published by the Healthcare Financial Management Association), *The Group Practice Journal,* and more. He was instrumental in the CMS Innovation Award of a $20.75 million grant which Phytel, VHA Inc., and TransforMED received from The Center for Medicare & Medicaid Innovation (CMMI). In addition to his leadership position at Phytel, Dr. Hodach also serves on the board of directors of the American College of Medical Quality. Before joining Phytel, he held senior leadership positions at Matria Healthcare and Accordant, and co-founded MED.I.A. Dr. Hodach has a Ph.D. in Pathology and an M.D. with Board Certification in Neurology and Electrodiagnosis, as well as a Master's Degree in Public Health.

**Paul Grundy, MD, MPH,** is Global Director, Healthcare Transformation at IBM, and President of the Patient-Centered Primary Care Collaborative. Dr. Grundy is known as the "godfather" of the patient-centered medical home. An active social entrepreneur and speaker on global healthcare transformation, he concentrates his efforts on driving comprehensive, linked, and integrated healthcare. Dr. Grundy's work has been covered by *The New York Times, BusinessWeek, Health Affairs, The Economist, The New England Journal of Medicine,* and other newspapers, radio, and television stations across the U.S. He is a healthcare ambassador for the nation of Denmark and adjunct professor at the University of Utah Department of Family and Preventive Medicine. Dr. Grundy is a member of National Academy of Science's Institute of Medicine, director of the ACGME, and member of the national advisory board of the National Center for Interprofessional Practice & Education, Mayo Clinic Center for Connected Care. He is a retired senior diplomat with the rank of Minister Consular U.S. State Department. Dr. Grundy graduated as valedictorian from the Southern California College, earned an M.D. from the University of California–San Francisco Medical School, and received a Masters of Public Health from the University of California–Berkeley.

**Anil Jain, MD, FACP,** is Senior Vice President and Chief Medical Officer, IBM Watson Health, previously serving as Chief Medical Officer of Explorys (now part of IBM Watson Health), formed in 2009 based on innovations that he developed while at the Cleveland Clinic. In this role, Dr. Jain directs the informatics and analytics innovations, product management, and software development, as well as leading the life sciences business unit. In addition to serving on state and national committees focused on driving quality and research through health IT, he has authored more than 100 publications and abstracts and has delivered numerous talks on the benefits of sustainable health IT innovation, clinical informatics, and big data analytics. Dr. Jain also continues to practice and teach medicine part-time in the Department of Internal Medicine at Cleveland Clinic and had previously served as an Attending Staff and Senior Executive Director of IT. He is a former leader at Better Health Greater Cleveland and had served as co-Director of Informatics of Case Western School of Medicine's CTSA. Dr. Jain is an active member of the Health Information Management & Systems Society (HIMSS) and the American Medical Informatics Association (AMIA), and is a Fellow of the American College of Medicine (ACP), and is also a Diplomat of the American Board of Internal Medicine (ABIM). He received a degree in Biomedical Engineering and a degree in Medicine from Northwestern University prior to his post-graduate training in Internal Medicine at the Cleveland Clinic.

**Michael Weiner, DO, MSM, MSIST,** is Chief Medical Information Officer at IBM. Prior to his current position with IBM, Dr. Weiner served as the Chief Medical Information Officer and Director of Clinical Informatics for the DoD VA Interagency Program Office, where he was responsible for creating a unified Interagency Electronic Health Record for more than 125,000 providers and 18 million beneficiaries worldwide. He is an active member of the American College of Physicians and the American Osteopathic Association, and is a former NASA Space Shuttle takeoff and landing physician. Dr. Weiner serves on the Philadelphia College of Osteopathic Medicine Alumni Board and the board of the American Medical Informatics Association, as well as having served on the Health and Human Services' Office of the National Coordinator Health Information IT Policy Committee, helping create Meaningful Use Stage 1. He has received numerous awards from the President of the United States, for his service in the Navy, including two Meritorious Service Medals, and two Air Medals. Dr. Weiner is an adjunct professor of Health Information Technology at the George Washington University and is one of only a few physicians ever to have been certified as a Chief Information Officer by the U.S. General Services Administration. He is a graduate of the U.S. Naval Academy and attended medical school at the Philadelphia College of Osteopathic Medicine. Dr. Weiner is a board-certified practicing physician in Internal Medicine, and holds a Master's degree in Management and a Master's degree in Information Systems Technology from George Washington University.

# Credits

**Associate Publisher:** Jim Minatel

**Vice President, Professional Technology & Strategy:** Barry Pruett

**Editorial Manager:** Rev Mengle

**Project Editor:** Paul Levesque

**Copy Editor:** Becky Whitney

**Production Editor:** Barath Kumar Rajasekaran

**Special Help:** Camille Graves

**Cover Designer:** Michael Trent

# ACKNOWLEDGMENTS

We would like to thank the extraordinary group of people who made significant contributions to this book. Without them, this book would certainly not exist.

Bill Buck
Ted Courtemanche
Donna Daniel
Jerry Green
Jon Mark Harmon
Jeffrey Havlock
Guy Mansueto
Adam McCoy
Jorge Miranda
Russell Olsen
Marina Pascali
Mavis Prall
Kristy Sanders
Steve Schelhammer
Carly Sheppard-Knoll
Ken Terry

# CONTENTS

# FOREWORD

Health care in the U.S. does not function as an effective system for a variety of well-documented reasons, as I pointed out in my introduction to the textbook *Population Health: Creating a Culture of Wellness*. With a strong push from the federal government, as well as private payers, the U.S. health care industry is slowly pivoting toward value-based reimbursement. This transition to "income for outcome" will incentivize health care providers to pay more attention to non-visit care and will induce health care organizations to start managing the *health* of their patient populations, not just their health *care*. Only by doing so can they hope to reduce costs and improve quality enough to succeed financially under the new payment models. Moreover, to manage care properly, disparate health care providers and institutions will have to cooperate with each other to build a real health care system.

The premise of *this* book, contained in its title, is that population health management (PHM) cannot succeed unless physicians, their care teams, extended care networks, and community resources align with each other. It makes a whole lot of sense for doctors to play a leading role in population health management. Outside of friends and family, consumers trust physicians more than any other health care constituency, and certainly more than insurance or drug companies. The doctor-patient relationship is the key to patient engagement, which can lead to improved medication adherence, evidence-based guideline compliance, and lasting, sustainable health behavior change.

Written by the experienced team at IBM Watson Health, the book focuses sharply on the practical mechanics of how healthcare organizations can transition to population health management. While generous dollops of theory are also provided, the most germane parts of the book describe the practice of this new model (to most practitioners) of health care delivery.

For example, consider the chapters about consumer engagement and the social determinants of health. Individual engagement is a prerequisite of population health management; without it, people are less likely to make the lifestyle changes required to prevent or reduce the impact of chronic illnesses. But to get individuals engaged and support them in self-care management, health care providers must also be aware of the social determinants of each person's health. As noted in Chapter 13, clinical health care accounts for only 10%-25% of the variations in individual health over time. Health care's influence on the length of quality life would be markedly augmented, however, if it were combined with efforts to improve the social, economic, emotional, and physical environmental factors that contribute to health.

Research supports the need for population health management to extend beyond health care. Collaboration among providers on care coordination will ultimately need to incorporate social services, behavioral health, job placement and advancement, housing, and possibly spiritual and other community resources.

During my tenure in many population health leadership roles, including being the Global Medical Leader of GE and Corporate Medical Director for Truven Health Analytics, I learned the importance of paying attention to all health determinants, especially in engaging non-adherent individuals. Often their adherence can be supported by enlisting other domains for assistance. Many people are more inclined to manage their own care, for example, after establishing a home to live in and finding a steady job.

Another theme that runs through the book is the need to build a health IT infrastructure that can support population health management. Initially, many health care delivery systems assumed that they could simply rely on their EHR vendor to give them everything they needed. But experience has demonstrated that the EHR is only a starting point. It requires additional advanced data sources, cognitive analytics, secure, cloud-based platforms and mobile capabilities to establish a robust population health solution.

Moreover, PHM requires the ability to aggregate, normalize and analyze data from many different sources. Individuals receive their care across multiple care settings; many different care providers function inside a variety of delivery systems; and members of accountable care organizations (ACOs) utilize many different EHRs and patient portals. To connect these providers and health records requires the pursuit of interoperability, which is still largely lacking in health IT systems. These systems also lack the kind of clinical decision support and automation tools needed to facilitate care management and to make it efficient and effective. Longitudinal care coordination will ultimately require a personal health record that includes data from all care settings in which the patient has been treated.

The book's final chapter takes an in-depth look at the exciting developments in cognitive computing, which has the potential to take health care and PHM to a whole new level. A next-generation big data approach, cognitive computing can help health care organizations understand their populations better by providing insights into factors such as demographics, geographical location, behavioral health, transportation, lifestyle choices, consumer purchases, and socioeconomic status.

Cognitive computing can also search the medical literature in seconds, can use natural language processing to convert unstructured data into structured data, can improve predictive modeling, and can provide the analytic power to help physicians understand the genomic information about the people on their panel. This is what doctors will need in 21st century medicine. On their own, they will never be able to absorb more than a tiny fraction of the 1 million new published articles that come out each year. And with the emergence of genomics, proteomics, and microbiomics data, analytics will be an essential part of everyday medicine. Doctors will require significant learning — indeed, cognitive — computing resources to determine the relevance of all this data so they can provide highly personalized care, precision medicine, and the most appropriate care pathway for each person.

The most valuable lesson you will gain from this book, however, is that health care providers can impact the health status of the communities they serve. By doing so, they can improve the health of individuals and can also contribute to their performance as workers and as family and community members. The potential impact is enormous. This can lead not only to a higher quality of life for individuals, but also to enhanced productivity for employers and greater prosperity for communities.

Ray Fabius, MD
Co-founder, HealthNext
Former Chief Medical Officer, Truven Health Analytics,
and GE Global Medical Leader

# INTRODUCTION

The $3.2 trillion healthcare industry, as conventional wisdom has it, is a big ship to turn around. But employers, consumers, and government can no longer afford healthcare costs that, while growing more slowly than in past years, have reached stratospheric levels.[1] The fee-for-service payment system that rewards providers for the volume of services has been implicated in the high cost of health care.[2] So, with a concerted push from payers, the industry is in the midst of a rapidly accelerating shift from fee-for-service to various forms of pay-for-value.

The Centers for Medicare and Medicaid Services (CMS) has already taken a number of steps in its transition to value-based payments. To start with, the Medicare Shared Savings Program (MSSP) is rewarding accountable care organizations (ACOs) that create savings and meet quality goals.[3] Though most of the 434 ACOs participating in this program today are taking only upside risk in the form of shared savings, many of them will have to accept downside risk as well, starting in 2018, if they choose to renew their MSSP contracts.[4] Moreover, CMS has launched a Next Generation ACO program with 21 ACOs that have agreed to take financial risk in return for higher rewards.[5] CMS also has placed a small portion of hospitals' Medicare revenue at risk for achieving cost and quality goals, and it began applying a similar pay-for-performance program to physicians in 2015.[6,7]

By the end of 2018, half of Medicare payments are expected to go to alternative payment models (APMs) such as ACOs, patient-centered medical homes (PCMHs), and bundled payments.[8] Further, the new law that replaces the sustainable growth rate (SGR) formula with a different Medicare payment approach gives physicians involved in APMs a 5 percent annual bonus from 2019 to 2024.[9]

Private payers are moving in tandem with CMS. In March 2014, Anthem BlueCross BlueShield, one of the nation's largest health insurers, said that it had tied a third of its commercial reimbursements to pay-for-value quality programs.[10] UnitedHealth Group said it was expanding its incentive programs, with a goal of offering at least half of its network physicians the ability to earn bonuses for value, quality, and efficiency within a few years.[11] Aetna is paying incentives to practices that have achieved PCMH recognition and is working with scores of provider groups and health systems to create ACOs.[12]

About half of the 700-plus ACOs have contracts with private payers. Most of these contracts are based on shared savings rather than on capitation, which is a set monthly fee for each member of a patient population. But 45 percent of private-payer agreements include downside risk, meaning that providers can lose money if their healthcare spending exceeds their budget.[13]

What all of this means is that healthcare providers can no longer avoid the reality that their current business models are obsolete. As they transition to new care-delivery methods, they must stop basing business decisions on how their clinicians and facilities can produce additional, and ever more costly, billable services. Those services and facilities have been profit centers until now; but in the new world of value-based reimbursement and financial risk, they are becoming cost centers.

The fulcrum of profitability in this new world is maintaining or improving patients' health and delivering good outcomes. The only proven way to achieve these goals is to manage population health effectively and efficiently. To do that, healthcare organizations need advanced health IT, including analytics and automation tools that enable them to transform their mindset, culture, and work processes.

# Changing the Mindset

Except for group-model health maintenance organizations (HMOs) such as Kaiser Permanente and Group Health Cooperative, certain large groups and independent practice associations (IPAs) in California, and a few healthcare systems in other states, healthcare providers are not well positioned for population health management (PHM). While many healthcare organizations are creating new structures to prepare for value-based reimbursement, health care is still oriented to fee-for-service. Physician practices still organize care around office visits, and hospitals focus on acute care within their four walls.

One recent study found that physician practices of all sizes increased their use of evidence-based care management processes from 2006 to 2013. But, by the end of that period, even large groups used fewer than half of the recommended processes for chronic disease management, on average.[14]

The concept of caring for entire patient populations on a continuous basis, whether or not individual patients seek care, is only gradually seeping into the consciousness of healthcare managers and providers. And it is still difficult for many provider organizations to accept the idea that filling beds and appointment slots is less important than ensuring that all patients receive recommended preventive and chronic condition care.

To transform themselves, above all, organizations must have a leadership team that understands and embraces the implications of changing from a volume-based culture to a value-based one and the tenacity to stay the course. Health systems acknowledge the road to value is not smooth, but many report it is rewarding, even joyful for clinicians and staff at all levels.[15]

In terms of the work to be done, organizations must reduce two kinds of waste: first, the avoidable tests, procedures, and hospital admissions and readmissions that lead to high costs for employers and consumers; and second, the internal waste that inflates the cost of care delivery. The reorganization of care processes can address both kinds of waste simultaneously by improving the quality and efficiency of care.

Organizations that go down this path need to adopt consistent policies and procedures, starting with a common set of clinical protocols. They must form care teams that can coordinate care for every patient, tailoring their approach to the individual's health risks and conditions; restructure workflows so that each member of the care team is working up to the limit of his or her training and skill sets; and use their care managers as efficiently as possible in order to provide appropriate support to all patients who need help.

Electronic health records (EHRs) are essential to any PHM strategy. But EHRs are not designed to support PHM. Though they can supply much of the data required to track and monitor patients' health and identify care gaps, they must be combined with claims data to provide a broad view of population health and to track individual patients across care settings. Moreover, providers need electronic registries to identify care gaps and provide the near-real-time data required to intervene with subgroups of patients efficiently and in a timely manner. Although some EHRs include such registries, they're not as complete, flexible, or usable as those available from third-party developers.

The IT infrastructure for PHM must also include applications that automate the routine, repetitive work of care management. These automation tools offer several advantages: First, they can lower the cost of care management by taking over time-consuming chart research and outreach work. Second, they free up care managers to devote personal attention to high-risk patients who urgently need their help. Third, they allow providers to do essential pre-visit planning and post-visit follow up on a consistent basis. Fourth, they can bring noncompliant patients back in touch with their personal physicians. And fifth, these tools enable organizations to quickly scale up their care management efforts so that they can continuously care for all patients in their population.

Most important, the combination of these tools offers a mechanism for engaging patients in their own health care. Without patient engagement, population health management is impossible.

## Current Trends

The rise of accountable care organizations in recent years reflects the concurrent emergence of value-based reimbursement and financial-risk contracts. Composed of physicians and hospitals that are committed to lowering costs and improving quality, ACOs must be able to deliver high-quality care within a budget. Strategies such as admitting patients to lower-cost hospitals and de-emphasizing expensive tests can help them do this in the short term; but in the long term, ACOs will have to manage population health well to be successful.

The patient-centered medical home — a holistic approach to primary care that includes a whole-person orientation and integrated care coordination — is considered an essential building block of ACOs. The National Committee for Quality Assurance (NCQA) has awarded medical home recognition to more than 10,000 practices, composed of over 48,000 providers, and the number of PCMHs is growing rapidly.[16]

The growth of patient-centered medical homes bodes well for the transformation of health care through ACOs and other APMs. But to coordinate care effectively across care settings, the primary care physicians who have built medical homes must gain the cooperation of specialists, hospitals, and other healthcare players in the medical neighborhood.

This might seem like a no-brainer at a time when healthcare organizations are trying to prepare for value-based payments. But during this transitional period, when most specialists and hospitals still depend to a large extent on volume-based reimbursement, it is not easy for primary care doctors to persuade them that their future success depends on working with medical homes to coordinate care and reduce costs. Physicians employed by healthcare systems will follow organizational directives to some extent, but at least half of physicians are still in independent practices.[17]

Some healthcare organizations, including hospital systems and independent practice associations (IPAs), have formed clinically integrated networks (CINs) that facilitate the collaboration of providers across care settings and business boundaries under value-based contract mechanisms. These networks, which depend on health IT for communications and data sharing, can connect providers who otherwise might not collaborate with one another. By improving coordination among these providers, they can provide the foundation of effective ACOs.

# Patient Engagement

As mentioned earlier, patient engagement is the sine qua non of population health management. At a population-wide level, this is about ensuring that patients take good care of themselves and comply with doctors' recommendations for proper preventive and chronic care as well as better health behavior. Fully half of disease prevention is up to patients, including their diet, exercise, and smoking behavior.[18]

But acute care, especially in hospitals and ambulatory surgery centers, also requires patient engagement for optimal outcomes. Patients must not only prepare for procedures but also follow their post-discharge care plans and take the medications that have been prescribed for them.

It is unrealistic to expect certain patients — especially those who are elderly, very ill, poorly educated, or suffering from mental health conditions — to comply fully with their discharge instructions. Even if they want to, they may be unable to comply, because they cannot afford their medications or can't obtain appointments with their primary care physicians. So in a world of accountable care and value-based payments, providers must learn how to help these patients and get them involved in their own care after they leave the hospital.

The government's Meaningful Use EHR incentive program encourages providers to engage patients in several ways. In Stage 2 of Meaningful Use, eligible professionals (EPs) and eligible hospitals must share records with patients online. EPs must also communicate with patients via secure online messaging and must send them reminders about preventive care.[19] The final rule for Stage 3 requires that patient-generated data be incorporated into the EHR for more than 5 percent of all patients seen by an EP or discharged from an eligible hospital or emergency department during a reporting period. These may include a variety of inputs, including data from home health monitors, wearable devices, and patient-reported outcome data.[20]

Meanwhile, technology offers several other avenues for engaging patients. Automated patient-outreach programs can message patients by email, text, or phone, reminding them to make appointments with their doctors for needed preventive and chronic care.[21] Text messaging has been shown to help certain kinds of patients, such as people with diabetes and pregnant women, take better care of their health.[22] Educational materials tailored to individual patients can be made available online. And personal health records (PHRs) — which can be used to download, store, and transmit health records — can help patients keep track of their care plans and medications and communicate with their providers.[23]

Recent advances in home telemonitoring and telehealth using mobile devices not only provide the opportunity for remote consultations but also generate data that can keep providers and care managers apprised of patients' conditions between visits.[24] Of course, these new data streams could easily overwhelm providers; the information must be carefully screened so that caregivers see only relevant data for decision-making and intervention.

# A Roadmap for Population Health Management

No two healthcare organizations are exactly the same or operate in the same environment with the same population. Nevertheless, as this book makes clear, provider organizations can follow a common roadmap that will take them close to where they want to go.

That map begins with the risk stratification of their population to identify which patients have the greatest health risks (and therefore, pose financial risks to the organization). Health-risk assessments administered to patients and analytics applied to clinical and claims data enable organizations to classify their populations.

Organizations should also reengineer their work processes, using Lean/Six Sigma methods wherever possible, and then apply automation tools to make those processes more efficient.[25] The first step is to automate patient outreach, applying clinical protocols to registries that are either standalone or part of EHRs. These registries can be used to launch outbound messages to patients who have care gaps.

Another type of automation involves running reports on registry data to classify patients by subgroup. Care managers can then design campaigns to improve the health of specific subgroups, such as patients with Type 2 diabetes and hypertension.

Many organizations make a mistake when they try to perform care management manually. They end up hiring a large number of nurses to search medical records and call patients individually. This process is not only a waste of time and money but also wastes the skills of these highly trained professionals.

Another common error is a failure to complete pre-visit planning and post-visit follow up. With the help of automation, it's relatively easy to find out what patients should do before office visits, such as get tests done so that physicians can see the results. Similarly, tracking patient compliance after visits is not a big chore if the practice uses its EHR for automated tracking of orders for tests and referrals. Providers can find out whether patients filled prescriptions, by getting online medication histories from Surescripts.[26]

With the help of certain health plans, a growing number of providers are using claims data to identify their patients' care gaps and do predictive modeling. Claims data shows all services that a plan member received from any provider, but it is out of date and often contains errors. By feeding a registry with integrated EHR and claims data and applying analytics to this information, organizations can identify care gaps and high-risk patients in near-real-time. Moreover, that actionable information can be supplied to providers at the point of care and to care managers as they plan their work and prioritize their cases. That allows them to intervene proactively with the patients who need help the most.

# What This Book Is About

As the foregoing comments suggest, this book draws connections among the new care delivery models, the components of population health management, and the various types and applications of health IT that are required in order to support those components. Two key concepts tie all of this together: 1) Advanced analytics must be applied to comprehensive data to understand all the factors involved in population health and to make the data actionable for providers and care teams and 2) PHM requires a high degree of intelligent automation to assess and reach everyone in a population, engage patients in self-care, and maximize the chance that each person will receive the proper preventive, chronic, and acute care when they need it.

In the course of explaining how to do this, we also describe how healthcare organizations are transforming themselves to manage population health and prepare for value-based reimbursement. The ACO, CIN, and PCMH models have already been discussed, and the advent of bundled payments will also have a major impact on hospital and post-acute care. But at its core, the transition to accountable care focuses on care teams that take responsibility for managing and coordinating the services provided to individual patients. These care teams must also engage patients in caring for themselves and improving their health behavior. And as care teams become more sophisticated, many of them will use Lean thinking to continuously improve their own work processes.

The book is laid out in three sections that progress from the general to the particular aspects of population health management. Section 1, "New Delivery Models," first explains what PHM is and why it's important. Ensuing chapters cover ACOs, patient-centered medical homes, and clinically integrated networks, which are the favored vehicles for PHM.

Section 2, "How to Get There," discusses the health IT infrastructure that PHM requires. This section starts with the impact of the government's Meaningful Use program on EHR development and adoption. It also explains what is known about the new EHR incentive program being developed under the Medicare Access and CHIP Reauthorization Act of 2015 (MACRA).[27] Other chapters in this section address the extended data infrastructure needed to support PHM, predictive modeling applications, and the return on investment (ROI) in automation and analytic solutions designed for PHM.

Section 3, "Implementing Change," describes how organizations can use health IT to manage population health. This discussion begins with the basics of care coordination and moves on to advanced methods of care management that utilize Lean thinking. Following a chapter on overall methods of patient engagement, we discuss post-discharge automation, which is another way to involve patients in their own care.

The final pair of chapters covers the new trends that are becoming important in population health management. Chapter 13 explains why social determinants of health (SDH) are now on the agenda of many organizations involved in PHM and shows the best way to make a difference in this area. Chapter 14 describes the strides that cognitive computing is making in health care and explains why it is integral to the future of PHM.

Although this book is intended for healthcare executives and policy experts, anyone who is interested in health care can learn something from its exploration of the major issues that are stirring health care today. In the end, the momentous changes going on in health care will affect all of us.

# Section 1
## New Delivery Models

# POPULATION HEALTH MANAGEMENT

**EFFECTIVE POPULATION HEALTH MANAGEMENT DEPENDS ON ENGAGING PATIENTS AND COORDINATING CARE ACROSS SETTINGS AND OVER TIME.**

Accountable care organizations (ACOs) and patient-centered medical homes (PCMHs) are among the key building blocks of Population Health Management (PHM). PHM starts with strong primary care and spans the entire care continuum to improve health and health outcomes of a defined population.

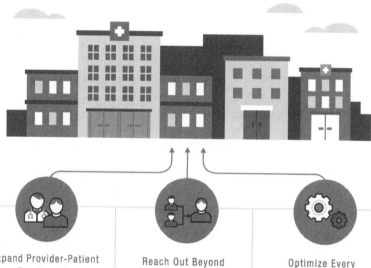

### Expand Provider-Patient Relationship

**SUCCESSFUL PHM BEGINS WITH STRONG PHYSICIAN-PATIENT RELATIONSHIPS**

- Extend patient relationships through the care team and across the continuum

- Motivate patients to engage in their healthcare between visits

### Reach Out Beyond Practice Walls

**ACOs AND PCMHs SERVE AS THE FOUNDATION OF PHM**

- Facilitate better health outcomes through coordinated patient care

- Leverage health IT to connect providers and community resources across the continuum of health care

### Optimize Every Encounter

**AUTOMATING PROCESSES CAN IMPROVE EFFICIENCY AND REDUCE COSTS**

- Use data analytics to identify high-risk patients, reduce care gaps, and measure outcomes

- Improve patient outreach and education by maintaining communication between visits

# 1

# Population Health Management

- *Introduction:* Healthcare reform has not solved the major problems of our healthcare system with cost, quality, and access. To do that, we'll need to achieve the Triple Aim, including finding a way to manage population health efficiently.

- *Definition of PHM:* Population health management (PHM) addresses the care of populations and the engagement of patients across care settings and over time. Above all, it requires an organized system of care.

- *Barriers to PHM:* In the United States, the biggest barriers to population health management are the fragmentation of care delivery, misaligned financial incentives, a lack of managed care knowledge, and insufficient use of health information technology.

- *The beginnings of change:* Pay-for-performance and disease management have had little impact on population health improvement. But newer models such as patient-centered medical homes (PCMHs) and accountable care organizations (ACOs) are more promising as they begin to change incentives. The widespread adoption of electronic health records (EHRs) also opens many new possibilities.

- *The crucial role of automation:* To have an impact on population health, health care organizations must manage their entire patient populations. To do that effectively, they need various technology applications in addition to EHRs.

- *The three pillars of PHM:* Physicians should lead PHM using three complementary approaches: Strengthening and expanding the

**11**

doctor-patient relationship through the care team, reaching out beyond the four walls of their offices, and optimizing patient visits. Analytic and automation tools make this possible.

The protracted debate over healthcare reform has highlighted the shortcomings of our healthcare system. Through June 2015, nearly 17 million people gained insurance coverage as a result of the Affordable Care Act, including 6.5 million who became eligible for Medicaid.[1] But with the primary care workforce declining and a big increase in the demand for care anticipated, patient access to care is likely to shrink in the coming years.[2]

Quality is also an issue. The U.S. has a "sick care" system that is not designed to take good care of chronically ill patients, who generate about three-quarters of health costs, and it does a poor job of preventing people from getting sick.[3] According to a famous RAND study, American adults receive recommended care only 55 percent of the time.[4] The gaps in treatment lead to unnecessary complications, ER visits, and hospitalizations — a major component of the waste in the system. So even if we had enough healthcare providers, the rising costs of chronic disease care would soon exceed our collective ability to pay for it.

The fragmentation of our delivery system and the poor communication among providers are prime reasons for the poor quality of care that many patients receive. For example, the 30-day readmission rate of Medicare patients with congestive heart failure (CHF) fell slightly after 2012 because of Medicare penalties on hospitals, but still averaged 22.7 percent from 2010 to 2013.[5] Some researchers have speculated that the high rate of CHF readmissions may be related to shorter lengths of stay in the hospital.[6] But other studies show that better care management on the outpatient side could eliminate the majority of these readmissions.[7] In many cases, that care is not being provided because of poor hand-offs from inpatient to outpatient care and the lack of primary care follow-up with the patients after discharge. In addition, physicians have no financial incentive to engage in the home care of patients, beyond the general supervision of home health nurses. In the case of heart failure, this continuous care is required in order to prevent emergencies that can lead to readmissions.

Except in a few large, integrated healthcare systems and government systems that take financial responsibility for care, physicians are not generally paid to treat patients outside of office visits or to coordinate their care across care settings. Partly as a result, the continuity of care is disrupted at many points.[8]

At the same time, nonmedical determinants of health — which have a far greater impact on health than does medical care — are not being properly addressed. Overeating, smoking, unsafe sex, lack of exercise, and other personal health behaviors are major components of health spending, yet physician counseling of patients is poorly reimbursed and usually confined to office visits for other problems. In addition, social determinants of health, such as access to care, health literacy, cultural barriers, income, and health insurance affect the overall health of individuals and populations. (See Chapter 13.)

For these and many other reasons, the United States spends twice to three times as much per capita on health care as most other advanced countries do, yet the outcomes of patients are inferior in many respects.[9] Despite the Affordable Care Act, health care has become unaffordable for many people even with insurance coverage.[10] Both private and public payers are wrestling with medical costs that, while rising more slowly than before, are still growing 50% faster than the rate of inflation.[11]

Clearly, a radical change is in order. We must reorganize the financing and the delivery of health care to provide greater value to both patients and society.

Myriad proposals to restructure the system have been made. One of the most promising is the *Triple Aim* of the Institute for Healthcare Improvement, formerly headed by Donald Berwick, MD, who first articulated this model. The Triple Aim program seeks to

- Improve the experience of care
- Improve the health of populations
- Reduce the per capita costs of care[12]

This chapter addresses the second aim — to improve the health of populations. By applying population health management principles, physicians and other providers can also improve the healthcare experience for patients while reducing cost growth to a manageable level.

# What Is Population Health Management?

As Berwick and his colleagues pointed out in a paper on the Triple Aim, much of the current quality-improvement efforts — such as pay-for-performance and Medicare's quality-reporting programs — focus on single sites of care, including acute care hospitals and physician practices.[13] To truly make a difference in outcomes, however, reformers must try to raise the quality of care and improve care coordination across all care settings. Also, this approach must be applied over a much longer period than that of a single episode of care.

These concepts lie at the core of population health management, which has been defined as a healthcare approach focusing on "the health outcomes of individuals in a group and the distribution of outcomes in that group."[14] Former Kaiser Permanente CEO David Lawrence, MD, observes:

> Patients are just one of many such groups within a community. At any given time, most people do not worry about illness or wonder if they have one. They are not under treatment, and they see a physician infrequently. Yet for all people, lifestyles and behavior; race, culture, and language skills; and the environment in which they live are all important determinants of their individual health . . . . Effective population health care includes interventions to moderate the impact of these powerful determinants [of health].[15]

## Key components

Population health management, or PHM, as we hereafter refer to it, addresses not only longitudinal care across the continuum of care for all conditions, including mental health, but also personal health behaviors that may contribute to (or prevent the healing of) disease. Based on the experience of Kaiser Permanente and other organizations that are dedicated to PHM,[16] here are some of the other aspects of this approach to care:

- *An organized system of care.* Healthcare providers must be organized, even if that only means that they've been electronically linked and have agreed to follow certain clinical protocols to improve the quality of care.

- *Care teams.* Physicians and other clinicians work in care teams to provide multiple levels of patient care and education consistently.

- *Coordination across care settings.* Patients have a personal physician who coordinates their care and guides them through the system.

- *Access to primary care.* Primary care is vitally necessary to make sure patients receive necessary preventive, chronic, and acute care.

- *Centralized resource planning.* Resources are allocated to ensure that individual patients receive all necessary care and that available resources are optimally applied across the population.
- *Continuous care.* Providers are available to patients during *and* between office visits, and all forms of communication, including secure electronic messaging, are appropriately utilized.
- *Patient self-management education.* With the help of printed and online materials, care teams help patients learn how to manage their own conditions to the greatest extent possible.
- *Focus on health behavior and lifestyle changes.* Providers and the educational materials they offer reinforce the need for healthy lifestyles across the population.
- *Interoperable electronic health records.* Electronic health records are used to store and retrieve data, on not only individual patients but also the status of the population. These records are also used to track orders, referrals, and other care processes to ensure that patients receive the care they need. And by exchanging data with other clinical systems, interoperable EHRs — systems capable of communicating with disparate EHRs — provide physicians with information that helps them make better decisions.
- *Electronic registries.* Whether or not registries are part of EHRs, they are important components of PHM because they enable caregivers to track and manage all services provided to, or due for, their patient population as well as subgroups of that population.

In addition, shared decision-making has become an important tool in population health management. This includes providing and explaining information to patients about treatment options to help them make informed decisions about their care.

Until recently, major components of PHM were found mainly in group-model health management organizations (HMOs) like Kaiser Permanente and Group Health Cooperative of Puget Sound; large integrated delivery systems like Intermountain Healthcare, Geisinger Clinic, and the Henry Ford Health System; and the Veterans Affairs Health System and the Military Health System. But accountable care organizations, the Medicare Shared Savings Program, and commercial risk contracts are all increasing interest in PHM among other healthcare organizations as well.

# Obstacles to PHM

In the United States, the biggest barriers to population health management are the fragmentation of care delivery, perverse financial incentives, a lack of managed care knowledge, and insufficient use of health information technology.

According to the Institute of Medicine's 2001 report, *Crossing The Quality Chasm*, "The current health care delivery system is highly decentralized . . . . In a population increasingly afflicted by chronic conditions, the health care delivery system is poorly organized to provide care to those with such conditions . . . The challenge before us is to move from today's highly decentralized, cottage industry to one that is capable of providing primary and preventive care, caring for the chronically ill, and coping with acute and catastrophic services."[17]

The fee-for-service reimbursement system is the opposite of the payment approach that is suited to PHM. Fee-for-service incentivizes physicians to perform more services rather than to help patients get well or to prevent them from getting sick. Because third-party payers usually pay doctors only for services performed in their offices, the hospital, or another institutional setting, physicians have no incentive to communicate with patients online or on the phone or to care for them at home. Other payment approaches also have perverse incentives, including *capitation,* which motivates doctors to do as little for patients as possible, and *straight salary,* which doesn't encourage them to work hard.[18]

Because most physicians are accustomed to practicing in the fee-for-service system, they have no idea how to manage care within a budget.[19] (Budgeting is part of the central resource planning referred to earlier.) Healthcare resources are limited, so physicians must learn how to order tests and perform procedures more appropriately, consistent with evidence-based guidelines. Many doctors will object that they must practice defensive medicine to guard against malpractice suits. Because physicians are quite concerned about this issue, malpractice reform could help accelerate the evolution of PHM.

Finally, the healthcare industry needs to make much better use of information technology and improve the quality of data in the system if PHM is to become a reality. This includes not only EHRs and health information exchanges but also registries and applications that use clinical protocols and sophisticated algorithms to identify individuals with care gaps and to trigger communications to those patients and their physicians.[20]

The government's Meaningful Use incentive program has helped boost the adoption of EHRs, which are now used by 78 percent of physician practices.[21] Most physicians are still not using EHRs for quality improvement or for tracking patient health between office visits. However, Meaningful Use, particularly the Stage 2 and Stage 3 criteria, encourages physicians to take advantage of EHRs and other kinds of certified applications to manage population health.

# The Beginnings of Change

Over the past 15 or 20 years, approaches such as pay-for-performance and disease management have had a very limited effect on quality improvement. Pay-for-performance programs focus on a relatively small set of measures, confuse physicians with conflicting goals from multiple health plans, fail to reward improvement, and often use sample sizes that are too small to show how well individual physicians are doing on particular metrics.[22]

*Disease management*, a systematic approach to caring for patients with chronic diseases, has taken two different forms:

- The *chronic care* model, a method of integrating all the care for particular chronic conditions across providers and over time,[23] requires the resources of a large organization, such as a group-model HMO, and cannot be readily applied in small practices, although they can undertake parts of it.[24]
- The *insurance-based* model tries to overcome the fragmentation of the market by taking a more patient-focused approach. The insurers and third-party disease management firms rely on nurse care managers, who telephonically interact with patients to educate them about their condition and their health risks and work with them over time to effect behavior change. The major flaw in this model is that physicians are involved in the process only peripherally, if at all.

More promising models have emerged in the past few years. These include the patient-centered medical home and the accountable care organization.

The PCMH is designed to help primary care practices of all sizes provide comprehensive primary care. Among its key components are a personal physician who is responsible for all of a patient's ongoing care; team care; a whole-person orientation; care coordination facilitated by the use of health

IT; a care-planning process based on a robust partnership between physicians and patients; and enhanced access to care, including non-visit care.[25]

Though thousands of practices have been recognized as patient-centered medical homes, practices that try to become medical homes encounter some significant obstacles. First, small primary care practices may lack the time and the resources to transform themselves and acquire the necessary information technology;[26] second, they may find it difficult to gain the cooperation of specialists and hospitals; and third, most physicians do not receive adequate financial support from payers for coordinating care.[27] However, a growing number of health plans are paying care-coordination fees to primary care practices that are recognized as medical homes.

ACOs consist of hospitals and physicians that take collective responsibility for the cost and quality of care for all patients in their population. Though related in some respects to the original HMO concept, the ACO grew from the ideas of Elliott Fisher, MD, a professor at Dartmouth Medical School; Donald Berwick, MD, then president of the Institute for Healthcare Improvement; and Karen Davis, then president of the Commonwealth Fund.[28] It is complementary to the PCMH in the sense that it could enable primary care physicians to benefit financially from improving care coordination. Conversely, ACOs cannot function without a strong foundation of primary care.[29]

An ACO may be a single business entity, such as a group-model HMO or an integrated delivery system. But it could also involve an "extended medical staff" or a contracting network that includes a healthcare system. Independent practice associations (IPAs) that have evolved into clinically integrated networks could also serve as ACOs.

Partly because of the Medicare Shared Savings Program (MSSP), ACOs have grown rapidly in recent years, and there are now more than 700 ACOs.[30] Many healthcare organizations have formed ACOs to participate in the MSSP and/or commercial risk and shared savings contracts.

The widespread development of ACOs and PCMHs could provide a powerful impetus for a shift from the current care-delivery model to PHM. With the backing of large organizations and the introduction of financial incentives that encourage an outcomes-oriented, patient-centered care model, PHM could become the dominant model of health care.

## Examining the crucial role of automation

Some observers have raised serious objections to this rosy scenario. Consultant and healthcare expert Jeff Goldsmith, for example, points out that the effort of insurance companies to shift financial risk to providers proved to be the Achilles' heel of managed care in the 1990s.[31] This doesn't necessarily doom ACOs, however, because they will have to be accountable for quality as well as for cost. This should prevent a public backlash similar to the one that defeated HMOs. In addition, information technology has advanced to the point where all patients in a population can be identified, risk-stratified, and provided with advanced self-management tools to prevent exacerbation of their illnesses. Physicians did not have these tools in the heyday of HMOs.

David Lawrence, the former CEO of Kaiser Permanente, points to another problem: the difficulty that primary care physicians would have in making the transition to the new delivery model. (Though he cites this difficulty in regard to the medical home, the same criticism could be applied to ACOs, because primary care physicians are the linchpins of care coordination in both models.) Lawrence believes that, to increase access to primary care, we need to make use of "disruptive innovations," including retail clinics, employer-based wellness programs, home telemonitoring of patients with chronic conditions, and new methods of educating patients in self-management.[32]

## Managing the entire population

To be able to manage all aspects of health from wellness to complex care, healthcare organizations must assess the entire population, taking advantage of new Software as a Service (SaaS) analytics platforms that run continuously with near real-time data feeds. Patients can then be stratified into various stages across the spectrum of health. Those who are well need to stay well by getting preventive tests completed; those who have health risks need to change their health behaviors so that they don't develop the conditions they're at risk for; and those who have chronic conditions need to prevent further complications by closing care gaps and also working on health behaviors. Technology can be quite helpful in assessing and stratifying patients and targeting interventions to the right people. The automation of the processes provides a more efficient and effective way to do population health management.

What's greatly needed for successful PHM is an electronic infrastructure that performs much of the routine, time- and labor-intensive work in the background for physicians and their staffs. Fortunately, most of the tools for building such an infrastructure already exist, although they tend to be scattered and underused. When these tools are pulled together and applied in a coordinated, focused manner, they will be a powerful force for change.

Technology is not a substitute for the physician-patient relationship, which is the basis of continuous care. In fact, physicians and their care teams can have a major, positive effect on patient experience, compliance, and behavior change. But to the extent that automation tools are used to strengthen that relationship and enable physicians and care teams to provide value-added services that help patients improve their health proactively, these technologies can help drive population health management.[33]

# The Three Pillars of PHM

To do PHM properly, physicians and their care teams must strengthen their relationships with patients in a variety of ways, including making sure that they come in for needed preventive and chronic care. Care teams — which include physicians, mid-level practitioners, medical assistants, social workers, and nurse educators — must optimize the services they provide to patients during office visits. And they must extend their reach beyond the four walls of their offices to provide a continuous healing relationship. The appropriate IT tools can facilitate achievement of all three goals while lessening the burden on practices.

One of the best ways to strengthen the doctor-patient relationship is to combine an electronic registry with an automated method of communicating with patients who are overdue for preventive and/or chronic care services. The patient demographic and clinical data in the registry can come from billing systems or electronic health records, or from labs and pharmacies. The registry provides lists of patients with particular health conditions and shows what has been done for them and when. By continuously running evidence-based clinical protocols and a communications engine, the registry can trigger outbound calls or secure online messages to patients who need to make appointments with their doctors for particular services at specific intervals.

Besides improving the health of the population, this automated messaging also brings patients back in touch with their physicians — in some cases, after long intervals of non-contact. Without requiring any effort from the doctors or their staffs, this combination of tools enhances the doctor-patient relationship and helps to close gaps in care while also increasing practice revenues as a byproduct.

Optimization of visits requires preparation by both the patient and the care team. The first thing patients should do is complete a health risk assessment

(HRA) that shows the state of their health and what they're doing about it. The patients should also receive educational materials, including online multimedia tools, to prepare them for the office visit.

Physicians and other care team members need actionable, patient-specific reports that combine data from their EHRs with data from registries, other providers, and HRAs to show what has been done for the patient, the gaps in their care that need to be filled, and nonmedical issues that may be impeding patients' abilities to manage their health and health risks. Care teams also require population-level reports that can help them figure out how to improve the quality of care. Though advanced EHRs include health maintenance alerts, they may lack clinical dashboards that present key markers of the patient's status; they may be unable to compile data across a patient population to support quality improvement: and they may be unsuited for patient care by a multidisciplinary care team.[34]

What's needed is a sophisticated rules engine that can incorporate disparate types of data with evidence-based guidelines, generating reports that provide many different views of the information. For example, the entire patient population could be filtered by payer, activity center, provider, health conditions, and care gaps. The same filters could be applied to patients with a particular condition, such as diabetes, to find out where the practice needs to improve its diabetes care.

The same approach could be used to produce reports for care teams at the point of care. For a diabetic patient, a report related to that condition would show the patient's blood pressure and body-mass index, whether the person had received an HbA1c test within a certain period, and the person's HbA1c level. Such a report should also include information about the patient's other conditions and care gaps that might be relevant to the patient's diabetes and his or her ability to manage it.

If the reports were combined with the registry and the patient messaging software, the physician or mid-level practitioner would be able find out whether and when the patient had been contacted to make an office visit or get a test done and whether an appointment had been made. In addition, the care team could use these reports to reach out to patients who needed educational materials or one-on-one educational and goal-setting sessions to learn how to manage their conditions.

Extending the reach of the care team beyond the office requires both the willingness of providers to stay in touch with the patient and modalities that help patients care for themselves. Automation can help both sides achieve those goals without excessive effort. For example, patients who fill out HRAs could receive educational materials tailored to their conditions, and they could be directed to appropriate self-help programs for, say, smoking cessation or losing weight. And if physicians had automated methods to contact patients and remind them of what they needed to do to improve their health, the practice would be more likely to perform that component of PHM.

# Conclusion

To create a sustainable healthcare system that provides affordable, high-quality health care to all, we will have to adopt a population health management approach. Though the transition to PHM will be difficult for providers and patients alike, the change could be facilitated and accelerated through the use of health information technology, self-management tools, and automated reminders that are persistent in changing behaviors.

The current generation of EHRs lacks many of the features required to improve population health. But by combining EHRs with supplemental technologies that already exist, physicians can rapidly move to PHM strategies that will benefit all their patients and enhance the physician-patient relationship.

These new technologies are important to the new accountable care organizations that are sprouting everywhere. The next chapter describes the kind of IT infrastructure that ACOs need in order to do population health management.

# HOW ACOs CAN MANAGE POPULATION HEALTH

Accountable Care Organizations (ACOs) have strong incentives to improve population health to meet quality goals and reduce costs.

## 2010

### The Patient Protection and Affordable Care Act

Authorized the creation of ACOs.

 **MEDICARE SHARED SAVINGS PROGRAM (MSSP)**

ACO participants can include organizations such as independent practice networks, federally qualified health centers, and hospitals and their employed physicians.

## 2015

### The Medicare Access and CHIP Reauthorization Act (MACRA)

Provides new incentives for providers to join "Alternative Payment Models" like ACOs.

**MORE RISK**

Medicare and commercial insurers alike are requiring ACOs to take more financial risk as they manage defined populations through value-based payment arrangements.

**MORE REWARD**

The better organizations are at population health management, the more they stand to gain in shared savings and incentive payments.

**THE MORE RISK THAT PROVIDERS TAKE, THE MORE IMPORTANT IT IS THAT THEY MANAGE PATIENT POPULATIONS EFFECTIVELY.**

### Health IT Drives ACO Success Through:

**CLINICAL INTEGRATION**
and shared data access

**CONTINUOUS RISK STRATIFICATION**
and performance measurement

**TOP OF LICENSE CARE TEAMS**
with electronic communication channels

**DYNAMIC PATIENT ENGAGEMENT**
delivered through multiple modalities

# 2

# Accountable Care Organizations

- *Introduction:* In 2010, the Affordable Care Act authorized a Medicare Shared Savings Program (MSSP) for accountable care organizations (ACOs), and the Medicare Access and CHIP Reauthorization Act (MACRA) of 2015 will continue to advance ACO models. Private payers are also contracting with ACOs. To succeed, ACOs must learn how to manage population health effectively.

- *The ACO environment:* Physicians and hospitals must learn how to work together in ACOs, regardless of who runs these organizations. Those ACOs that have mastered population health management are doing well. Though payers don't want to push financial risk on providers too rapidly, some advanced ACOs have already accepted global capitation contracts.

- *ACO snapshots:* The history of four large-scale ACO programs shows that this approach can have a significant impact on cost and quality.

- *Population health management:* ACOs have strong incentives to improve population health to meet quality goals and reduce costs. To do that, they must stress non-visit care and disease management, build care teams, and work with patients to improve their health behavior.

- *The role of information technology:* Population health management requires clinical integration, which cannot exist without a robust information technology (IT) infrastructure. In addition, a range of automation tools is needed for cost-effective care management and patient engagement.

The Patient Protection and Affordable Care Act (PPACA) of 2010 focuses mainly on regulating health insurance and expanding coverage. But the legislation also addresses the role of the healthcare delivery system in health spending growth.

In this area, the law's major thrust is to change how providers are paid. Among the approaches that Congress authorized the government to undertake is one that involves accountable care organizations (ACOs), which are healthcare provider groups that are designed to be accountable for the cost and quality of care.

Specifically, the PPACA authorized the Centers for Medicare and Medicaid Services (CMS) to launch a shared-savings program with ACOs in 2012. Under this approach, an ACO that meets specified quality goals can split with CMS any savings that surpass a minimum level.[1]

ACOs that participate in the Medicare Shared Savings Program (MSSP) must consist of providers that "work together to manage and coordinate care for Medicare fee-for-service beneficiaries." Among the ACOs in the MSSP are organizations based on individual practice networks, group practices, partnerships of hospitals and physicians, hospitals and their employed doctors, and federally qualified health centers.

ACOs must meet thresholds on 33 quality measures and cut costs by more than a minimum percentage to qualify for payments equal to 50 percent of savings above a benchmark related to their historical performance. A few ACOs have elected to take *downside risk* — that is, to take financial responsibility for spending more than the benchmark — in return for a higher percentage of savings.[2]

The MSSP, which is not a pilot, potentially affects all patients covered by traditional Medicare. As a result, the ACO provision has generated strong interest among group practices and healthcare organizations.

The ACO initiatives of certain commercial insurers are also attracting attention from providers. Some of the private ACO contracts involve financial risk, and others are limited to gainsharing. About half of the 700-plus existing ACOs hold private contracts; 36 percent have only Medicare contracts; and 16 percent have agreements with both Medicare and private payers.[3]

In the first performance year of the MSSP, 54 of the 114 participants that joined the program in 2012 had total costs that fell below their budget benchmarks, but only 29 reduced spending enough to qualify for a total of $126 million in shared savings. The other 60 ACOs generated costs above their benchmarks.[4]

The next year, 86 of the 333 ACOs in their second performance year, or 26 percent, earned shared-savings payments. Total savings equaled $777 million, and these ACOs received $341 million. In general, analysts noted, ACOs with more experience in the MSSP were more likely to reap shared savings.[5]

Meanwhile, CMS's Pioneer program, which requires ACOs to take more financial risk, has lost half of the 32 organizations that originally enrolled in it. Some of the 16 dropout Pioneers joined the MSSP; the rest left the CMS program entirely.[6]

Note that the ACO concept dovetails with other new reimbursement methods that payers are piloting, including payment bundling and patient-centered medical homes (PCMHs). Further down the road, shared savings will likely transition to some type of payment bundling and, eventually, global *capitation* (a fixed payment for all care provided to each patient). A recent study found that 56 percent of health-plan contracts with ACOs feature downside risk of some kind.[7] But the government and private insurers are still proceeding with caution because they know that the vast majority of providers are not ready to assume very much financial risk. Moreover, there are questions about how much limitation on provider choice the public is willing to accept.

The more risk that providers take, the more imperative it is for them to do population health management (PHM). In the case of ACOs, the reasons are transparent: These organizations must manage the full spectrum of care and must be accountable for a defined patient population.[8] Unless an ACO is capable of tracking the health status of, and the care provided to, every one of its patients, it is unlikely to produce significant savings or meet the quality benchmarks of CMS. And when organizations take on financial risk, it is absolutely essential that they learn how to prevent illness and manage care as well as possible. The more risk that providers assume, the better they have to be at managing population health.

## The ACO Environment

A growing number of healthcare organizations have partnered with health plans to implement ACOs.[9] Though most insurance companies are still reluctant to offer global capitation contracts, they see opportunities in working with ACOs to lower costs and improve quality.

Meanwhile, hospitals and doctors that are partnered in ACOs must find ways to share revenue. After emerging from a regulatory deep freeze a decade ago,[10] gain-sharing between hospitals and physicians got a shot in the arm from CMS' Bundled Payments for Care Improvement (BPCI) initiative.[11] But those bundled payments cover either inpatient care or hospital and post-acute care, not the chronic disease care that ACOs focus on.

The ownership of practices is another important factor in how revenues are shared and how ACOs are organized. While the percentage of physicians employed by hospitals doubled in the first decade of this century,[12] there are signs that direct hospital employment has leveled off in recent years. According to the latest statistics of the American Medical Association (AMA), 60 percent of physicians practice in doctor-owned organizations, and only 20 percent work in practices owned by hospitals or are direct hospital employees.[13] A 2014 survey by the Medical Group Management Association (MGMA), similarly, found that 68 percent of MGMA member organizations were physician owned and 20 percent were part of a hospital or an integrated delivery system.[14]

Nevertheless, hospitals are still trying to get physicians aligned with them, both for competitive reasons and because they believe that they will need physicians' cooperation when reimbursement methods change. Many healthcare systems are moving toward clinical integration with their physicians, whether or not the latter are employed by the system. (See Chapter 4.) The MGMA survey, in fact, found that from 2012 to 2014, 11 percent of MGMA members had integrated clinically with a hospital but retained their clinical independence.[15] The increasing reliance of healthcare on information technology is expected to accelerate this process.[16]

Some observers question whether ACOs can succeed in most areas unless hospitals take the lead in organizing them. Yet nothing in the CMS regulations requires hospitals to lead or to even be a direct participant in ACOs. The only requirements are that ACOs include primary care physicians and serve at least 5,000 Medicare patients each.[17] But, because an ACO must coordinate care across all care settings, it must secure the cooperation of one or more hospitals. So, although both physician organizations and hospitals would prefer to be in charge, they will have to learn how to work together.

## Government support

While all of this is happening, the government is increasing its support for the ACO movement. Beyond the MSSP and the Pioneer ACO programs, CMS has established a Next Generation ACO model that offers more risk and reward than either of the other models. The Next Generation program also allows

ACOs to prospectively (rather than retrospectively) take responsibility for Medicare beneficiaries, allows patients to choose ACOs, and encourages the use of telehealth and care coordination services. According to CMS, 121 organizations are participating in this program.[18]

In 2015, the Department of Health and Human Services (HHS) announced that by the end of 2016, 30 percent of Medicare payments would go to "alternative payment models" (APMs) such as ACOs, patient-centered medical homes (PCMH), and healthcare organizations that accept bundled payments.[19]

These APMs form one of two Medicare payment tracks that physicians can choose, starting in 2019, under the Medicare Access and CHIP Reauthorization Act of 2015 (MACRA).[20] This legislation, which is further discussed in Chapter 5, gives physicians a clear incentive to join an ACO and/or form a PCMH.

## ACO snapshots

Some ACOs have done very well in the MSSP. For example, Mercy Health Select, the ACO of Mercy Health, a 24-hospital system based in Cincinnati, saved Medicare $15.4 million and received $6.5 million as its share in 2014.[21] Emboldened by this achievement, Mercy Health Select has switched to track 3 of the MSSP, which includes downside risk and yields a higher percentage of savings. In addition, the ACO has risk contracts with several commercial and Medicare Advantage plans. In total, 20%–30% of Mercy Health's primary care panels consist of patients covered by risk contracts.[22]

Mercy Health Select executives attribute the ACO's success to its ability to manage population health. As Mercy Health was forming the ACO, the healthcare system also started building patient-centered medical homes; currently, 125 of its 200 primary care practices are NCQA-recognized PCMHs. Another key facet of the ACO's approach has been a care management program that is available to — and appreciated by — both the healthcare system's employed physicians and independent doctors who belong to the ACO. The ACO has also worked hard to improve cooperation between its specialists and primary care doctors and is expanding its network to include post-acute-care providers.

Integrating data from multiple EHRs, along with claims data, has been a challenge for Mercy Health Select. Because Mercy's data warehouse recognizes only identification numbers of patients who have records in its own EHR, the organization uses tools from two outside vendors to aggregate and analyze the ACO's data. But the system works well enough that the ACO can present comprehensive, timely data on patient care gaps to providers at the point of care.

On the private sector side, the biggest ACO experiment is the "alternative quality contract" of Blue Cross and Blue Shield of Massachusetts (BCBSM). This is actually a global capitation agreement with two features that differentiate it from the old HMO risk contracts: First, participants can qualify for graduated quality incentives, and second, the insurer pledges not to reduce their budgets in future years. In return, the contract holders promise to gradually cut cost growth to the rate of inflation.[23]

Eighty-five percent of the physician practices and hospitals that belong to BCBSM's Blue Cross HMO network now participate in the alternative quality contract. They range in size from Partners Healthcare in Boston to the physician-hospital organization of Lowell General Hospital in Lowell, Massachusetts.[24] Though these organizations are not ACOs, strictly speaking, the goals they must meet are similar to those of ACOs, and some of them have formed ACOs that participate in the MSSP or the Pioneer program as well.

A Harvard Medical School study found that, compared with a control group of patients in several other Northeast states, patients whose providers participated in the BCBSM alternative quality contract had lower spending growth, and the quality of their care improved more over a four-year period.[25]

Though there has not yet been a comprehensive study of the hundreds of ACOs formed in recent years, some have been quite successful. For example, Hill Physicians, a large IPA based in Sacramento, California, developed an ACO with Dignity Health, a San Francisco-based hospital system, and Blue Shield of California for a two-year pilot that was funded by the California Public Employees' Retirement System (CalPERS). The ACO was formed to provide care to the 41,000 public sector employees and retirees covered by CalPERS and enrolled in Blue Shield's health plan in Sacramento.

Through a combination of approaches, including PCMHs, improved transitions of care, and intensive care management for patients with complex needs, the ACO reduced spending by $20 million in its first year. Of that amount, $15.5 million was used to achieve zero growth in Blue Shield's premiums for CalPERS members. The remainder of the savings was shared among the three ACO partners. At the end of the ACO's second year, premium reductions for CalPERS members totaled $37 million, and the ACO partners shared another $8 million.

Since then, Hill Physicians has formed three more commercial ACOs, some with local partners. In one of these ACOs, it has reunited with Dignity and Blue Shield to deliver care in San Joaquin County, using a population-based payment model that resembles full capitation.[26]

Healthcare Partners, a multistate physician group and IPA based in Los Angeles, engaged in another ACO pilot with Anthem Blue Cross, starting in 2012.[27] This pilot, which used a shared-savings approach, generated an estimated $4.7 million in savings in the first six months of 2013 by shortening hospital stays and reducing the number of ER visits. The ACO managed to do this even though its patients were members of a preferred provider organization (PPO), rather than an HMO, and were allowed to go out of network.[28]

With this success under its belt, Healthcare Partners' ACO contracted to take care of Anthem PPO members with two or more chronic conditions. This initiative produced $1.8 million in savings from July 1, 2013, through June 30, 2014. In addition, the ACO surpassed Anthem's quality benchmarks on several measures.[29]

## Population health management

As noted in the Introduction, U.S. health care costs much more per capita than the systems of other advanced countries but does not deliver better results.[30] The reasons are well known: The U.S. has a fragmented, chaotic care-delivery system; healthcare providers are incentivized to provide high service volume rather than high-quality care; there are too few primary care physicians and too many specialists; and the system is provider-centered rather than patient-centered.[31]

To turn around this bloated, wasteful healthcare system, policy makers and health policy experts are focusing on population health management. As noted in Chapter 1, PHM has been defined as a healthcare approach that emphasizes "the health outcomes of individuals in a group and the distribution of outcomes in that group." It addresses not only longitudinal care across the continuum of care but also personal health behavior that may contribute to the evolution or exacerbation of diseases.[32]

Among the key characteristics of health organizations that conduct PHM are an organized system of care; the use of multidisciplinary care teams; coordination across care settings; enhanced access to primary care; centralized resource planning; continuous care, both in and outside of office visits; patient self-management education; a focus on health behavior and lifestyle changes; the use of interoperable electronic health records (EHRs); and the use of registries and other tools essential to the automation of PHM.[33]

As ACOs gain traction, the providers that belong to them are increasingly focusing on PHM. Whether the financial incentive is shared savings or global budgets for all patient care, ACOs have a strong motive to maintain health, prevent disease, and control chronic conditions so that they don't lead to ER visits and hospitalizations. To achieve these goals, ACOs have to stress non-visit care and disease management, including home monitoring of the sickest patients. They have to build care teams that are capable of tracking patients' health status and ensuring that they receive recommended care. And they have to incentivize providers to work with patients to improve their health behavior and their compliance with care plans.

ACOs share many of these objectives with patient-centered medical homes. (See Chapter 3.) For example, a physician whose practice serves as a medical home must coordinate care, improve patient self-management skills, track the services provided to patients, and maintain contact with patients between visits. Medical homes also use electronic tools such as EHRs and registries.[34] Patient-centered medical homes are generally much smaller than ACOs and may lack the ability to induce specialists and hospitals to cooperate with them.[35] Nevertheless, a practice that qualifies as a medical home has gone a long way toward being able to function within an ACO.

An effective ACO must not only take excellent care of patients who present for care, but must also try to monitor and stay in contact with people who do not have contact, or who rarely have contact, with healthcare providers. The importance of communicating with this segment of the population is profound because it includes many individuals who are or will become sick and need acute or chronic care at some point. Therefore, an ACO that proactively addresses the health needs of this cohort will be able to control costs better than one that does not.

## The role of information technology

To be successful, an ACO must be clinically integrated, which means that physicians and other providers must communicate and exchange key clinical information with each other. Until a few years ago, this was quite difficult because most clinical data was locked up in paper files that were inaccessible to providers outside of a particular hospital or practice. Even the delivery of lab results was still done mostly by fax, courier, or mail. Now that EHRs have become widespread because of the government's Meaningful Use incentive program, all of this is changing.

EHRs are crucial to clinical integration. Not only can they make it easier for caregivers to document and retrieve patient data, but they also hold the key to health information exchange with other providers — if and when they become interoperable.

Despite the enormous increase in the amount of digitized health information, however, most EHRs are still incapable of exchanging structured data. The clinical summaries that certified EHRs must be able to exchange in Meaningful Use Stage 2 use a specially formatted document known as the consolidated CDA (C-CDA). EHRs from different vendors can exchange these summaries, but the data in them often cannot flow into the data fields in electronic charts; even when an EHR can extract the data from a C-CDA, it is a laborious, lengthy process for the provider.

The federal government has spent more than half a billion dollars to help states develop health information exchanges (HIEs). Though it is unclear that this effort has substantially improved the ability of providers to exchange patient data, a report shows that in 2013, more than six in ten hospitals exchanged health information with outside providers. Fifty-seven percent of hospitals exchanged data with ambulatory providers outside of their system — although only about a quarter of them notified outside primary care providers when their patients entered one of their ERs.[36]

Meanwhile, regional HIEs are still searching for a business model,[37] and an increasing number of healthcare organizations are building private exchanges.[38] Clinician-to-clinician messaging using the Direct secure messaging protocol — a method of exchanging documents as attachments to messages sent over the Internet — is also growing as the Direct infrastructure evolves.[39]

The Interoperability Roadmap of the Office of the National Coordinator for Health IT (ONC) states that the "movement to alternative payment models will naturally stimulate demand for interoperability." ONC points out that "a supportive payment and regulatory environment must lower real and perceived costs of interoperability," including a loss of competitive advantage among healthcare systems in the same market.[40] Whether that will happen remains unclear.

## Automation and analytic tools

EHRs have some drawbacks as tools for performing PHM. Though some vendors are starting to move ahead in this area, most EHRs are not designed for tracking populations, providing actionable reports on care gaps, or sending alerts to patients.[41] ACOs will need not only EHRs but also supplemental applications that automate the work of monitoring, educating, and maintaining contact with the patient population.

These tools, which should be used in conjunction with EHRs, include electronic registries; multiple outreach and communications methods; software that can stratify a population by health status; and health risk assessment programs that trigger alerts and provide educational materials to patients. Automated PHM tools ensure that the routine, repetitive work of managing population health is done in the background, freeing up doctors and nurses to do the work that only they can do.

For example, registries can be programmed to generate reports on the care gaps of patients for care coordinators and care managers in practices. The care managers can use the information to prepare care teams for patient visits and to ensure that patients are receiving recommended services across the continuum of care. By automating patient communications, registries combined with outreach tools also make it easy to send alerts to every patient who needs to be seen for follow up.

These supplemental technologies can also aid ACOs in managing population health at the macro level. A sophisticated rules engine can integrate disparate types of data with evidence-based guidelines, generating reports that provide many different views of the information. As explained in Chapter 1, for example, the entire patient population could be filtered by payer, activity center, provider, health condition, and care gap. The same filters could be applied to all patients with a particular condition to find out where the ACO needs to improve its care for that disease.

ACO management could also use this type of information to pinpoint where the coordination of care is breaking down. For example, if an unusual number of patients with a particular condition were being readmitted to the hospital, that might indicate a problem with outpatient follow-up.

Another important determinant of population health is the degree to which patients are coached on improving their health behavior. Automation tools can also help in this area. For example, when a patient fills out a health risk assessment online or in a practice computer kiosk, that person can receive educational materials tailored to his or her condition and can be directed to appropriate self-help programs for, say, smoking cessation or losing weight.

# Conclusion

Because of the Medicare shared-savings program and other government and private-sector programs, ACOs are generating excitement among healthcare providers. As ACOs become more widespread, they could be a powerful force for establishing population health management as the primary approach to quality improvement and cost containment in the United States.

To do PHM properly, ACOs must use a range of information technologies. These include not only electronic health records but also supplemental applications that automate the routine work of tracking, educating, and communicating with patients. These tools make it possible to do PHM comprehensively and cost-effectively, allowing ACO members to benefit economically from shared savings, bundled-payment, and global capitation programs.

Many healthcare organizations are setting up ACOs. But only the ACOs that achieve clinical integration and learn how to do population health management will succeed. Therefore, information technologies, including automation and analytic tools, are essential components of ACO success.

Patient-centered medical homes, often considered the building blocks of ACOs, also need EHRs and other health IT tools to perform their primary task of care coordination. The next chapter explains what medical homes are and why health IT is essential to their mission.

# POPULATION HEALTH WITHIN THE MEDICAL NEIGHBORHOOD

To take advantage of financial incentives from federal and commercial payers, many primary practices are forming patient-centered medical homes (PCMHs). The PCMH model is centered on the physician-led care team, which coordinates care with others in the "medical neighborhood."

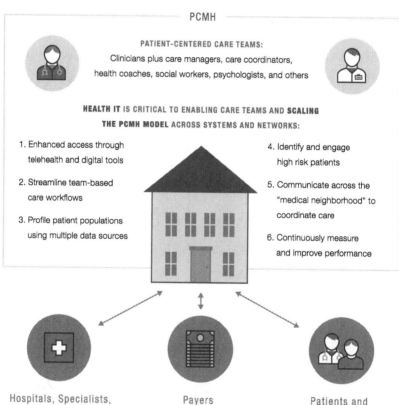

## PCMH

**PATIENT-CENTERED CARE TEAMS:**
Clinicians plus care managers, care coordinators, health coaches, social workers, psychologists, and others

**HEALTH IT** IS CRITICAL TO ENABLING CARE TEAMS AND **SCALING THE PCMH MODEL** ACROSS SYSTEMS AND NETWORKS:

1. Enhanced access through telehealth and digital tools

2. Streamline team-based care workflows

3. Profile patient populations using multiple data sources

4. Identify and engage high risk patients

5. Communicate across the "medical neighborhood" to coordinate care

6. Continuously measure and improve performance

**Hospitals, Specialists, Long Term Care Facilities**

- Care coordination across all settings facilitated by technology and health information exchange

**Payers**

- Recognized PCMHs earn tangible economic rewards through bonuses and incentives

**Patients and Caregivers**

- Whole patient focus to improve experience and outcomes

# 3

# Patient-Centered Medical Homes

- *Introduction:* The patient-centered medical home (PCMH) movement is growing rapidly, with support from both private insurers and the government. While medical homes can't achieve their full potential until they integrate with the medical neighborhood and start automating care management, new financial incentives will support PCMH evolution.

- *PCMH background:* The PCMH model is essentially holistic primary care in which physician-led care teams coordinate and manage care. The criteria for PCMH recognition from the National Committee for Quality Assurance (NCQA) emphasize health IT and mirror some of the requirements of Meaningful Use Stage 2.

- *Challenges and solutions:* Primary care practices must completely reengineer themselves to become PCMHs. Though small practices can do much of this, even large multispecialty groups lack many of the requisite components of the PCMH. The cost of creating and maintaining a medical home could be much lower if PCMH functions in the practices were highly automated.

- *The role of information technology:* Electronic health records (EHRs) are necessary but not sufficient for practices that aim to become PCMHs. They have some of the necessary tools but fall short in the area of population health management. External registries, analytics, and automation tools can fill the gap.

Because of the current national focus on accountable care organizations (ACOs), attention has shifted away from the patient-centered medical home, an approach designed to rebuild primary care and improve care coordination. Nevertheless, the PCMH model is continuing to grow rapidly and to attract support from providers, payers, and consumer groups.

The National Committee for Quality Assurance (NCQA) has recognized more than 10,000 practice sites with 48,000 providers as patient-centered medical homes.[1] One reason why practices seek this recognition is that payers provide tangible economic rewards to recognized PCMHs.

NCQA says it "has established formal relationships with a large number of public and private payer organizations who sponsor programs that offer incentives to clinical sites to become NCQA-recognized medical homes. Most of these sponsoring organizations pay a regular bonus or offer enhanced reimbursement to recognized clinical sites or their clinicians."[2]

As of 2014, more than 90 health insurers had embraced the PCMH approach. These include such major carriers as Aetna, Anthem, CIGNA, Humana, and United.[3] Altogether there are more than 160 PCMH initiatives in 48 states, Puerto Rico, and Washington, D.C.[4]

The Centers for Medicare and Medicaid Services (CMS) is participating in multi-payer projects in several states.[5] Meanwhile, 42 state Medicaid programs are involved in PCMH demonstrations.[6] And the Veterans Health Administration (VHA) has rolled out what it calls patient aligned care teams — essentially, the same concept as PCMHs — across its primary care clinics.[7]

# Initial Results Are Promising

Early evidence shows that the patient-centered medical home can improve access to high-quality care and the management of chronic conditions. For example, one study of care provided under PCMH principles found that patients with diabetes had significant reductions in cardiovascular risk; patients with congestive heart failure had 35 percent fewer hospital days; and asthma and diabetes patients were more likely to receive appropriate therapy.[8]

A study of seven PCMH demonstration projects reported that the strategy resulted in reductions in ER visits ranging from 15 percent to 50 percent, and decreases in hospital admissions ranging from 10 percent to 40 percent.[9]

Another paper based on the experience of Group Health Cooperative, a large, integrated delivery system, showed that the PCMH model resulted in 29 percent fewer emergency visits and 6 percent fewer hospitalizations.[10]

In fact, the PCMH model has been shown to reduce overall costs. The Patient-Centered Primary Care Collaborative (PCPCC), a stakeholder organization that advocates for the PCMH, recently reported on 30 peer-reviewed, industry, and state and federal evaluations of PCMHs in 2014 and 2015. Most of the studies, the PCPCC noted, found reductions in one or more measures of cost and utilization. Here are a few details of the PCPCC-reported studies:

- Blue Cross Blue Shield of Michigan derived $512 million in savings from PCMHs over six years. The patients who belonged to PCMHs had a 26 percent lower rate of hospital admissions for common conditions than other patients did; they also had an 11 percent lower rate of adult ER visits, and a 16 percent lower rate of pediatric ER visits.

- Community Care of North Carolina (CCNC), a public-private partnership, organized a network of PCMHs nine years ago to improve quality and lower costs in the state Medicaid program. The program has had reductions in ED visits, inpatient admissions, and readmissions. The average cost reduction has been $312 per recipient per year, or 9 percent, according to a state audit.

- CareFirst BlueCross BlueShield of Maryland has a unique PCMH program that connects non-affiliated providers via nurse care managers. The program resulted in $345 million in savings in 2014 and $609 million from 2011 through 2014. The savings came mainly from 19 percent fewer hospital admissions (5 percent in 2014), 15 percent fewer days in the hospital (11 percent fewer in 2014), and 20 percent fewer readmissions (9 percent in 2014).

One of the PCPCC's conclusions was that the more experience that PCMHs gained, the more likely they were to lower costs. "Most studies did not assess the total cost of care, but the trend across these 17 peer reviewed studies suggests that the longer the PCMH program had been implemented and subsequently evaluated, improvements in cost or utilization were demonstrated."[11]

# Managing the Medical Neighborhood

For medical homes to be successful in improving the quality and reducing the cost of care, they need the cooperation of outside specialists and hospitals. Yet the other providers in a PCMH's "medical neighborhood" may not be inclined to cooperate, because their incentives are not necessarily aligned with PCMH goals.[12] Though the PCMH is designed to manage population health and avoid unnecessary care, the revenue of specialists and hospitals depends on the volume of services they provide. That will not change until value-based reimbursement becomes the dominant method of payment.

Because of this barrier, some experts say, PCMHs cannot achieve their full potential unless they are incorporated into ACOs.[13] The latter organizations not only have the same incentives as medical homes but are also composed of both primary care physicians and specialists. So, whether multispecialty groups, independent practice associations, or healthcare systems sponsor ACOs, they should, in theory, foster cooperation between the PCMH and its medical neighborhood.

Conversely, some observers view the PCMH as an essential building block of ACOs. That is because ACOs must be primary care-driven and patient-centered — two key characteristics of PCMHs — in order to succeed in a risk-bearing environment.[14]

Another key to the success of both PCMHs and ACOs is the automation of population health management. The goal of population health management is to keep patients as healthy as possible, thereby reducing the need for expensive ER visits, hospitalizations, and procedures.[15] As will be explained later in this chapter, it is impossible for providers to manage population health effectively without the use of automation tools, including patient registries and analytic and care management applications.

# PCMH Background

There are many definitions of the patient-centered medical home. One of the best comes from David Nash, MD, Dean of the Jefferson College of Population Health at Jefferson University in Philadelphia:

> The patient-centered medical home (PCMH) is essentially delivery of holistic primary care based on ongoing, stable relationships between patients and their personal physicians. It is characterized by physician-directed integrated care teams, coordinated care, improved quality

through the use of disease registries and health information technology, and enhanced access to care.[16]

A March 2007 joint statement by medical societies representing pediatricians, family physicians, and internists calls the PCMH "an approach to providing comprehensive primary care for children, youth, and adults."[17] The chief components of the PCMH include

- A personal physician who is the first contact for a patient and who provides continuous and comprehensive care
- A physician-led care team that takes collective responsibility for care
- A whole-person orientation, in which the personal physician provides for all of a patient's health needs and arranges referrals to other health professionals as needed
- Care coordination across all care settings, facilitated by information technology and health information exchange
- An emphasis on delivering high-quality, safe care in partnership with patients and their families
- Enhanced access to care through open scheduling, expanded hours, and improved communication among physicians, staff, and patients via secure email and other modes
- Additional reimbursement to reflect the value of the PCMH's activities and the costs of setting up the necessary infrastructure.

NCQA has further defined the PCMH by establishing a set of criteria that practices must meet to become NCQA-certified medical homes. (This is not the only PCMH certification program — the Joint Commission has one, for example — but it's the one that recognizes most medical homes.) These criteria have become increasingly important because most PCMH demonstration projects use them as a measurement tool,[18] and some health plans require NCQA certification for incentive payments to practices.[19]

## Medical home certification

NCQA's medical home certification process grew from another NCQA program that recognizes physicians for effectively using information technology and managing population health,[20] and the PCMH certification criteria also focus on health IT. The NCQA standards measure access and communication, patient tracking and registry functions, care management, patient self-management support, electronic prescribing, test tracking, referral tracking, performance reporting and improvement, and advanced electronic communications.[21]

Specifically, the NCQA's 2014 criteria for recognition as a PCMH consist of these 26 elements, in six domains:

- Patient-centered access
  - Patient-centered appointment access
  - 24/7 access to clinical advice
  - Electronic access
- Team-based care
  - Continuity
  - Medical home responsibilities
  - Culturally and linguistically appropriate services
  - The practice team
- Population health management
  - Patient information
  - Clinical data
  - Comprehensive health assessment
  - Use data for population management
  - Implement evidence-based decision support
- Care management and support
  - Identify patients for care management
  - Care planning and self-care support
  - Medication management
  - Use electronic prescribing
  - Support self-care and shared decision-making
- Care coordination and care transitions
  - Test tracking and follow up
  - Referral tracking and follow up
  - Coordination care transitions
- Performance measurement and quality improvement
  - Measure clinical quality performance
  - Measure patient/family performance

- Implement continuous quality improvement
- Demonstrate continuous quality improvement
- Report performance
- Use certified EHR technology[22]

A quick glance at these criteria shows the importance of health IT in gaining recognition as a PCMH. In fact, several of the requirements, such as sending an electronic summary of care records to other providers in more than 50 percent of referrals, mirror the criteria for Meaningful Use Stage 2. It's also notable that "must-pass" NCQA requirements, such as "use data for population health management," "care planning and self-care support," and "referral tracking and follow up," all necessitate the use of robust EHRs and ancillary applications.

NCQA has a specialty practice recognition program that encourages specialists to work more closely with primary care practices to coordinate care — in other words, to make the medical neighborhood friendlier to medical homes. Again, health IT plays a prominent role in the criteria, many of which are aligned with the Meaningful Use Stage 2 requirements.[23]

## Challenges and solutions

To do population health management, a patient-centered medical home must build a number of core competencies. The care team in the practice must ensure that patients receive the preventive and chronic care recommended in evidence-based guidelines; that patients' conditions are tracked in a systematic way; that the practice reaches out to noncompliant patients and those who don't regularly see their doctors; that the practice provides patient education and self-management coaching; and that steps are taken to address poor health behaviors.

Because relatively few physician practices operated in this mode until recently, the systematic application of population health management has been largely left to employers, health plans, and disease management companies. The patient-centered medical home represents, in part, an effort to make physicians and patients central to this process. The Agency for Healthcare Research and Quality (AHRQ) has even coined a term for this new approach: practice-based population health (PBPH).[24]

A 2007 study of the preparedness of large group practices to become medical homes showed that most lacked key elements of the required infrastructure and practice approach.[25] A follow-up study found that, by 2013, the large groups were still using less than half of the requisite processes and that small- and medium-size groups were using fewer than 30 percent of them.[26]

This is not to say that small, independent practices cannot become medical homes. Some have achieved amazing feats of self-transformation. But, even if they already have EHRs, small practices may not be able to afford other PCMH components, such as dedicated care coordinators and care managers. To expand their hours and provide after-hours access to patients, they must incur additional labor costs. And, as noted earlier in this chapter, they may find it difficult to persuade specialists and hospitals to cooperate with them on care coordination unless their incentives are aligned with the PCMH.

Experts have made several suggestions about how smaller practices might be able to turn themselves into medical homes.[27] For example, they could hire practice transformation consultants who are experienced in working with such practices. Also, the government might create regional extension centers — similar to the health IT regional extension centers that were used successfully in the Meaningful Use program — to help doctors over the hump. And both North Carolina and Vermont have successfully used community resource centers to supply shared care coordination services that small practices could not afford on their own.[28]

Meanwhile, larger medical groups, including those owned by health systems, have made rapid progress toward transforming their primary care practices into PCMHs. These groups have a big advantage in bringing about the requisite culture change, especially if their doctors are employed. In addition, they generally have greater resources to hire care coordinators and to establish the kind of health IT infrastructure that medical homes require. The biggest challenge that these organizations face is figuring out how to scale up their efforts quickly without incurring excessive costs.

## Building the medical neighborhood

Though these approaches can help practices build medical homes, their success as PCMHs will still be determined by how well they can establish communication and collaboration channels with other providers. The potential role of ACOs in this area has already been mentioned, but it may not be necessary to wait until ACOs are widespread to begin improving the ecosystem in which the PCMH operates.

Under a $20.75 million grant from the Center for Medicare and Medicaid Innovation, VHA Inc. (a national healthcare network), TransforMED, and Phytel, a technology company (now part of IBM) that specializes in automated, provider-led population health improvement solutions, worked together from 2012 to 2015 on a project to expand the PCMH concept to the patient-centered medical neighborhood. The goal was to connect PCMHs in 15 communities with acute-care hospitals and specialty practices to deliver higher-quality, more patient-centered care at an affordable cost.[29] The results of the demonstration had not been announced at the time of this writing.

## How much will it cost?

Most health plans use a mixed or hybrid payment model to reimburse physicians for the extra work and expense of providing a medical home. They pay physicians fee-for-service for the clinical work they do, plus a fixed care coordination payment for each patient and some kind of quality incentive. Though other approaches have been suggested, little data exists on how well they might work in encouraging PCMH activities.[30]

There's also no agreement on how high the care coordination fee should be in the hybrid model. For example, the North Carolina Medicaid program paid primary care doctors a coordination fee of $2.50 per patient per month.[31] In contrast, in a multi-payer pilot in Pennsylvania, the state required payments of $4 per patient per month to practices that had attained Level 3 NCQA certification as medical homes.[32] The PCPCC report cited a *Health Affairs* study that found the average national payment was $4.90 in 2014.[33]

One reason for the wide range of these fees is that not much is known about the costs of establishing a PCMH. A study of federally funded community health centers found that a fully functioning PCMH was associated with an operating cost per patient per month that was 4.6% higher than the cost of operating a similar center without a PCMH. The costs of tracking patients and improving quality — both health-IT-intensive tasks — were particularly high. In total, the community health centers that functioned as medical homes added $2.26 per patient per month in operating costs, or about $500,000 per month for the average clinic.[34]

But the authors observed that another study of an integrated delivery system's use of a PCMH showed that it saved $18 per patient per month in averted hospitalizations and ER visits. Most of those savings accrued to payers, indicating the need for reimbursement sufficient to cover the infrastructure costs of PCMHs.

A more recent study looked at the cost of establishing medical homes in Colorado and Utah. The authors found that the PCMH-related costs per full-time equivalent primary care clinician varied across practices, averaging

$7,961 per month in Utah practices and $9,658 in Colorado practices. The average estimated cost per member per month (PMPM) was $3.85 in Utah and $4.83 in Colorado.[35]

As noted earlier, some PCMHs that are part of integrated delivery systems have lowered costs and achieved a return on investment. But it's unclear whether that model would work for smaller, unaffiliated practices. What is clear is that the cost of creating and maintaining a medical home could be much lower if the practices were highly automated.

This approach requires the intelligent use of health information technology. By linking together some currently available health IT tools, physician groups can automate much of the work that might otherwise be too costly and difficult for them to do. Moreover, automating the manual processes of care coordination and care management makes it possible to scale the medical home to practices of every size.

# Role of Information Technology

Observers agree that information technology, including the EHR, is essential to the patient-centered medical home's success. But EHRs lack many of the features required to do practice-based population health. AHRQ cites the inability of most EHRs to generate population-based reports easily; to present alerts and reminders in such a way that providers will use them rather than turn them off; to capture sufficiently detailed data on preventive care; and to interoperate with other clinical information systems.[36]

EHR vendors are moving to correct these deficiencies. For example, some applications allow users to adjust the level of alerts to their own needs and tolerance levels. And, though another report points to the difficulty of using the registries embedded in some EHRs,[37] those are also being improved to help physicians meet the Meaningful Use criteria.

Nevertheless, practices need a variety of health IT tools beyond EHRs to meet AHRQ's original requirements for PBPH.[38] These requirements include the ability to

- Identify subpopulations of patients
- Examine detailed characteristics of identified subpopulations
- Create reminders for patients and providers
- Track performance measures
- Make data available in multiple forms

Speak to store staff or visit indigo.ca/plum for full program details.
*Conditions and exclusions apply.
This paper is sustainably sourced. 100% BPS and BPA free, printed on FSC paper.
We cannot provide an exchange or refund on magazines or newspapers.
or refunded onto a credit note for the value of the item at the time of purchase.
store-bought condition with a receipt. Items with a gift receipt may be exchanged
Refunds or exchanges may be made within 30 days if item is returned in

external, web-based registries to
compile lists of subpopulations
and chronic care, such as annual
HbA1c tests at particular intervals
updated data in the registries comes
s, labs, and pharmacies.

ich can be customized by physician
. When a registry is linked to an
notified by automated telephone,
physicians for appointments. Some
care teams prior to patient visits.[39]
on health management, a registry
. It should also have a sophisticated
ypes of data with evidence-based
vide many different views of the

portant include online health risk
ion materials and health coaching,
ms, automation of care management
reports, and biometric home monitoring of patients with serious conditions. Table 3-1 shows how information technology can be used to automate population health management.

| Care Team Process Step for At-Risk Patients | Manual Tasks | Automation Opportunities |
| --- | --- | --- |
| 1. Identify at-risk patients. | * Review charts of patients scheduled for upcoming office visits. <br> * Review charts of patients associated with a specific payer contract with pay-for-performance incentives. | * Utilize algorithms and data mining to identify all patients within provider panel with care gaps, irrespective of visit date or payer. <br> * Stratify and prioritize patients based on risk evaluation algorithms. |

*(continued)*

| Care Team Process Step for At-Risk Patients | Manual Tasks | Automation Opportunities |
|---|---|---|
| 2. Document gaps in care. | * Review multiple screens and fields within EMR and patient-management system to identify care gaps and appointment dates.<br>* Review paper charts for additional information. | * Create reports across multiple sources of data for entire provider panel population to identify care gaps based on evidence-based algorithms.<br>* Flag patients with upcoming visits. |
| 3. Communicate gaps in care to treating providers. | * Discuss gaps in care with the provider as part of the visit preparation process.<br>* Prepare a cover sheet for the paper chart. | * Automate provider-level reports on patients with care gaps.<br>* Automate the creation of patient care summaries for use in visit and between-visit management. |
| 4. Communicate treatment needs to patients. | * Make phone calls to patients, often by nurses as well as other staff, which reach only a limited number of patients.<br>* Mail reminder letters for preventive care. | * Utilize automated technologies to generate outreach by phone, email, and/or text message according to patient preference for all patients in the provider panel with preventive and/or chronic care gaps. |
| 5. Assess at-risk patients. | * Conduct assessments during office visits or by phone using paper or another tool that may or may not integrate with EHR. | * Send all patients the online health risk assessment tool; the results can be used for individual and population management activities.<br>* Offer online health risk assessment part of patient portal. |
| 6. Educate patients about treatment plan and care needs. | * Generate a printout of the patient treatment plan at the end of the visit; the plan may be handed to the patient or mailed.<br>* Make phone calls to patients for treatment plan follow up. | * Offer patient treatment plans and education tools through secure patient portal for ongoing patient support.<br>* Push reminders and other communications to individual and subpopulations of patients through patient portal as well as by phone, email, and text message. |

**Table 3-1** *Identification of Automation Opportunities in Manual Care Management Process*

A health risk assessment is fundamental because it is a key source of data for the analytics used in population health management. HRAs, along with other information, enable practices to sort their patients into four categories: healthy people, people at risk of or in early stages of chronic diseases, people with advanced chronic diseases, and people who are highly complex and at high risk for acute or adverse events. These groups are always changing. Those who are well today may be sick tomorrow, and those who have an early stage of disease today may have be in a more advanced stage tomorrow. Regular administration of HRAs can help keep medical homes apprised of which patients are likely to need additional care in the future.

To reinforce the lifestyle modification messages delivered in the office visit, medical homes should use tailored communications and interventions to achieve and sustain behavior change. These include online educational materials that may be linked to HRAs, along with automated reminders to patients. Practices can also take advantage of the new mobile technologies, such as smartphones and texting, as well as patient web portals that may be attached to EHRs.

Medical homes can also use automation tools to support the efficient functioning of care teams. These include accurate and usable patient data summaries to minimize the need for chart reviews. The summaries, generated by registries, will remind providers of a patient's care gaps and the need to work with them on modifying health behavior. Care teams can also streamline the visit preparation process by identifying care opportunities and having patients complete tests before visits.

To support the workflow of care managers, medical homes can deploy software that automatically sets priorities for their communications with patients, based on the severity of their conditions. Using data from EHRs and registries, this type of application can tell care managers whether they need to call patients directly or whether electronic messaging will suffice.

The benefits of using these health IT tools include the ability to track, monitor, and engage patients; to tailor interventions to different segments of the population; to measure performance for quality reporting; to automate care coordination; to ensure that care gaps are filled; and to do all of this without increasing the workload of doctors or staff members.

# Conclusion

After 10 years of experience, the patient-centered medical home has gone beyond the pilot phase. The PCMH movement has picked up a lot of momentum and credibility, along with financial support. According to NCQA, however, health insurers need to pay PCMHs considerably more than they do today: Instead of an average of $5 PMPM, they should be paying $6-$8 PMPM to support practice transformation and achieve the desired goals. That shouldn't be too challenging for health plans that are seeing an ROI of 6:1 by the third year of a PCMH's development, says Margaret O'Kane, president of NCQA.[40]

With all that has been discovered in the past decade, we now know that medical homes must achieve three key goals to be successful: They must learn how to perform population health management; they must acquire and implement a variety of health IT tools to do that and to coordinate care effectively; and they must develop relationships and workflows with the other providers in their medical neighborhoods.

Major changes in practice workflow and work roles must accompany the proper use of information technology. In the end, practices must be completely reengineered to provide effective, patient-centered medical homes — and the environment in which they operate must also change to permit seamless care coordination. But all this change can be less painful and lead to more productive results if practices use the right combination of technologies to do population health management.

To fully implement population health management, a PCMH must be part of something bigger than an individual practice. That might be an ACO, but the medical homes that comprise such an ACO must first learn how to work together as a unit. Similarly, practices owned by a healthcare system must learn how to work with independent practices to achieve the scale and build the care coordination capability required by PHM. One way for them to do that is to form a clinically integrated network, the subject of the next chapter.

# Section 2

## How to Get There

# CLINICAL INTEGRATION

Clinical integration across providers and care sites is a prerequisite for building Accountable Care Organizations (ACOs). Successful integration requires a population health management technology infrastructure.

## The Clinically Integrated Network (CIN)

- Community of hospitals, health systems, independent and employed physicians, and other community providers who work together to improve care and lower costs

- Permitted to jointly contract with payers and employers on shared-savings or financial-risk basis

- Require analytics for views across the network to manage ACO and other value-based contracts

Here's what health information technology (HIT) can do for CINs:

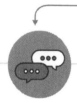  

| **IMPROVE COMMUNICATION** | **TURN DATA INTO ACTIONABLE INFORMATION** | **INCREASE PATIENT ENGAGEMENT** |
|---|---|---|
| • Allow secure texting for provider-patient communication | • Integrate data from disparate EHRs and other data systems | • Empower patients through the use of mobile health apps |
| • Create patient portals for record sharing, results delivery, medication refills, etc. | • Aggregate and organize data in a data warehouse or data lake | • Provide online health risk assessments to ascertain which patients are in greatest need of care |
| • Automate patient outreach via phone, email, or text | • Stratify patients based on needs and reduce care gaps to achieve better outcomes | • Offer patients convenient alternatives to office visits |

# 4

# Clinically Integrated Networks

- *Introduction:* Clinical integration across providers and sites of care must come before ACOs and population health management. But most organizations lack the key components of clinical integration, including a robust IT infrastructure.

- *Clinically integrated networks (CINs):* The Federal Trade Commission (FTC) and the Justice Department allow these networks to negotiate with payers if they're designed to raise quality and lower costs. This is important to healthcare organizations that want to build ACOs that include outside physician groups and services. If they form a CIN first, it must be able to integrate data from multiple EHRs and other systems to manage cost and quality.

- *Automation tools:* To manage population health successfully, CINs must deploy automation tools that allow them to use their care managers effectively. They must also have solutions that enable them to engage all of their patients and follow up on those who have been recently discharged from the hospital. Finally, they must be able to measure the performance of their providers.

- *Need for speed:* A successful CIN, like Advocate Health Care in Chicago, took many years to develop. Healthcare organizations that are preparing for value-based reimbursement don't have that much time. They should take advantage of the latest health IT solutions to accelerate the process.

- *Conclusion:* The ability of providers to integrate clinically depends on many factors, most notably physician governance, cultural change, shared financial incentives, and a robust health IT infrastructure.

More and more healthcare organizations are recognizing that clinical integration of providers is a prerequisite to care coordination, population health management, and accountable care organizations. They also know that patient-centered medical homes — the building blocks of ACOs — can thrive only in patient-centered medical neighborhoods where specialists collaborate with primary care physicians. For this cooperation to be truly effective, all these providers must be clinically integrated.

The Premier Healthcare Alliance in 2012 published a study of the capabilities of organizations in its ACO collaborative. According to the study, most of these healthcare providers lacked the clinical integration they needed for ACO success.

Given that clinical integration is the ability to coordinate appropriate care for the population served, this capability represented a significant gap across all organizations. Those organizations that did score higher definitely exhibited a greater ability to foster coordination and collaboration across the multiple healthcare providers during the patient's episode of care. Disease management programs are one example of such care coordination.[1]

The backbone of clinical integration is a robust health IT infrastructure. To enable care teams to deliver efficient, high-quality care, this infrastructure must consist of far more than networked electronic health records. Provider organizations must also deploy analytics and automation tools that make the data actionable in clinical workflows and that facilitate population health management. When properly integrated with EHRs and financial systems, these applications can enable organizations to scale up quickly for care management at a population-wide level and can provide them with the insights they need to take financial risk.

This chapter explains the components of clinical integration and summarizes the kinds of information technology required for its implementation. Case studies of organizations that are building the necessary infrastructure are also included.

# Clinically Integrated Networks

Until a few years ago, except in group-model HMOs such as Kaiser Permanente and Group Health Cooperative, and big multispecialty groups like the Mayo Clinic and the Cleveland Clinic, clinical integration was viewed primarily as a legal concept that allowed unrelated fee-for-service providers to negotiate joint contracts with payers. These providers often came together through vehicles such as physician-hospital organizations (PHOs) and independent practice associations (IPAs).

The Federal Trade Commission (FTC) and the Department of Justice initially regarded efforts by providers to negotiate together as per se violations of antitrust law that would lead to price fixing. But in the early 2000s, the agencies began to issue statements and rulings that carved out a legal space for clinically integrated networks to bargain with payers if their stated purpose was to improve quality and reduce costs. These opinions have continued to grow in scope over the years.[2]

In February 2013, for example, the FTC issued an advisory opinion permitting the operations of the Norman (Oklahoma) Physician Hospital Organization, a partnership between the Norman Regional Health System and the Norman Physicians Association. Although this clinically integrated network (CIN) planned to negotiate prices with payers, the FTC said that was unlikely to lead to a restraint of trade, because the independent physicians were free to contract with health plans on their own.[3]

The FTC and the Department of Justice define a permissible CIN as "an active, ongoing program to evaluate and modify the clinical practice patterns of physician participants to create a high degree of interdependence and collaboration among the physicians to control costs and ensure quality."[4] Among the criteria for such a program, the agencies state, are the selection of high-quality providers, ownership and commitment by providers, physician investment in the program, appropriate use of health IT, collaboration in the care of patients, quality and cost-improvement initiatives, data collection and dissemination, and accountability.

As healthcare organizations prepare for accountable care, these requirements have taken on a new importance. That is because few organizations encompass all the providers they need to deliver comprehensive, integrated care to a population across all care settings. Even if healthcare systems employ physicians, they usually need help from private-practice doctors and other unrelated providers in the community. This means that their clinically integrated networks must cross business boundaries and that unrelated providers will be bargaining with health plans on shared-savings and bundled-payment arrangements. To do that legally, they must abide by the federal rules.

## Current definition

A *clinically integrated network* is a jointly governed group of providers — including independent physicians, physician groups, employed physicians, and hospitals or health systems — that work together to

- Develop mechanisms to monitor and improve the utilization, cost, and quality of healthcare services provided
- Develop and implement protocols and best practices
- Furnish higher-quality, more efficient care than could be achieved by working independently
- Pool infrastructure and human and financial resources
- Jointly contract with commercial and government payers and employers on a shared-savings or financial-risk basis[5]

This approach is especially important to healthcare systems because their employed physician groups often do not include enough primary care physicians (PCPs) for a successful ACO. The CIN approach allows them to integrate outside PCPs with their employed doctors to create the proper balance of specialties. For example, Orlando Health in Orlando, Florida, employs 500 physicians, the bulk of them non-primary care specialists. To align community PCPs with its goals, Orlando Health has created a 400-doctor CIN that includes both employed and independent physicians, and it has partnered with the largest primary care group in central Florida. (See the accompanying case study.)

According to the Premier ACO collaborative study, having more employed physicians was not associated with a more successful ACO strategy. "In fact, some of the highest performers had the lowest proportion of employed physicians."[6] So a clinical integration approach can be the best way to gear up for accountable care and value-based reimbursement.

## Basic requirements

Successful clinical integration requires a tightly aligned, physician-governed network that uses a single set of performance metrics. Engaging physicians and getting them to agree on clinical protocols is not easy, but it is essential to clinical integration and a common approach to care management. The organization must also agree on how to measure utilization of resources and network financial performance.

# Case Study: Orlando Health

Orlando Health is a large healthcare system that includes eight hospitals with a total of 1,800 beds. It employs 500 physicians, the majority of them specialists. To achieve its goal of becoming the highest-quality, lowest-cost provider in central Florida, Orlando Health needed to get additional primary care physicians on the team. So it formed a clinically integrated network (CIN) that included its employed doctors, independent primary care physicians, and practitioners employed by the University of Florida healthcare system. It also became aligned with the largest primary care group in the region.

Meanwhile, Orlando Health got most of its ambulatory care offices recognized as patient-centered medical homes (PCMHs). And it used the CIN to form an ACO that now has shared-savings contracts with CMS and three private payers.

Early on, Orlando Health recognized that its clinical integration strategy required the use of automation tools for care management and patient engagement. After completing onsite demos and site visits with ten population health management vendors, it chose a company that offered an easy-to-use provider interface, snapshots of patient care gaps, the ability to interface with multiple EHRs, the ability to integrate pharmacy and lab data, and integrated patient outreach/education capabilities.

To do population health management across the continuum of care, Orlando Health's CIN had the same vendor build a health information exchange that pulled data from the disparate EHRs that its many unrelated practices used. The CIN's physicians agreed on the clinical protocols that they were willing to follow and be evaluated on. In addition, the CIN developed a health IT infrastructure capable of reporting on quality measures to Medicare and commercial payers.

Orlando Health depended on its population health management vendor to do the heavy lifting, including data integration and workflow assessments, data mapping to protocols, system configuration, training, and implementation. The software developer also identified and addressed problems with data integrity, including those that originated in the clinical workflow.

An early win for Orlando Health came from its use of the vendor's patient outreach program. This ongoing automated messaging campaign persuaded many patients who needed preventive or chronic care to make appointments with their doctors. Orlando Health also used it as the basis for a local school system's campaign to increase the use of breast cancer screening. Many women are now getting mammograms as a result.

In addition, Orlando Health is using an automated care management program to identify care gaps and intervene with patients who have hypertension, high cholesterol, and/or diabetes. And it employs a different form of outreach provided by the same firm to follow up with patients after hospital and emergency-department discharges.

For Orlando Health, automation was the key to both clinical integration and population health management.

*(continued)*

(*continued*)

By automatically risk-stratifying the population, identifying care gaps, engaging patients, managing care for high-risk patients, and evaluating performance, Orlando Health was able to scale up its CIN quickly without spending a huge amount of money on care coordination and care management.

Leveraging the CIN as the linchpin of this massive endeavor, Orlando Health has improved population health in a number of ways. In the first year, the organization increased the number of diabetic patients with current HbA1c tests by 7 percent; increased the number of patients who received appropriate mammograms by 10 percent and the number who got colorectal cancer screening by 9 percent; and increased the number of patients who closed care gaps by 22 percent. Partly as a result of these successes, Orlando Health generated $6.6 million in shared savings from its first two ACO contracts.

The health IT infrastructure has to support not only performance measurement and reporting but also the operational requirements of improving performance on cost, quality, and patient experience. To achieve these goals, it must be able to

- Interface multiple EHRs to a population health management platform, either directly or through a health information exchange
- Integrate lab, pharmacy, imaging, and other ancillary data
- Apply business and clinical intelligence to data in near-real-time
- Provide a single view of patient data to providers and care managers
- Enable managers to pull up data quickly on subpopulations of patients
- Generate performance assessments of individual providers, sites, specialties, and the entire organization

## Automation tools and CINs

Today's clinical integration networks must be able to do population health management to demonstrate their value to payers. CINs may use nurse care managers to perform tasks that require human intervention, such as working with high-risk patients and calling discharged patients who don't understand their discharge instructions. But to manage population health effectively, CINs need a high degree of automation that allows them to provide appropriate care to every patient. Organizations cannot hire enough care managers to track, monitor, contact, and intervene with every patient who needs help if they rely on manual methods.[7]

The first step in creating a CIN health IT infrastructure is to aggregate data in a data warehouse or a data lake. (See Chapter 6.) That is no different from what any healthcare enterprise or group practice must do to gain value from the data. But, unlike an integrated group, a CIN consists of many different business entities that use disparate EHRs. So the CIN must have a strategy and the appropriate tools for mapping the data from many different sources to a single, normative database or a single view of data.

This mapping process must overcome numerous obstacles. For example, patients must be uniquely matched to the available data on them, and they must also be attributed correctly to their primary providers. This attribution is not easy when patients have multiple providers or frequently move from one physician to another. Also, the data has to be made actionable for patient engagement. That requires cleaning up the demographic data and contact information.

CINs must also verify and ensure the integrity of the clinical data, using special analytic tools. Part of the data aggregation and normalization process involves the identification of gaps and errors in the information. If the informaticians who do this see that certain data elements are missing or clearly out of range, they have to go back to the practice or the hospital that generated that data and find out why.

The health IT staffers in most healthcare organizations are neither trained for, nor have time to do, this kind of work. Yet it is essential to clinical integration and population health management. So CINs may have to retain outside specialists who have the expertise and the proper tools to complete this key step successfully.

Healthcare organizations have some problems with paid claims data, which is out-of-date and often flawed. But at least for now, it is difficult for most organizations to form an accurate idea of how much care delivery costs them without some claims data from payers. In addition, this data can be useful in tracking out-of-network referrals. And, when claims data is combined with clinical data, it provides the most comprehensive picture of all the care that a patient has received.

## Risk stratification

To automate population health management, support providers at the point of care, and increase the effectiveness of care management, CINs must apply analytics to the data in their repositories and registries. This starts with the risk stratification of patients into high-, medium-, and low-risk categories. Risk stratification can be used to assign patients to different kinds of interventions; in combination with predictive modeling software, it can also forecast which patients are most likely to get sick.[8]

## Patient outreach

By applying clinical protocols to a registry, analytic tools can identify patients' preventive and chronic care needs. CINs can connect those analytics with automated outbound messaging to remind patients when it is time for them to make appointments with their providers for necessary care. Such an approach has been shown to increase the likelihood that patients will seek the care they need.[9] It also provides value by reconnecting patients with their physicians after a long hiatus.

The same approach can be used as the basis of campaigns to get patients more engaged in their own care so that they will not have to see a provider. For example, automated messages could suggest that patients take specific steps to stop smoking or lose weight. This kind of outreach could be coordinated with public health campaigns directed at the same behavior change.

In terms of population health management, automated outreach is critical for preventing people from getting sick or sicker. All patients of the CIN's providers must be monitored and encouraged to seek appropriate care or to take better care of themselves to optimize population health.

## Care management

The automation of care management offers several advantages. First, outreach to keep low-risk patients on track can be done with a minimum of effort. Also, care managers can use automated care gap identification to draw up work lists of high-risk individuals who need their attention. As for those at medium risk — chiefly, people who have chronic diseases — care managers can use automation tools for not only outreach but also targeted interventions such as educational campaigns, disease management, and group visits.

In a mature CIN that has used these tools for some time, care managers initiate hundreds of such campaigns by using the software to set parameters for people with different conditions and for subcategories of those populations. This approach can multiply, by many times, the effectiveness of a single care manager. Early-stage CINs may want to start with priority conditions and expand from there to make sure that their care teams are prepared for the influx of patients. The worst thing organizations can do is to tell patients they need care and then not be able to provide it to them in a reasonable time frame.

A CIN must create a unified care management structure on behalf of all its member practices. Though patients will view the care managers as an extension of their providers' practices, those nurses will actually perform care-management and patient-engagement tasks for the entire network. Similarly, the data that forms the basis of the care managers' work lists will come from a central database, and all the care managers will use the same analytic and automation tools.

## Patient engagement

This middle layer of technology between individual practices and the CIN can also be used to increase patient engagement. We have already mentioned automated patient outreach and educational campaigns. But that is only the beginning of the modalities that technology can facilitate. Among the other tools CINs can use to get patients more involved in their own health are online health risk assessments, mobile health apps, secure texting, and patient portals.

Patient portals can be used for record sharing, results delivery, appointment and refill requests, and online communication with providers. The use of these websites has soared because providers need them to meet the requirements of Meaningful Use Stage 2 by sharing health records with their patients.[10] But portals attached to EHRs in physician practices can pose a problem because patients would prefer not to download multiple records from different providers. Various methods, including personal health records on a third-party website and the government's Blue Button application, have been used to help patients assemble their records in one place.

CINs should not base their patient engagement strategies on portals. Many providers do not yet have them, and many patients don't use them. Even at Kaiser Permanente, which has had a portal since 2005, only about 60 percent of members with website access use it regularly.[11] Automated messaging to patients — by phone, text message, or email — will continue to be an essential method of contacting patients who have care gaps or who need to be further engaged in their own care.

# Case Study: Jackson Health Network

The Jackson Health Network (JHN) is a clinically integrated network in Jackson, Michigan. Affiliated with Allegiance Health, JHN includes about 75 percent of the local physicians. The CIN was formed to improve community health and to enable the area physicians — most of whom are in small practices — to negotiate value-based contracts with payers.

The CIN's contracting ability has grown recently because of two factors: First, Allegiance Health in 2015 joined with five other Michigan healthcare systems to form a super-CIN governed equally by physicians and hospitals. Second, Allegiance in November 2015 agreed to be acquired by the Henry Ford Health System in Detroit.

Several factors have aided JHN on its road to clinical integration. First, 60 percent of its primary care practices have been recognized as patient-centered medical homes. Second, more than 150 JHN physicians, including employed and community doctors, use the same electronic health record (EHR), known as the Jackson Community Health Record (JCHR). Third, the county health department uses that EHR too, and is aligned with JHN's health improvement goals. And fourth, the CIN uses a suite of automated tools designed for population health management, including automated patient outreach.

JHN has a "clinical performance reporting system," or a patient registry, that extracts patient data from the JCHR. Analytics applied to the registry data enable JHN to create reports on individual care gaps that facilitate outreach to patients. A quality reporting system based on the same registry is enabling physicians to see how they compare with their peers and to identify the care gaps of individual patients. Each specialty has its own report card, which is used to determine incentive payments to physicians.

The JCHR is integrated with the Allegiance health information system. That allows the automation of test ordering and result reporting and the automated provision of hospital reports to ambulatory care physicians. In addition, the access of most doctors to the community record reduces redundant testing and improves the patient experience.

Like every other CIN and accountable care organization, JHN has had to work hard to clean up its data and preserve data integrity. Clinicians don't always enter the information in the correct fields, and JHN has encountered difficulties in importing data from labs and imaging centers outside the CIN. In addition, they have the customary problems with patient identification and provider attribution. Nevertheless, JHN's managers are fairly confident that they've worked through these challenges.

With the help of its automation and analytic solutions, JHN has improved its clinical quality scores on several indices. Annual screening for depression rose from 51% of patients seen in 2012 in 66% in 2014. Breast cancer screening increased from 55% of appropriate patients in 2013 to 59% in 2014. LDL cholesterol screening for patients with cardiovascular disease jumped from 49% in 2012 to 75% in 2014. And the percentage of diabetic patients with an HbA1c <7% grew from 39% in 2013 to 42% in 2014. Most primary care practices also had drops in hospital length of stay and readmissions of their patients.

## Post-discharge care

CINs must also have a way to follow up with patients after discharge from a hospital or an emergency department. One efficient way of doing that is to use automated messaging to survey patients within the first 24 hours after their discharge to home. Using feedback from the survey calls, care managers can contact patients who have questions about their discharge instructions or their medications or who have not made an appointment with a primary care provider. (See Chapter 12.)

If hospitals want, they can use the same mechanism to notify providers that their patients have been discharged and are in need of follow-up care. If a patient is having difficulty scheduling a doctor appointment, a care manager can contact the physician's practice and find out what the problem is.

## Performance evaluation

Just like any healthcare system or group practice, a CIN must be able to measure performance in order to improve it. This requires analytic tools that can evaluate performance at the level of individual providers and offices as well as for the entire organization. Among the parameters that must be measured are quality, cost, utilization, and patient experience. In addition, CINs must be able to analyze adherence to protocols in the care of subpopulations such as patients with Type 2 diabetes or patients who have both Type 2 diabetes and hypertension.

Before a CIN can measure performance, the providers in the network must agree on a set of clinical protocols that they will follow. This is a difficult but not insuperable challenge. As one study of clinical integration (CI) points out:

> For a new CI program, it can be difficult enough just to get physician buy-in for performance measurement, let alone for care pathways. But as CI programs develop stronger physician engagement, clinical standardization seems to become easier. Indeed, the challenge becomes less about winning physician buy-in and more about how the program can accelerate the standardization process across hundreds of conditions or diagnoses, many of which cut across specialty areas and care settings.[12]

After a CIN has its protocols and its physicians have committed to following them, it can begin to measure how closely they hew to those guidelines and the associated measures that must be reported. CIN managers can also use dashboards based on clinical analytics to see how well their approaches to caring for certain subpopulations are working. If the percentage of diabetic patients with HbA1c >9 does not fall over time, for instance, the medical director of a CIN can drill down into the data to find out why and do something about it. That might include talking to doctors who are outliers or creating automated campaigns to increase the engagement of patients who have diabetes.

Physicians must be able to view data on their own patient panels so that they can see how well various segments of that population are doing and assess their own performance. A dashboard designed for providers should also give them access to data on individual patients so that they can see which ones have care gaps and/or need interventions to improve their health.

# The Need for Speed

Clinically integrated networks are still fairly new, although a few IPAs and PHOs have had success with this strategy for years. Among them is Advocate Physician Partners (APP), a cluster of PHOs associated with Advocate Health Care in Chicago. APP has long held risk contracts from local payers, and its ACO has cut costs for Illinois Blue Cross and Blue Shield. The organization has also improved quality, safety, and patient satisfaction.[13]

Founded in 1995, APP took nearly a decade to fully develop its CIN. Lee Sacks, MD, chief medical officer of Advocate, told *The New York Times*, "It's hard to imagine you could start from scratch and do this and be successful in three years."[14]

Healthcare organizations gearing up for accountable care must move faster than Advocate did. So they will have to figure out new ways to do it. Part of the solution is for every provider in the CIN to use electronic health records — something that APP emphasized early on. But in addition, they need automation and analytic tools that can enable the CIN to scale up quickly for population health management.

# Conclusion

Ultimately, the ability of providers to integrate clinically depends on effective physician governance and culture change. Financial incentives must be aligned, and doctors must be willing to give up some of their autonomy to work with other care providers as a team.

A robust health IT infrastructure is also a prerequisite for clinical integration. Solutions now exist to automate most of the routine tasks involved in population health management. CINs that use these tools can accelerate the process of becoming more tightly integrated and providing value in the marketplace.

Before a CIN, an ACO, or a PCMH can begin to build this infrastructure, however, physician practices and hospitals must acquire government-certified EHRs and meet the requirements of the Meaningful Use program. Fortunately, the criteria of that program are designed to promote population health management. The next chapter looks at how healthcare providers can use Meaningful Use as a catalyst to accelerate their PHM initiatives.

# MEANINGFUL USE & POPULATION HEALTH MANAGEMENT

**BY 2019, THE FEDERAL GOVERNMENT'S MEANINGFUL USE (MU) PROGRAM WILL TRANSITION INTO THE MEDICARE ACCESS AND CHIP REAUTHORIZATION ACT OF 2015 (MACRA).**

MU's incentives, penalties and requirements will continue under MACRA, including increased use of:

### CERTIFIED EHR TECHNOLOGY

- Capture patient health information electronically
- Use patient data to track clinical conditions and coordinate care

### CLINICAL DECISION SUPPORT TOOLS

- Alerts to align care with evidence-based guidelines
- Analytics identify risks, such as drug-drug interactions

### TECHNOLOGY THAT IMPROVES PATIENT ENGAGEMENT

- Increase participation of patients in their own health care
- Increase number of patients who have online access to their health records and care plans

### HEALTH INFORMATION EXCHANGE TOOLS

- Share summaries of care for every patient in all settings
- Utilize technology that incorporates patient-generated health information like health-risk assessments and functional status reports

# 5

# Meaningful Use and Population Health Management

- *Introduction:* The government's electronic health records (EHR) incentive program is designed to transform healthcare delivery and dovetails with other healthcare reform initiatives.
- *Meaningful Use overview:* From the beginning, the requirements for showing Meaningful Use of EHRs have emphasized population health management (PHM), as this brief description of the Meaningful Use (MU) program shows.
- *Transition to MIPs:* As Meaningful Use transitions to the Merit-Based Incentive Program (MIPS), what the meaningful use component of MIPS will include is not yet known. But it will certainly support value-based care and PHM.
- *PHM components of MU:* The MU Stage 2 criteria and proposed Stage 3 criteria have specific components related to PHM.
- *Patient-generated data:* One of Stage 3's objectives requires the incorporation of patient-generated data, such as health risk assessments (HRAs) and functional status reports. Even if Stage 3 is canceled, this kind of data is essential to patient engagement and risk management.

- *Health information exchange:* Both MIPS and CMS' alternative payment models will require providers to exchange patient data with one another. Many physicians and hospitals find this challenging because interoperability is still a work in progress.

The government's EHR incentive program, which has disbursed more than $30 billion, has greatly increased the adoption and use of EHRs by doctors and hospitals.[1] Because of the criteria used to reward providers for the meaningful use of EHRs, the initiative has also promoted the use of that technology to transform healthcare delivery.

The Meaningful Use (MU) program, as it has to come to be known, did not evolve in isolation from other aspects of healthcare reform. The Patient Protection and Affordable Care Act of 2010 (ACA) includes a number of provisions that presuppose the widespread adoption of EHRs and some degree of interoperability among disparate systems.

Among these are the provisions that set up the Medicare Shared Savings Program (MSSP) for accountable care organizations (ACOs) and the Centers for Medicare and Medicaid Services (CMS) Innovation Center, which is charged with testing, evaluating, and expanding new care delivery models.[2] Among the innovation center's initiatives are a bundled-payment demonstration and a Comprehensive Primary Care Initiative (CPCI). In addition, CMS is involved in multiple pilots of the patient-centered medical home.[3] All these initiatives are oriented to population health management and require the use of advanced health IT.

# Meaningful Use Overview

As this book was going to press, it appeared that the current Meaningful Use program would end this year and would be replaced by something else. The program's successor, to be announced in the spring of 2016, will almost certainly be one of four components in the Merit-Based Incentive Payment System (MIPS), one of two Medicare physician payment tracks established by the Medicare Access and CHIP Reauthorization Act of 2015 (MACRA).[4]

We discuss MACRA and MIPS at greater length later in this chapter. For now, the key point is that the main goals of both the EHR incentive program and MACRA are to provide physicians with the IT tools they need to manage population health and the incentives to use those tools as intended.

For example, the HITECH provisions of the 2009 American Recovery and Reinvestment Act (ARRA), which established the Meaningful Use program, have these objectives:

- Improve quality, safety, and efficiency while reducing health disparities
- Engage patients and their families in their health care
- Improve care coordination
- Ensure privacy and confidentiality for personal health information
- Improve population health[5]

The HITECH legislation did not describe how these aims were to be achieved. But it did direct the Department of Health and Human Services (HHS) to include electronic prescribing, the health information exchange, and quality data reporting among the requirements for receiving EHR incentives.[6]

The initial Meaningful Use regulations, published in July 2010, included a framework for moving toward PHM, although some of the PHM-related requirements were made optional or were postponed to Stage 2 or 3 of Meaningful Use. Examples of PHM-related criteria in Stage 1 include showing the ability to exchange data with other providers, generating lists of patients with specific conditions to use in quality improvement activities, and sending reminders to patients for preventive or follow-up care.[7]

Overall, the Stage 1 criteria focus on electronically capturing health information in a coded format; using that data to track key clinical conditions; communicating that information for purposes of care coordination; implementing clinical decision support tools; and reporting clinical quality measures and public health information.

In Stage 2, the requirements for eligible professionals (EPs) and eligible hospitals (EHs) were expanded, HHS says, "to encourage the use of health IT for continuous quality improvement at the point of care and the exchange of information in the most structured format possible, such as the electronic transmission of orders entered using computerized provider order entry (CPOE) and the electronic transmission of diagnostic test results."

As originally conceived, the criteria for Stage 3 (now likely to be replaced) were to "focus on promoting improvements in quality, safety, and efficiency, focusing on decision support for national high priority conditions, patient access to self management tools, access to comprehensive patient data, and improving population health."[8]

# Meaningful Use nuts-and-bolts

The basics of the Meaningful Use program are fairly well known at this point. But we will briefly summarize its essential provisions to clarify the discussion for those who are unfamiliar with the program.

Both eligible hospitals (EHs) and eligible professionals (EPs) — a group that includes physicians as well as other types of healthcare professionals — must show Meaningful Use of certified EHR technology to receive incentive payments and avoid penalties. There are two Meaningful Use (MU) programs — one for Medicare and one for Medicaid. EPs who participate in the Medicare MU program are eligible to receive nearly $44,000 in total incentive payments, and nearly $64,000 is available to EPs who show Meaningful Use in the Medicaid program. Providers cannot receive payments from both programs at the same time.[9]

The timelines for the two programs are different. Under Medicare, EPs have been allowed to attest to Stage 1 of Meaningful Use since April 2011. They attest each year to receive incremental payments for up to five years and to avoid penalties in the form of lower Medicare payments. The last year in which providers could attest to Meaningful Use for the first time was 2014.[10]

Medicaid providers can receive a first-year payment if they adopt, implement, or upgrade EHRs without showing Meaningful Use. They must begin to demonstrate Meaningful Use in 2016.[11]

In the Medicare EHR incentive program, Meaningful Use Stage 2 began in January 2014 and extends through 2017. Stage 3 will begin January 1, 2018, but eligible professionals and hospitals can voluntarily begin to attest in that phase in 2017.[12]

The penalty phase for those who did not attest to MU by 2013 and did not qualify for a hardship exception started in 2015. The reductions in Medicare reimbursement began at 1 percent and will grow to a maximum of 5 percent in future years.[13]

The requirements for Meaningful Use were initially divided into core objectives and an optional menu from which providers had to select a certain number of objectives. In MU Stage 1, for example, EPs had 15 core objectives and had to select five of ten menu items.[14] In a 2015 final rule that also covered Stage 3, however, CMS reduced to 10 the number of EP objectives in Stages 1 and 2. The number of objectives for eligible hospitals in those stages dropped to nine.[15] There are no longer any menu items.

Certification bodies approved by the Office of the National Coordinator for Health IT (ONC) can certify both complete EHRs and modular components of EHRs as meeting ONC's criteria.[16] This regulation allows the certification of various nontraditional EHRs and supplemental technologies that can aid physicians in improving quality and obtaining government incentives.

The certification requirements adopted in 2011 reflected the MU Stage 1 criteria. Since 2015, providers who attest in MU Stage 1 or Stage 2 have been required to use EHRs that meet ONC's 2014 edition requirements.[17]

## Upping the ante in Stages 2 and 3

The MU Stage 2 requirements are considerably stiffer than those of Stage 1, but were watered down substantially in 2015. For example, EPs were originally required to ensure that 5 percent of patients seen during the reporting period viewed, downloaded, or transmitted health records that were available online. That requirement has been reduced to just one patient. Similarly, instead of attesting that 5 percent of their patients exchanged secure messages with them, EPs only have to attest that they have the capability to do this messaging.[18]

In the same rule that altered the Stages 1 and 2 requirements, CMS also finalized the criteria for Stage 3. In this phase, eligible providers must meet eight objectives, including five that have components of interoperability between disparate EHRs. The objectives include protection of patient health information, electronic prescribing, clinical decision support, computerized provider order entry, patient electronic access to health information, coordination of care through patient engagement, health information exchange, and public health and clinical data registry reporting.[19]

# PHM Components of Meaningful Use

EHRs were not originally designed for population health management. They were supposed to help physicians document better, reduce recordkeeping costs, and justify higher evaluation and management charges. Although EHRs always had some safety and quality features such as drug interaction checkers and health maintenance alerts, these were very limited. Moreover, the lack of interoperability among disparate EHRs has made it difficult for providers to exchange information with each other.

The 2014 certification rules have forced vendors to augment their systems in certain ways, and some leading EHR companies have added population health management features. But ancillary applications can still make a big difference in the ability of providers to show Meaningful Use and improve the quality of care.

Bear in mind that only certified EHR technology can be used to show Meaningful Use. Some care management tools such as automated patient messaging applications have been certified. But even if a supplemental application cannot be used to show Meaningful Use, it could help healthcare organizations improve population health.

The following section describes areas where the latest Meaningful Use requirements support the transition to population health management.

# Clinical decision support

In its latest iteration, MU Stages 2 and 3 require EPs to use five clinical decision support (CDS) interventions related to four or more clinical quality measures or high-priority health conditions. They must also turn on drug-drug and drug-allergy interaction checks for the entire reporting period.[20]

Health maintenance alerts in EHRs can meet the criteria for CDS alerts to improve preventive and chronic care, but they fall short of what's needed for PHM. For example, these alerts often cannot be customized; in some applications, users must build them from scratch; and they usually are not linked to automated messaging or PHM dashboards. Use of an outside registry and protocol-linked software would give providers the tools they need for PHM and to help them meet the CDS requirement of Meaningful Use.

# Patient engagement

In Stage 2, more than 50 percent of patients seen during the reporting period must be able to view, download, or transmit their health information online within four days after it becomes available to the EP or within 36 hours after a hospital discharge. But, as noted earlier in this chapter, only one patient per EP or EH must actually do so until 2017, when the threshold rises to 5 percent of patients seen.

In Stage 3, the percentage of patients who must have online access to their records rises to 80 percent, and more than 10 percent of patients seen must either view, download, or transmit their data or must access their health information through an ONC-certified application programming interface (API).[21]

In 2016, EPs have to use secure electronic messaging to communicate with at least one patient; in 2017, that will rise to 5 percent of patients seen. In Stage 3, the threshold jumps to 25 percent of patients. This objective is important in PHM because it provides a key vehicle for follow-up care between visits.[22]

The new Stage 2 rules require that 10 percent of patients seen be provided with educational materials about their conditions. In Stage 3, that percentage rises to 35 percent.[23]

The selection and provision of these resources should be automated to save time and effort. The EHR can use clinical protocols to identify the correct materials, and patients can be sent secure messages with links to the websites where those resources can be found. Where the EHR doesn't have this end-to-end capability, outside applications may be utilized.

In another Stage 3 measure related to patient engagement, EPs and EHs have to incorporate patient-generated health information into their EHRs for at least 5 percent of patients seen during the reporting period. The information could include screening questionnaires, medication-adherence surveys, intake forms, health-risk assessments (HRAs), functional-status surveys, or other data sources.[24]

# A leap forward for PHM

The patient-generated health data requirement represents a big leap forward for population health management. Not only will it be easier to track the health status of patients who have not recently visited their providers, but the inclusion of HRAs could also help organizations measure the health risks of individuals.

The inclusion of patient-generated data in MU Stage 3 is controversial. Healthcare providers are not accustomed to considering patient-generated data beyond the items that patients fill out on a clipboard during the intake process. By and large, physicians are not amenable to the idea of having patients correct or update their health information. And many questions remain about how best to integrate patient-entered data in the EHR.

Yet increasing the participation of patients in their own health care is a key element of Meaningful Use and of population health management. Without patient engagement, it is doubtful that population health can be significantly improved.

Some organizations, such as Group Health Cooperative of Puget Sound, are having patients fill out health risk assessments, and Dartmouth Hitchcock

Spine Center collects health status information from patients before every visit. But, even though this concept is spreading, it is not yet a mainstream approach.[25]

An ONC report on patient-generated health data notes that it can be very important for the new care-delivery systems, including ACOs and patient-centered medical homes. These new delivery models depend on patient engagement and on care teams working with patients between office visits, the report notes. "It therefore becomes more critical to value the patient as a source of vital information."[26]

The American Health Information Management Association (AHIMA) also weighed in on the inclusion of patient-generated health data. In addition to the use of patient-entered data, as one AHIMA blog post pointed out, "one growing source of patient-generated data is from an expanding array of eHealth tools that patients and their families are adopting to aid them in the management of their health." These include both remote patient monitoring and mobile health applications, AHIMA noted.[27]

## Health information exchange

When a patient is discharged from a hospital or an emergency department or is referred to a specialist, the EP or EH that transitions or refers the patient to another provider is required to provide a summary of care in both Stages 2 and 3. This summary record must be generated for every patient, and it must be transmitted electronically for 10 percent of transitions of care and referrals in Stage 2.[28]

In Stage 3, the ante is raised considerably. The EP or EH must

- Electronically transmit the summary of care for 50 percent of transitions and referrals
- Incorporate into the EHR the summary of care for more than 40 percent of transitions received and new patients
- Reconcile information on medications, medication allergies, and health problems in 80 percent of transitions or referrals received[29]

The summary of care exchange requirements is designed to improve handoffs of patients from one provider to another. These handoffs are essential for good care coordination and for the ability of medical homes to function well within their medical neighborhoods. They can also help prevent readmissions.

Healthcare providers have had difficulty, however, in meeting even the fairly limited requirements for health information exchange (HIE) in MU Stage 2. One reason is that the mechanisms for information exchange are still being developed in many areas. Despite having received more than half a billion dollars in federal aid, statewide HIEs and the regional exchanges that some of them support have not gained much traction outside of a few states such as Delaware, Indiana, Michigan, and New York. In contrast, private HIEs created by healthcare organizations have grown dramatically in recent years.[30]

Nevertheless, a 2014 survey revealed that more than six in ten hospitals were exchanging data with providers outside of their enterprises — a 51 percent increase since 2008. Though many of those hospitals were only exchanging lab and radiology reports with outside providers (57 percent and 58 percent, respectively), 42 percent exchanged clinical care summaries, and 37 percent exchanged medication histories.[31]

Whether healthcare organizations are doing this because it saves money or improves quality or because of Meaningful Use is beside the point. What is important is that increased electronic connectivity will help them manage population health.

HIEs are also essential to PHM, because they allow care teams to look up information on their patients in other providers' systems and, conversely, to obtain data on patients they've never seen. The latter ability is especially important in emergency departments that treat many patients who have not been seen by anyone else in their organizations. In addition, providers can use HIEs to find out what services other providers have provided for their patients.[32]

Providers can also exchange health information by using the Direct secure-messaging protocol, which allows them to send messages and attached documents directly to one another. Direct messaging is becoming more popular as the health information service providers (HISPs) that convey the messages get accredited and start to form a national network.[33] But Direct only allows data to be pushed from one point to another. The HIE or another mechanism, such as that of the CommonWell Health Alliance, is necessary for data to be pulled out of multiple databases.

HIEs can support or enhance many of the functions required by the Meaningful Use program, notes a report from the Health Information Management and Systems Society (HIMSS). Most significant from the viewpoint of MU is the ability of HIEs to exchange care summaries at transitions of care.[34]

# MIPS and MACRA

As mentioned earlier, CMS is transitioning the Meaningful Use program into MACRA, which includes MIPS and alternative payment models (APMs) such as accountable care organizations (ACOs) and patient-centered medical homes. Under MACRA, which will take effect in 2019, physicians who choose the MIPS pay-for-performance track will have their Medicare payments adjusted up or down, depending on how they perform in four areas: quality, efficiency, practice improvement activities, and meaningful use of EHRs. The annual adjustments will start at 4% in 2019 and will rise to 9% in 2022. Qualified participants in APMs will receive 5% pay increases each year for five years.[35]

In a January 19, 2016 blog post, Andy Slavitt, Acting Administrator of CMS, and Karen DeSalvo, National Coordinator for Health Information Technology, explicitly paired MACRA with the Administration's goal of applying 30% of Medicare payments to various kinds of value-based care by the end of 2016, and 50% of those payments by 2018. MACRA is clearly going to be the next step in this strategy for eligible professionals, most of whom are physicians.[36]

The government's IT plans are increasingly tied to the development of application programming interfaces (APIs) that use the draft HL7 standard called Fast Healthcare Interoperability Resources (FHIR). Slavitt and DeSalvo stated that the government will encourage the use of these APIs to plug a variety of outside apps into EHRs to help providers deliver better patient care. In addition, they said, providers will be given the "flexibility to customize health IT to their individual practice needs"— another apparent reference to the nascent APIs.

The two officials also made it clear that, despite Slavitt's stated intention to end Meaningful Use in 2016, the program's incentives and penalties will continue, as prescribed by law. Moreover, they said, the Meaningful Use Stage 3 requirements will continue in force until they are superseded by new MACRA regulations.

As of this writing, the draft MACRA regulations have not yet been promulgated. However, providers should expect that CMS will introduce MIPS in 2017, measuring the performance of physicians for payment adjustments in 2019. Meanwhile, there have been no changes so far in the Medicare or Medicaid EHR incentive programs for hospitals.

# Conclusion

Meaningful Use may be at a crossroads, with some observers expressing doubt that a substantial percentage of providers will continue on to Stages 2 and 3, even if the latter phase isn't canceled.[37,38] Yet, to the extent that doctors and hospitals persevere and that EHR vendors provide them with the means to do so, Meaningful Use — in its present form or as it may be folded into MACRA regulations — has the potential to create much of the infrastructure needed for population health management.

Whether physicians choose MIPs or the APM route in coming years, healthcare organizations will need sophisticated IT tools. The basic ingredients of PHM — patient engagement, care coordination, health information exchange, and automated care management — all require a health IT infrastructure that includes not only EHRs but also other types of applications designed for this approach.

The next chapter explains how to build a comprehensive, flexible data infrastructure. By using big data techniques and the latest, most powerful computer technology, organizations will be able to handle the volume, velocity, and variety of data that they will encounter as they make the transition to population health management.

# THE DATA LAKE FRAMEWORK

THE "DATA LAKE" APPROACH TO POPULATION HEALTH MANAGEMENT ALLOWS HEALTH SYSTEMS TO COLLECT, ORGANIZE, COMBINE, AND NORMALIZE ALL TYPES OF DATA ON AN AS-NEEDED BASIS.

Organizations that combine a data lake with massively parallel computing capabilities can quickly turn data from disparate sources into actionable information they can use to improve care.

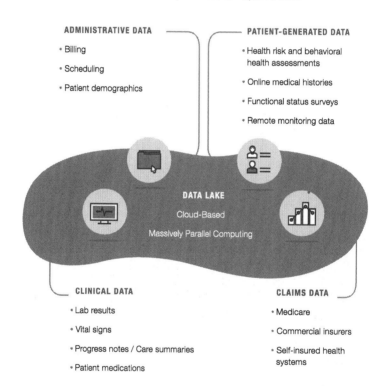

**ADMINISTRATIVE DATA**

* Billing
* Scheduling
* Patient demographics

**PATIENT-GENERATED DATA**

* Health risk and behavioral health assessments
* Online medical histories
* Functional status surveys
* Remote monitoring data

**DATA LAKE**

Cloud-Based

Massively Parallel Computing

**CLINICAL DATA**

* Lab results
* Vital signs
* Progress notes / Care summaries
* Patient medications

**CLAIMS DATA**

* Medicare
* Commercial insurers
* Self-insured health systems

| WITH THE INFRASTRUCTURE IN PLACE AND DATA AT THE READY, ORGANIZATIONS CAN THEN USE ANALYTIC TOOLS FOR: | | |
| --- | --- | --- |
| Building patient registries | Stratifying by risk | Benchmarking |
| Identifying gaps in care | Creating predictive models | Automating work queues |

# 6

# Data Infrastructure

- *Introduction:* The use of data warehouses in combination with analytic tools falls short in the context of population health management (PHM), which requires comprehensive, scalable, and flexible health IT. To address the volume, velocity, and variety of data needed to support the manifold components of PHM, a big data solution is required. But this approach must be combined with other forms of IT to optimize care management, care coordination, and patient engagement.

- *Data sources:* Administrative, clinical, claims, and patient-generated data all have advantages and disadvantages in population health management. The best approach is to combine these data types as needed. Provider attribution, patient matching, unstructured data, and data governance also need to be considered when building a data infrastructure.

- *Big data's role:* A "data lake" framework, combined with massively parallel computing, offers the best solution to the challenge of answering queries and generating reports quickly enough to support care teams as they manage population health. This scalable approach pulls in all data types, structured and unstructured, and allows reports to be assembled without customization or the rewriting of business rules.

- *Analytics:* After the requisite infrastructure is in place, organizations can start to use analytic tools. Among these are applications for registries, care gap identification, risk stratification, predictive modeling, utilization management, benchmarking, clinical dashboards, and automated work queues.

- *Timely response:* To be useful and relevant in patient care, data analysis must be timely. The data lake approach can produce ad hoc reports and populate registries in less than 24 hours, much faster than conventional data warehouses. Organizations that seek to integrate remote monitoring data must remember that they cannot supply providers with data faster than they can react to it. Screening mechanisms are required in order to find the relevant data.

- *Other big data directions:* Natural language processing (NLP), an approach that enables computer programs to "understand" language in context, is being used to extract valuable insights from unstructured data. Geographical information systems hold promise for producing additional insights related to where patients live and work. Meanwhile, genomic research, aided by big data tools, offers the prospect of precision medicine, which could greatly improve the diagnosis and treatment of patients.

Largely because of the government's EHR incentive program (see Chapter 5), the majority of healthcare providers have certified EHRs. These systems give them the foundational elements of the IT infrastructure needed in population health management. For example, the structured data in these EHRs supplies part of the information needed to identify individual care gaps, alert providers about them, and stratify a population by health risks. Certified EHRs can generate and exchange care summaries at transitions of care (such as hospital discharges and specialist referrals), although more work needs to be done on actualizing that capability. And, they include patient portals that are essential components for patient engagement.

Nevertheless, healthcare organizations need a much more sophisticated data infrastructure to do PHM effectively and at scale. Among other tasks, their systems must be able to

- Aggregate comprehensive, timely, and accurate clinical and financial data

- Attribute this data accurately to the correct patients and their accountable providers

- Generate insights into the total cost of care, utilization of services, and out-of-network costs

- Identify high-risk and rising-risk patient cohorts using predictive analytics

- Alert providers and other stakeholders about high-risk patients

- Aid care managers with workflow support, clinical content, decision support, and information on community resources

- Track care plans and make them accessible to all stakeholders

- Coordinate care in real time, including notification of care transitions

- Support medication management across care settings

- Track chronic disease prevention and management

- Provide wellness and disease management reminders at the point of care

- Engage patients with educational content and lists of community resources

- Manage patient-entered and/or device-uploaded data

- Integrate other patient-generated data, including health risk assessments

- Evaluate the performance of the organization, its care delivery sites, and its individual providers

- Perform financial modeling to support contract negotiations

- Calculate payment distributions and track disbursals[1]

Healthcare organizations face several major challenges in developing this kind of data infrastructure. To start with, their data may be "siloed" in dozens of separate systems that can't communicate with one another. If an organization serves as a hub for a clinically integrated network (CIN), that network usually includes community providers that are using many different kinds of EHRs, some with limited interoperability.

Moreover, a large healthcare system, clinically integrated network (CIN), or accountable care organization (ACO) will generate a huge amount of data as it scales up to full population health management. As the organization moves down that road, it quickly discovers that the sheer volume of data exceeds the capabilities of its traditional information systems.

"Once the volume of data increases, the need to scale exists, and if funding is available, the organization can upgrade to a more sophisticated, automated, and integrated solution," noted Jacquelyn S. Hunt and her colleagues in a recent article in *Population Health Management*.[2]

The conventional response to these challenges is to build an enterprise data warehouse that usually includes analytic applications. As of 2013, a HIMSS Analytics survey found more than half of healthcare systems used either a data warehouse or a more limited type of data aggregation system, called an operational data store. Forty-six percent of the organizations used clinical and business intelligence applications, and half of those entities had data warehouses.[3]

Initially, most organizations use enterprise data warehouses to analyze data retrospectively — that is, they harness analytics to find out how patients and subpopulations have fared in the past. That can be useful in constructing a baseline for quality improvement and utilization management, but it has limited value in care management because patients' health needs are constantly evolving. Neither can the retrospective approach be employed to predict the future health status of patients or the cost of their care. This kind of forecasting is essential to any organization that plans to take financial risk.

The more advanced data warehouses include predictive modeling software that can forecast the health risks of patients as well as dashboards that are able to show up-to-date population health trends. Such data warehouses also include (or are linked to) registries that can help providers and care managers address the emerging needs of individual patients.

But, as you'll see, most of these platforms fall short in comprehensiveness and flexibility. So when healthcare organizations reach the stage where they need to address the full range of PHM requirements, it may be time for them to consider a big data solution.

The volume of data is one of three dimensions that necessitate the use of big data techniques in population health management. The other dimensions are

- *Velocity*, or how fast organizations must deal with new data
- *Variety*, which refers to the many kinds of data needed to inform PHM and financial risk management[4]

One source adds a fourth *v*: veracity, defined as the "uncertainty of data," or judgments about the accuracy of data.[5]

Whatever form a big data solution takes, it does not eliminate the need for "small data" approaches to care management, care coordination, and patient engagement. In many cases, these may be registry-based solutions that can be linked to automation programs. Automation tools, such as patient outreach applications, can enable care teams to improve quality rapidly and inexpensively while creating some of the return on investment that organizations are seeking.[6]

As this chapter explains, healthcare organizations must build a data infrastructure that will enable them to jump into population health management as quickly and as efficiently as possible. The infrastructure must enable the organization to adapt to changing business models in reimbursement, care delivery, and partnerships with other providers and health plans. Most important, it must supply the insights the organization needs in order to deliver value, defined as higher-quality care at lower cost.

# Data Sources

The first step in building a data infrastructure is to determine what data an organization needs, where that data resides, and how it can be accessed and aggregated with other information. Data acquisition also involves other issues such as data accuracy, provider attribution, and patient matching, as well as difficulties in accessing the information locked in unstructured data.

The main types of healthcare data are administrative, clinical, claims, and patient-generated. The inclusion of each of these data types has advantages and disadvantages; but for population health management purposes, it is best to have as much data as possible and to be able to combine different data types as needed. An organization must also be able to convert the raw data stream into actionable information in as close to real time as possible.

## Administrative data

Billing, scheduling, and patient demographic data are stored in many ambulatory care, acute care, and post–acute-care systems. Demographic information is necessary — though not sufficient — for accurate patient matching. It is also required for data analysis that involves age, gender, or place of residence as well as for patient engagement.

Scheduling information is essential to determine when a patient last came into the office or had a procedure done and the date of the patient's next appointment. By combining this kind of data with diagnostic and procedure codes and other data, it is possible to discover care gaps and provide decision support for care management consistent with evidence-based guidelines.

Billing data has been used to create registries that help physician practices identify and reach out to patients with gaps in preventive and chronic care. But billing information has inherent limitations. It cannot be used to identify certain subpopulations, such as patients with certain clinical findings (for example, elevated blood pressure or patients with abnormally high HbA1c values). In addition, not all clinical activity is billable, and, even when it is, physicians do not always submit a code for every service they perform. Poor charge capture not only reduces revenue but also decreases the value of administrative data in population health management.

## Clinical data

EHR data is richer than billing or claims data. It contains clinical information not found in billing records, such as laboratory test results and vital signs. EHR data is also more timely than claims data. Ambulatory care notes, including updated medication and problem lists, are available as soon as they're entered into the system, although occasionally they may require the physicians to "sign and close" them. Lab results that come into the EHR electronically are also available without delays.

Because of the lack of interoperability between disparate EHRs, EHR data is generally limited to the organization in which it's recorded. If a patient receives a service outside that organization or network, that service will usually be documented in a different EHR or practice management system (PMS) rather than in the enterprise EHR system. Because data on that care event is missing, it cannot be used in clinical decision support and is not part of the database used in registries or for analytic purposes.

Recently, it has become possible to exchange summaries of care between providers with disparate EHRs. When that happens, some clinical data from outside the organization may be added to the enterprise EHR. Health information exchanges (HIE) may also provide additional clinical data that can be useful in patient care. Nevertheless, this kind of information exchange has evolved more slowly than has the adoption of the EHR.

## Claims data

Paid claims data from health plans provides the broadest view of the care that a patient has received from all providers. This data is typically available from several sources. Self-insured health systems may find that their third-party administrators are willing to provide the paid claims data for employee patients. The Centers for Medicare and Medicaid Services (CMS) provides claims data periodically to ACOs that participate in the Medicare shared savings program. Finally, commercial insurers collaborating with a particular healthcare organization may provide their claims data to the health system. Health plans with which the organization has contracts that require PHM are those most likely to share claims data.

By informing clinicians about the care that a patient has received outside their enterprise, claims data can improve medical decision-making, fill treatment gaps, and prevent redundant testing. This data can also aid organizations in contract negotiations. Moreover, it can tip off ACOs and other risk-bearing organizations whenever a patient seeks care outside the network, either because of lack of access in-network, physician referral patterns, or patient convenience. This out-of-network care can impact profitability, patient loyalty, and the ability to manage costs.

The most significant disadvantage of claims data is that it is not timely. Commercial claims data is usually not complete until 30 days after the date of service; the time lag for Medicare varies, but may be as long as three months for complete claims. So, whereas claims data can fill in the retrospective picture, it is not helpful for care managers trying to manage a high-risk patient who has just been released from the hospital.

Claims data often contains errors because the billing information is inaccurate or because the charges are bounced back and forth multiple times between the health system and the payer. It is therefore important to reconcile claims data with clinical data to weed out incorrect information. In addition, because it is not as rich as clinical data, claims data alone fails to provide a granular picture of clinical situations.

# Patient-generated data

Patient-generated data includes many different kinds of information, ranging from health risk assessments, behavioral health assessments, and online medical histories to functional-status surveys and remote monitoring data. Although this kind of data has not traditionally been an important source of information on the health of a patient, that is rapidly changing.

Health risk assessments can help predict a patient's health risk, which is a basic building block of population health management. Behavioral health assessments such as the PHQ-9 and M3 tests measure depression, anxiety, bipolar disorder, and PTSD. Online medical histories can increase the efficiency of provider documentation and provide additional information about patients. A functional-status survey, which measures the ability to perform the activities of daily life, is one of the best sources of outcomes data. And, as mobile health apps and wearable sensors proliferate, clinicians' interest in remote patient monitoring is starting to grow.[7]

The CMS Stage 3 Meaningful Use final rule specifically mentions patient-generated data. The rule — which is likely to be supplanted by new criteria — would require 5 percent of patients seen during the reporting period to contribute patient-generated health data or data from a nonclinical setting into an EHR.[8] Monitoring data from home and mobile devices is already being entered into EHRs through platforms such as Apple HealthKit and Validic.[9]

# Provider attribution

Without a method of attributing patients to a particular physician, it would be impossible for an ACO, a CIN, or a healthcare system to evaluate the provider's performance or to apportion any financial gains or losses to that provider from a shared-risk or bundled payment contract. Moreover, correct attribution is necessary to risk-stratify the patients on a primary care physician's panel and to assign patients to care teams.[10]

Attributing a provider to a patient can be challenging. Perhaps a patient doesn't have a regular primary care doctor but regularly sees a nurse practitioner or sees various primary care providers in a practice, depending on availability. Also, some patients see internal medicine subspecialists who double as primary care physicians. And, certain high-risk and other types of patients seek "primary care" in the emergency department.

To prevent incorrect attribution, some practices have schedulers ask patients for the name of their primary care physician every time they call for an appointment. In addition, some insurers attribute patients to particular providers. Unfortunately, the provider who has the relationship with the patient may not necessarily be the accountable provider assigned by the health plan, creating challenges for physicians.

Provider attribution rules may follow a certain set of steps. For example, a health system may be asked to choose the primary care provider who most frequently sees the patient. However, if a patient has seen two physicians an equal number of times, the health system must choose the provider who had the most recent encounter with the patient.

Another issue that is very important in accountable care is that of prospective vs. retrospective attribution. Because it is difficult to forecast from which provider or organization a patient will seek care in a given year, attribution is likely to be more accurate if it is based on claims data for the performance year. Computer modeling bears this out. Applying Medicare data to simulated ACOs, researchers determined that 57% of patients who visited providers in the ACOs during a performance year were attributed retrospectively to those providers; in contrast, just 45% of those who visited these ACOs were prospectively attributed. This is important to participants in the Medicare Shared Savings Program (MSSP), because CMS mainly uses retrospective attribution in determining payments.[11]

On the other hand, being unable to forecast which patients will be attributed to ACOs in advance makes it difficult for providers to determine which patients should be managed within the quality and cost parameters of the MSSP. These ACOs are like health plans that don't know who their members are until the end of the enrollment year.[12]

CMS has begun moving to correct this problem. Under the latest MSSP rules, effective January 1, 2016, it is permitting prospective attribution for ACOs that sign up for track 3 of the program, which includes enhanced risk sharing.[13]

## Patient matching

Another prerequisite of a PHM data infrastructure is a reliable method of matching patients accurately with their health data. This is not simple, because each provider has different medical record numbers, and patient names may be entered in different ways that lead to errors. For example, a middle initial or *Jr.* may be omitted, resulting in one person being mistaken for another.

National estimates of matching accuracy rates within healthcare organizations range from 80 percent to 90 percent or higher. But those rates drop to 50 percent or 60 percent when data is swapped between organizations, according to one recent report.[14]

Some healthcare organizations have improved patient matching by using enterprise master patient index (EMPI) software. These applications, which are included in some EHRs, use probabilistic algorithms to raise the accuracy rate.

One drawback of EMPI algorithms is that they're limited to the data available within a single enterprise. When a probabilistic algorithm is applied to communitywide data, including claims data, the accuracy of patient matching can be much higher. A big data approach like the one described in the next section, *Big Data's Role*, can identify patients correctly as much as 98 percent of the time.

## Unstructured data

Roughly 80 percent of EHR data is unstructured, trapped in free text, textual documents, images, and other areas outside of discrete fields.[15] As a result, this information is currently unavailable for use in analysis or clinical decision support.

Much of this unstructured data is information that was not entered in the appropriate fields of the EHR. For example, the completeness of problem lists varies greatly,[16] and a study of EHR-derived quality data in primary care practices found that preventive care services had been undercounted by a significant margin.[17] Nevertheless, the missing data can often be found in unstructured progress notes that were dictated or typed into free text boxes.

Natural language processing (NLP) is being used to extract structured data from unstructured text in some organizations. (See Chapter 14.) NLP has improved significantly over the years, and some EHR vendors have used it with speech recognition to categorize certain kinds of medical terms in their EHRs.[18] NLP has also been helpful in specific clinical situations, such as recording the ejection fraction in echocardiograms.[19]

## Data governance

Data governance is a quality control discipline for assessing, managing, improving, monitoring, maintaining, and protecting organizational information. To achieve data governance, a healthcare organization or a network such as an ACO or a CIN agrees on a model that describes who can take what actions with what information, under what circumstances, using specified methods.

Data governance, which is also a formal set of processes for managing important data assets throughout an organization, seeks to ensure that data can be trusted and that people are held accountable for adverse events that occur because of poor data quality. It applies to data entry by individuals and to automated processes that bring data into a system.

Many healthcare organizations lack a data governance model, a recent Deloitte study found. Along with the lack of a clear strategy and an effective budgeting model, this is one of the gaps they need to fill before they can expand their use of analytics. "Organizations with a centralized strategy and governance structure will likely be best positioned to move from the promise of analytics to superior performance," Deloitte's report stated.[20]

## Big Data's Role

Population health management, as mentioned earlier in this chapter, requires a data infrastructure capable of delivering a vast amount of information to clinicians, care teams, financial managers, and others quickly and accurately and at the scale of a patient population that might include tens of thousands of people. Even the most advanced enterprise data warehouses may not be capable of doing this, because they lack the technical capabilities to handle the volume, velocity, and variety of data.

For example, a PHM-capable system must be able to respond quickly to a wide variety of queries. These might range from how many and which patients in the population have hypertension to how many ER visits were made in a given period by people with asthma who have inhaler prescriptions. However, the infrastructure in many healthcare organizations uses a type of report generation that is too inflexible to accommodate many of these queries.

In a conventional data warehouse, stored data is "bound" to business rules that are implemented as algorithms, calculations, or inferences. This data binding may be done for calculating lengths of stay, attributing providers to patients, or defining disease states that are included in patient registries. Data can be bound to patient identifiers, provider identifiers, service locations, gender, or specific diagnosis and procedure codes. Combinations of these bound data elements are used in responding to queries.

What this means is that programmers must prespecify the data elements needed to deliver analytic reports to users. If an organization could predict in advance all the queries it is likely to receive, such a data warehouse would suffice. But population health management is quite complex, and there will be a substantial number of requested reports that the system has not been programmed to generate.

To enable the system to respond to new queries and perform other functions not envisioned in the original business rules, the software programs must be modified. In a large healthcare organization, this process can take from 12 to 18 months to complete. And, by the time the changes have been made, the use cases may have changed, requiring a new set of modifications. This process is not only quite time-consuming, but it also may fail to meet the needs of users for information that can be acted on while it is still relevant to patient care.

## Data lake approach

Alternatively, a healthcare organization can select a big data infrastructure based on a data lake approach, which uses an ad hoc approach to gathering and running reports on data. In contrast to the relational databases used in most data warehouses, this approach often employs the Hadoop software framework for distributed storage and distributed processing of large datasets in cloud-based computer clusters. (Other non-relational database frameworks include NoSQL and Scale-Out MPP.[21]) Data can be aggregated much more quickly and cost-effectively than in traditional data warehouses because of the speed and low cost of massively parallel computing.

All data is stored in the data lake in its native format until it is needed, and each data element has a metadata tag for easy retrieval. This method allows far more flexibility than the conventional data warehouse approach because data is not bound to business rules or vocabularies when a particular query is received or a function must be activated. Consequently, the software program's data interface does not need to be rewritten to accommodate new kinds of queries or use cases. Any report can quickly be assembled by using configuration files that identify the business rules at runtime.

As a result, responses are ad hoc rather than predetermined, and reports based on new requirements can be delivered in days or weeks rather than in months or years. Moreover, a clinical data analyst or a tech-savvy nurse can format a report without requiring the assistance of a software developer or a database administrator. Because these professionals understand the subject matter better than developers or IT staff do, necessary adjustments can be made more quickly than in the prevalent method of report writing.

The data lake framework also has other advantages. First, data storage can be increased by simply adding more computer clusters. That process is easy to manage and makes the data lake approach quite scalable. Second, data doesn't have to be cleaned up until it is needed. So rather than clean an entire database in advance, data analysts can simply ensure that all data elements required for a particular use case are present and accurate. Also, the definition of clean data, which can vary from one type of analysis to another, need not be agreed on beforehand.

To deal with the velocity of data created in the course of population health management, the healthcare organization situates a health data gateway to the data lake cloud platform in its data center. The gateway identifies data across the enterprise and uses tools to map, collect, link, standardize, and add it to organization repositories and data marts on the cloud platform. If that platform is disconnected for any reason, the gateway continues to pull data from the organization's systems. When the cloud platform is reconnected, the gateway automatically sends it the data collected during the downtime.

## Data normalization

The data lake approach also allows the normalization of data (the mapping of different types of data to a standard format, in other words) from a variety of sources, including administrative, clinical, claims, and patient-generated. Specialized software engines can be used to integrate different kinds of data. For example, if data from disparate EHRs is aggregated, a particular kind of engine can normalize it by applying standard ontologies to a common nomenclature set. These may include RxNorm for medications, SNOMED for pharmaceutical subclasses, and NDC for medications dispensed by pharmacies. By comparing the data available in these three clinical languages, the engine can determine with a high degree of accuracy which medications were prescribed to a certain patient by providers using disparate EHRs.

Similarly, the organization can use CPT and HCPCS codes for procedures and ICD-9, ICD-10, and SNOMED for diagnoses. LOINC can be used for vital signs and lab tests as well as standardized tests for depression. By converting everything to these common nomenclatures, the engine can standardize 90 percent or more of clinical terms.

Because of the time lag between claims and clinical data, another kind of engine is needed to reconcile these two kinds of information. This engine looks at the dates of service associated with each piece of data, along with demographic data, the provider of record, and the type of service rendered to make ensure that the claims and clinical data apply to the same patient and the same service.

## Analytics

After an organization has built the data infrastructure it needs to aggregate, normalize, and query data efficiently, it can start to use analytic tools. Among these are applications for patient registries, care gap identification, risk stratification, predictive modeling, utilization management, benchmarking, clinical dashboards, and automated work queues.[22]

Big data analytics have a wide range of techniques for describing patient populations and evaluating how well organizations or providers perform against evidence-based guidelines. They can also be used to construct risk models that predict patient utilization and costs. Some healthcare organizations have used predictive modeling to forecast who is likely to be readmitted to the hospital.[23]

The first step in using analytics for PHM is to describe the population. For example, the organization may want to know how many patients have complex, chronic conditions such as diabetes and heart failure; the number of ER visits and hospitalizations by people with certain conditions or in particular age groups; how many of them are in the highest percentile for utilization; the differences among practice sites in the prevalence of certain diseases; or how the burden of disease is related to factors such as the payer mix or the age distribution of patients.

The next step is to combine different characteristics of the population to see what the cohort looks like. For example, an organization might want to see how many people who have a lab value of greater than 8 percent on an HbA1c test have been diagnosed as diabetic. (In the United States, 28 percent of people with diabetes are undiagnosed.[24]) In some of these cases, the HbA1c test was performed when these patients went to the ER for another complaint, and the lab value went unnoticed or was reported to the patient, who did not seek follow up.

## Registries

An indispensable tool for population health management, a patient-centric registry contains data that enables providers to improve population health. Among other tasks, a registry lists the services that each patient has received, when the services were provided and by whom, the patient's recent lab values, and when the patient is due for preventive and/or chronic disease care.

Registries can also be used to compile lists of subpopulations that need particular kinds of care, such as annual mammograms for women in a particular age group or HbA1c tests for diabetic patients at specified intervals.

Analytics using evidence-based guidelines and applied to a registry reveal care gaps at both the individual and population levels. Patient-focused analytics can be used to alert providers and care teams so that they can ensure that a patient with a care gap receives the necessary care. Population-based analytics provide a management tool that population health managers can use to evaluate how the organization is doing in comparison with past performance or benchmarks based on data from similar organizations. Some PHM dashboards allow care managers to drill down into the data to see which patients need help immediately.

Registries may also be combined with outreach tools. These applications enable organizations to message patients automatically to tell them that they need to make appointments with their physicians to receive necessary care.

The leading EHRs include registries, along with some analytic and automation tools. But these applications are designed for use by a single healthcare organization, which may not have all the data on a patient when care occurred outside that health system. Moreover, EHR registries may not be designed to integrate non-EHR data such as claims data. Also, EHR registries are still not as robust or comprehensive as the best third-party registries, which may be standalone, part of a data warehouse, or linked to a cloud-based data lake platform.

The most advanced registries integrate a broad variety of data, including clinical, claims, and patient-generated data. Besides generating actionable intelligence for providers, they include financial and operational information that can help population health managers plan their strategies.

## Work lists

Providers and care managers need lists of patients who meet certain criteria. For instance, a registry can be used to identify every diabetic patient who hasn't had a foot exam so that care teams can queue up those services on the patients' next visits to their doctors.

Registry-based work lists can be used to alert care managers about high-risk patients who need a higher level of attention. For instance, a care manager might call these patients to identify their barriers in getting appropriate care, or the work list can be used to either trigger automated phone calls or send out letters to these people. The work list can also be cross-referenced with patients who have been readmitted to the hospital so that care managers can focus on preventing future readmissions.

For a work list to be useful, it must be integrated into the workflow of the care team so that all members of the team have their tasks queued up for efficient care delivery.

## Predictive modeling

As we explain more fully in the next chapter, predictive modeling is the front end of the data infrastructure for population health management. This type of analytics uses algorithms to predict who is most likely to get sick or sicker. Because many of the most common predictive algorithms were developed to support prospective payment, contracting, and benchmarking among payers, predictive modeling is still most often used with claims data. But the latest predictive analytics software can integrate clinical data, too. And some of these tools have been applied to large public databases to draw inferences about individual patients' health risks.

Because of the need for timely, rich data in predictive modeling, a combination of clinical, claims, and patient-generated data provides the best substrate for such modeling. Predictive modeling also benefits from advanced machine learning algorithms that data scientists construct using the massively parallel computing infrastructure found in big data implementations.

Predictive modeling is also essential to financial risk management. Organizations that take financial risk can use predictive modeling to project how many of their patients are likely to be high utilizers and how much their care is likely to cost. At the individual level, such forecasts are the most accurate for high-risk patients. But there are reliable methods of actuarially predicting the risk of entire populations.

It is also possible to predict the variability in costs using big data algorithms. The larger the data set, the more detailed these kinds of predictions can be. One model, for instance, has been shown to predict 70 percent of the variability in cost for any given Medicare patient, which is nearly twice as much as traditional models can forecast.[25]

The key to getting value from this kind of computation is to select the right model. Medicare and commercial insurance models are different from each other; so are models for financial and clinical risk. If one focuses on the likelihood that certain people will be readmitted to the hospital, a different kind of model is required.

## Risk stratification

*Risk stratification,* a subset of predictive modeling, classifies patients by their current or prospective health risk. This is important for organizations to know, because it forms the basis for deciding how to manage individual patients' health. High-risk patients will typically receive the personal attention of care managers between visits, whereas those at lower risk levels may receive only online educational materials about their conditions and alerts about the care they should seek from their providers.

Risk stratification can help organizations decide where to focus their resources. For example, if a large number of the sicker people in a population are obese and smoke cigarettes, those are two significant areas for the organization to concentrate on.

Risk stratification is tied closely to risk adjustment, which uses algorithms to make data sets comparable by adjusting for the severity of illness of the patients referenced in each data set. Risk adjustment can be used for the evaluation of provider performance and variations in care. It also is essential to any sophisticated analysis of costs or utilization. (For a deeper dive into this subject, see Chapter 7.)

## Performance evaluation

The population health database can be mined to show organizations how their physicians are doing in relation to evidence-based care guidelines, such as what percentage of their patients with diabetes had their feet checked at the last visit. When this data is fed back to providers, they're usually interested in comparing their performance with that of their peers. Often, this transparency leads to greater awareness and improvements in performance without significant investment and is a necessary first step for most quality improvement initiatives.

Organizations can also use analytics to measure the variations in care among physicians and sites, both internally and in comparison to national benchmarks. These variations are often markers for inefficiency; for example, some doctors may be ordering a test for patients with a particular condition that does not help them diagnose the condition any better or faster than other physicians who don't order that test. The *Dartmouth Atlas of Health Care* has documented huge variations in care for a number of conditions across the United States.[26]

# Timely Response

To be useful and relevant in patient care, data analysis must be timely. Timeliness is obviously not possible if a report must be customized to answer a query. Even if the query matches a prebuilt report in an enterprise data warehouse, the response will not be helpful to a clinician if the patient data in the warehouse is not up-to-date. For example, test results or information on patient outreach should be available within a day of being documented so that clinicians can receive timely alerts.

Conventional data warehouses can't aggregate and normalize clinical information this quickly. In ACOs and CINs that include many different business entities using multiple EHRs, the challenge is exponentially greater. For this reason, some healthcare organizations prefer to use standalone registries that can ingest and integrate the latest information more rapidly.[27]

The data lake approach, which encompasses registries, is even better for this purpose. The requested data can be quickly assembled in an ad hoc report in less than 24 hours, which is generally adequate for population health management. Admission/discharge/transfer alerts and certain other kinds of data need to be available in less time than that, however, so additional solutions may be required.

The opposite problem can occur when physicians receive data faster than they can react to it. Remote monitoring data, for example, needs to be screened so that doctors receive only alerts about relevant data regarding a patient's health condition. For example, if an insulin-dependent patient has a continuous blood sugar monitoring device, it might be measuring the level of blood sugar every minute or two. No physician would have the time to look at or respond to 60 readings an hour. All that the provider needs to know is whether the patient is fine or is about to go into a hypoglycemic crisis, or whether the sharp variations in blood sugar indicate that the provider should consider adjusting the patient's insulin dose.

# Other Big Data Directions

Big data techniques are starting to be applied in several other areas that are important in population health management. For example, natural language processing (NLP) is being used to extract valuable insights from unstructured data. It can also be used for pattern matching that may be useful in certain aspects of value-based care. NLP has already improved greatly in its ability to interpret medical terms within the context in which they're used. Big data computational techniques are continuing to boost NLP capabilities in health care. (See Chapter 14.)

Big data analytics can also be used to create various kinds of risk models. These models use patients' demographics, conditions, and medications; the procedures they've had done on them; and other variables to calculate risk scores that predict how much individual patients will likely cost in healthcare resources. By aggregating these risk scores, organizations can determine their staffing needs; risk-adjust their cost, quality, and performance data; or figure out whether they can live within the terms of a capitation contract.

Meanwhile, geographical information systems (GISs) are being rapidly developed in a number of industries.[28] Contemporary GIS, which uses a big data approach to derive insights from where people live and work, is expected to be valuable in health care someday. For example, it might show a correlation between residence in certain areas of a city where mold is a problem and the incidence of asthma in those areas. That kind of knowledge could be used in efforts to link social determinants of health with patient engagement strategies. (See Chapter 13.)

Big data is also being used in the rapidly growing field of precision medicine. Phenotypes based on EHR data are being correlated with genotypes derived from genomic sequencing. For example, researchers at Penn Medicine in Philadelphia recently found that small genetic differences among individuals can determine the varying effects on them of a particular antidiabetic drug.[29] Eventually, precision medicine will become mainstream. But first, physicians will need an automated mechanism to help them interpret the meaning of genomic data in the context of the medical literature.

# Conclusion

A healthcare organization's data infrastructure is critical to its success in population health management. Such an infrastructure must be comprehensive, scalable, flexible, and capable of meeting the organization's needs for many years. A comprehensive view of a patient is needed in order to support medical decision-making and avoid wasteful redundancy. Scalability is needed because of the huge data requirements of managing a large patient population. Flexibility is essential to provide a wide range of ad hoc reports quickly and with minimal customization. The data infrastructure must be adaptable to changing conditions and new types of data to future-proof the organization's health IT investment.

A data lake approach can meet all four of these requirements. Because it can aggregate and normalize a wide variety of data, including data from disparate EHRs, claims data, and patient-generated data, it affords a comprehensive view of patient care. A data lake architecture is quite scalable because the ability to store and process data can be quickly ramped up by adding computer clusters. The data lake's ability to generate ad hoc reports without the need to bind data to business rules in advance provides far more flexibility than conventional data warehouses offer. And the use of big data techniques that can accommodate data volume, velocity, and variety guarantees that organizations will be able to use this kind of infrastructure far into the future.

For both care management and financial risk management, predictive modeling is the most important analytic solution in the population health management toolkit. The next chapter explains how to do predictive modeling with the latest big data tools.

**BETTER MANAGEMENT OF CLINICAL AND FINANCIAL RISK**

As organizations learn to leverage the power of Big Data, they're turning
predictions into action to help improve outcomes and lower costs.

| **ADMINISTRATIVE DATA** | **CLINICAL DATA** | **PATIENT-GENERATED DATA** | **CLAIMS DATA** |
|---|---|---|---|
| ° Scheduling | ° Lab results | ° Health risk and behavioral health assessments | ° Medicare |
| ° Patient demographics | ° Progress notes/ Care summaries | ° Online medical histories | ° Commercial insurers |
| ° Billing | ° Patient medications | ° Functional status surveys | ° Self-insured health systems |
| | ° Vital Signs | ° Remote monitoring data | |

**RISK ADJUSTMENT**

Algorithmic tools combine and
analyze data to make predictions
for use in population health
management.

**PROVIDER ATTRIBUTION**

### Clinical Predictions

° Conduct risk stratification of patient populations

° Provide real-time alerts at the point of care

° Anticipate patient risk factors to avoid
readmissions and improve outcomes

### Financial Predictions

° Project financial impact of care delivery for
a patient population

° Use data to evaluate and negotiate risk contracts

° Make adjustments to lower costs

# 7
# Predictive Modeling

- *Introduction:* Predictive modeling forecasts which patients are likely to get sick or sicker in the near term. Predictive analytics should be combined with automation tools to help care teams improve outcomes and lower costs. It is also be used to help organizations manage financial risk.

- *Predictive modeling basics:* Predictive modeling can be used for risk stratification of a population or risk adjustment of outcomes. The approach, which grew out of health plans' actuarial forecasting, is now being applied by healthcare organizations to manage care and avoid readmissions. Predicting health events has limits, some of which are related to many organizations' inability to translate such insights into action.

- *Turning predictions into action:* Most predictive modeling tools from health plans and the applications built into some EHRs use claims data. To make health forecasting actionable, insights should be based to a greater extent on clinical data that is as current as possible.

- *Risk stratification:* Risk stratification is used to classify the population into high-, medium-, and low-risk categories so that care teams can deliver appropriate interventions to each group. It can also be refined to prioritize those high-risk patients who need help immediately. And it can enable care teams to address the needs of those most likely to become sick or sicker.

- *Provider attribution:* Correct provider attribution for patients is necessary for care coordination and performance measurement.

- *Risk adjustment:* Risk adjustment, which is used in refining performance metrics and negotiating contracts, uses different inputs than other kinds of predictive modeling.

- *Financial risk:* Predictive modeling is the key to calculating the financial impact of a risk-bearing contract on an organization. Whereas the positive predictive value of these applications varies for hospital and emergency department admissions, it is possible to predict with a fair degree of accuracy the likelihood that a particular patient will generate high costs.

- *Data sources:* The more data you have, the better you are able to predict outcomes. But every data source available today has shortcomings. Claims data is neither timely nor precise; clinical data is usually limited to a single organization; and patient-reported data, except for patient satisfaction surveys, is largely missing. Thus multiple sources of data are necessary for the best predictive models.

As the healthcare industry continues its transition to new care delivery and payment models, an increasing number of healthcare organizations are embracing population health management. (See Chapter 1.) By helping people manage their own health so that they seek needed preventive health care, and by proactively managing the care of chronically ill patients, these organizations seek to achieve the Triple Aim of improving population health, reducing the per capita cost of care, and enhancing the patient experience.

To manage population health, healthcare systems and group practices must build or acquire the requisite infrastructure, including software tools designed for data analysis and workflow automation. A key component of these tools is a type of analytic solution known variously as predictive analytics, predictive modeling, or health forecasting. In a population heath management context, these algorithmic tools predict which people are likely to get sick or sicker in the near term.

This information is crucially important to provider organizations and health plans that take financial and clinical responsibility for care. Ten percent of patients generate roughly 70 percent of health costs; 5 percent account for half of health outlays.[1,2] By identifying which people are high risk or likely to become high risk, risk-bearing entities can intervene with them to improve their outcomes and lower health costs.

Most health plans offer case management, disease management, and health coaching programs to these members. Some healthcare organizations — including those that own health plans — seek to ensure that high-risk patients receive necessary services and day-to-day support from care managers. To improve outcomes and lower costs, these organizations must connect predictive analytics with workflow automation tools that enable care teams to intervene with the right patients at the right time in the right way.

In this chapter, we explain what predictive modeling is and what it can and cannot do. We show how healthcare organizations can make the insights of predictive modeling actionable for clinical teams and their business leadership. We provide examples of how predictive analytics, population risk stratification, and risk adjustment are applied in practice. We also review the kinds of data required to support predictive modeling and compare the value of each data source for taking action.

# Predictive Modeling Basics

*Predictive modeling* is a branch of clinical and business intelligence (C&BI) that is used to forecast the future health status of individuals and to classify patients by their current health risk (risk stratification). It can also be used in risk adjustment to compare the aggregate health risks of one physician's or one organization's patients to those of another doctor or healthcare entity. Most important from the viewpoint of healthcare organizations that assume financial risk for care, predictive analytics can be employed to predict health costs for individuals and populations.

Although patients greatly vary from one another, the computer algorithms used in predictive analytics can recognize patterns of similarities and differences in the data. Based on those patterns, the applications draw inferences from the data about the likelihood of patients developing certain conditions or exacerbations of their existing conditions. In some cases, the developers of predictive analytics use large public databases as the basis of their models. Other models are built with data about specific patient populations.

To create a predictive algorithm, developers define a problem and then select and evaluate models to solve it. The model developer will identify baseline characteristics that act as "inputs" to a model and identify the outcome of interest that acts as the "output" of the model. After selecting the best model and validating it, they test it by applying it to a real-world database. They may also improve the accuracy of the predictive tool by using known patient factors and outcomes to "train" the algorithm.

Health plans have been doing predictive modeling for years, using paid claims data. The precursor of this approach is insurance underwriting, in which actuaries first identify insurance applicants who are likely to generate high costs and then calculate how much to charge individuals and employers for coverage. Over the past decade, health plans have also used their information on patients' health risks to identify those who might benefit from disease and case management programs. Because of the rapid turnover in their membership, most plans have limited the focus of these programs to the sickest people to ensure the best return on investment without sacrificing quality.

Few healthcare provider organizations put significant emphasis on health forecasting until the emergence of accountable care organizations (ACOs) and new payment models that put them at financial risk. In 2013, just 45 percent of healthcare systems had the enterprise data warehouses that, until recently, were required for this approach.[3] (As explained in Chapter 6, a data lake approach can also be used.) A 2015 HIMSS Analytics survey found that 52 percent of providers were using C&BI applications, including predictive modeling tools, compared to 46 percent two years earlier.[4] This suggests that a majority of healthcare organizations now do predictive modeling. And that's expected to increase significantly in the next few years as more organizations take on financial risk for care.

Another factor that is now driving the uptake of predictive analytics is the financial penalties that hospitals incur if they readmit too many Medicare patients. Moreover, the Medicare Shared Savings Program (MSSP) and Medicare's Value-Based Payment Modifier Program (VBPM) both include measures related to "ambulatory care-sensitive admissions" that could be avoided with better ambulatory care.[5,6]

To address this regulatory burden and to optimize clinical outcomes, studies of predictive models related to readmissions have proliferated. Not surprisingly, a number of vendors offer applications designed to predict which patients are most likely to be readmitted. Some of these vendors utilize the models published in the literature, and others use proprietary models.

Some of these readmission tools appear to be moderately accurate.[7,8] In addition, a predictive modeling application that calculates the odds of a patient developing a serious chronic condition or having a heart attack has been shown to be effective.[9] Nevertheless, a recent paper on health forecasting points out:

There is little evidence regarding how or whether forecasting improves healthcare value. This is due to both the modest level of research and what is termed the "impactibility" problem. That is, even if prediction algorithms accurately identify at-risk patients, intervening to achieve desired outcomes is often inhibited by limitations of current disease management approaches or the general state of medical science.[10]

To put it another way, fairly few organizations are using the insights of predictive modeling effectively to improve chronic disease care. But that is bound to change. Though financial forecasting and readmission prevention currently drive the use of predictive modeling in healthcare, the most important use of this approach will be in population health management because chronic diseases account for 75 percent of health costs.[11] Indeed, a recent study of Medicare data shows that improving care for patients with complex diseases is the most effective way to "bend the cost curve."[12] Therefore, the "consumers" of predictive analytics tools will have to expand from the CFOs to the frontline physicians and other care-team members.

# Turning Predictions into Action

Predictive analytics are only academic unless their insights prompt actions. In the area of population health management, these actions include alerts to providers at the point of care and information that enables care managers to prioritize their patient interventions. On the financial side, healthcare organizations can use predictive modeling to forecast the cost of care delivery so that they can better evaluate and negotiate risk contracts.

To be valuable in care management, predictive analytics must be timely. Claims data is necessary to predict the annual costs of caring for a patient population, but information that is three months old will not help clinicians intervene with patients to improve their outcomes or close care gaps. For that, organizations need the latest progress notes, lab results, and medications for a patient — in other words, the clinical data in an EHR. When this clinical data is combined with patient-reported data between visits, the information available for analytics is even more up to date.

Some EHR vendors offer predictive analytics that are capable of doing risk stratification. These analytics modules use claims data rather than EHR data.[13] Claims data can be used for this task because risk stratification at the broadest level does not require real-time data. But clinical information is required in order to predict health status accurately enough to design cost-effective interventions. Moreover, claims data reflects prior care events and patterns but does not capture recent changes in health behavior; for instance, a heart attack survivor may now be exercising, eating right, and no longer smoking.[14]

# Prescriptive analytics

The leading population health management solutions can now integrate clinical data with claims data for predictive modeling. In addition, some developers offer "prescriptive" analytics, which link predictive modeling with real-world clinical decision support. In other words, they help physicians make care decisions informed by the clinical and financial forecasts of predictive analytics.

Prescriptive analytics consists of algorithms that look at a health forecast from the viewpoint of what might be done to improve the outcome. The hypotheses generated by these algorithms are then measured against the evidence by reading clinical guidelines, textbooks, and/or the medical literature. When a match is found — say, a guideline stating that a heart failure patient should be seen by a physician within seven days of hospital discharge — the program recommends that course of action to the patient's provider or care team.

This is an example of cognitive computing, which is discussed in detail in Chapter 14. A branch of artificial intelligence, cognitive computing uses machine learning and natural language processing to understand medical concepts in the literature or other sources of information.

# Risk stratification

Predictive modeling forms the basis of risk stratification, which is used to identify the patients who will generate the majority of costs in the near future. Populations can be classified into high-, medium-, and low-risk patients with a fair degree of confidence. A common risk stratification strategy is to deem the healthiest 80 percent of patients as low-risk, 15 percent as medium-risk, and 5 percent as high-risk. Depending on which of those categories a patient is slotted into, they might receive intensive care management; online education and support in managing their own care so that chronic conditions do not worsen; or simply education and encouragement in maintaining a healthy lifestyle.

To prevent people from becoming high-risk, it is essential to keep track of and support those who are healthy today but could become sick tomorrow, referred to as the rising-risk population. Of the patients who generate the highest costs in a given year, only 30 percent had high costs a year earlier.[15]

As we explain later in this chapter, the accuracy of predictive modeling is lower for people who are currently healthy than for sick people. But as more comprehensive, varied, and granular data becomes available for analysis, the ability to predict which patients have a rising risk of getting sick will improve. Big data techniques have a role to play here: For example, they can compare the longitudinal medical histories of people who are similar to a particular patient with the care that patient is receiving. Eventually, that data will be compared with patient-generated outcomes data to risk-stratify patients more accurately than is now possible.

## Directing resources

At a population level, organizations can use risk stratification to decide how best to direct their resources. For the large number of patients who are obese and have high blood pressure, for example, organizations might decide to drill down further to identify patients within this group who have other chronic conditions and unhealthy behaviors that would increase the risk of an acute event.

With this kind of refined data set, organizations can tailor care-team alerts and patient interventions by risk cohort. Providers can use care alerts to ensure that the most urgent problems of patients are addressed during office visits. Other members of the care team can use the insights of predictive analytics to reach out to patients who need to be seen. Care managers can be prompted to intervene with certain patients and can also design campaigns to provide assistance to people with less urgent needs. For example, they might decide that group visits with an endocrinologist would be helpful to patients with diabetes who have not been able to lower their HbA1c levels.

## Making a difference

Other kinds of risk stratification can also be utilized in devising PHM strategies. For example, the Framingham Heart Study, a project of the National Heart, Lung, and Blood Institute (NHLBI) and Boston University, has devised cardiovascular risk models for 10-year and 30-year risk.[16] By incorporating predictors that include age, presence or absence of diabetes, smoking, treated and untreated systolic blood pressure, body mass index, and total and HDL cholesterol, it is possible to calculate risk scores for individuals. People with high cardiovascular risk scores can be systematically targeted to reduce their heart disease risk.

Similar to NHLBI's Framingham risk model, fairly accurate diabetes-prediction models have also been developed. And bone density scanning machines that detect osteoporosis often include software that can be used to calculate the risk of non-traumatic bone fractures in elderly patients. In both cases, early intervention could make a real difference in the lives of these patients and to the healthcare organizations that have taken on the financial risk of managing their health.

In contrast, although known risk factors can predispose an individual to gallstones, there is no reliable method of predicting when cholecystitis (an acute episode of a gallbladder attack) will occur. It is possible to predict the likelihood of heart disease, as noted above, but impossible to forecast whether someone will have a heart attack during a risk contract period. Consequently, most risk stratification models identifying future costs will weigh chronic conditions more than acute events.

## Automation tools

At a population-wide level, altering the outcomes of high- and rising-risk patients is time-consuming and labor-intensive. To make effective use of predictive analytics, healthcare organizations should couple these solutions with tools that automate the workflow of care teams. For example, predictive analytics can be applied to electronic care registries to give care managers the tools they need to intervene with patients based on their health status. High-risk patients and other patients with care gaps who have not seen their providers recently can be prioritized for outreach via automated messaging.

Automation can help organizations manage the majority of patients, because most people are generally healthy or have stable chronic conditions that do not require intensive care management. But it is crucially important to identify those rising-risk patients who are not yet very sick but may move into the high-risk category within the next year. By helping to ensure that these patients follow their providers' care plans, and by engaging them in managing their own health, care teams can help reduce the number of these people who become seriously ill.

Predictive modeling is also required to identify those who are already at high risk and to prioritize those who need help right away. The sickest patients can automatically be assigned to care management programs. Risk stratification can help identify others who could likely benefit from care management, based on rules such as their number of diagnoses, types and numbers of medications, and prior hospital admissions. But in a large population, thousands of patients might fit these definitions — far too many for care managers to handle personally with limited resources. So it may be necessary to use criteria such as prior costs from claims data and clinical risk status to further prioritize which patients need immediate attention. In addition, patient-generated data, including health risk assessments, functional status surveys, and remote monitoring data, may be employed to improve risk stratification. The number of patients identified by using such criteria should be aligned to the available care management resources.

Another key point is that a direct correlation exists between comorbidities and health risk. In 2010, for example, Medicare beneficiaries with multiple conditions accounted for nearly all readmissions. Average annual spending for Medicare patients with six or more conditions was $32,658, versus $12,174 for people with four or five conditions; $5,698 for those with two or three diseases; and $2,025 for people with one or no conditions. A good predictive analytics tool must factor in those comorbidities.[17]

## Clinical judgment and culture

When it comes to individual patients, predictive algorithms cannot predict with a high degree of accuracy who will be hospitalized or who will need to visit the ED. So the findings of predictive tools must be combined with clinical judgment to produce the best results in most cases.

For example, predictive modeling might indicate that an elderly patient who leaves the hospital with several conditions and is on multiple medications is at high risk for readmission. But one patient who has those risk factors might receive good home health care and be cognitively alert, whereas another with the same risk factors might have no support at home and might have little ability to understand discharge instructions. A physician who knows those two patients will be able to tell which of them is at higher risk of readmission and therefore a prime candidate for further intervention prior to discharge.

Predictive analytics are still limited in this respect. But when coupled with cognitive computing systems that can learn by observing real-world medical decision-making, these applications could evolve to the point where they are able to integrate a much larger number and greater diversity of factors into their predictions about individual patients. That would make them much more useful in clinical care.

To be of any use in improving the quality of care, predictive-modeling tools must also be adopted by clinicians. That requires some cultural change on the part of physicians. Some clinicians do not want to take "advice" from a computer; others may not have confidence in the underlying data; and some physicians may feel that their instinct trumps evidence.

Here again, the role of clinical judgment is paramount: If doctors believe that their judgment is being overridden by a computer algorithm, they'll rebel; but if they view predictive analytics as a kind of clinical decision support, they'll be more likely to use this tool, much as they use the most critical drug-interaction checks in electronically prescribing applications to avoid medication errors. As clinicians become more accustomed to predictive and prescriptive analytics and start to see them as an adjunct tool used in the decision-making process, they will adapt.

# Provider Attribution

As discussed in Chapter 6, a prerequisite of population health management is the correct attribution of patients to their primary provider and care team. Accurate provider attribution is required for both risk stratification and risk adjustment, which is used in comparing the performance of organizations and individual providers. Asaf Bitton, MD, an assistant professor of health policy at Harvard Medical School, explains that attribution takes effort but can be done properly:

> Attribution happens with about 60–90 percent fidelity, so some patients fall through the cracks. It is a key starting point for knowing generally who your clinicians care for, and getting to near-100 percent attribution within your EHR is an important milestone at the outset of your journey toward population management.[18]

However, it is not always clear which physician is a patient's primary provider. For example, a patient with severe diabetes may see an endocrinologist more often than his or her primary care physician, and that subspecialist may take on primary responsibility for the patient's care. An oncologist may do the same for a cancer patient.

Payers may also create attribution problems. The MSSP, for example, does not allow the attribution of patients until the year-end accounting with ACOs, making it difficult to attribute individuals to particular physicians when medical services are delivered. Moreover, a risk-bearing payer contract may specify that a provider is "accountable" during a particular contract year for some patients who are not in a provider's EHR. From this perspective, attribution is not only about connecting patients with the providers who managed their health during a particular period; rather, it is based on connecting patients with the providers and practices that assume both clinical and financial risk for managing them as deemed by the provider-payer contract.

# Risk Adjustment

Risk adjustment enables payers and provider organizations to compare the performance of clinicians, practices, or hospitals fairly by differentiating between the characteristics of the patients they serve, accounting for actual outcomes versus expected outcomes. This can be considered against internal performance or external performance baselines or targets and is often called *benchmarking*.

The most common type of risk adjustor is based on the severity of the health conditions in a particular population. The Adjusted Clinical Groups (ACG) predictive model from Johns Hopkins University, for example, is widely used in provider profiling. Based on diagnosis and pharmacy data, it describes the differences between providers' case mixes.[19] Verisk offers another commercial risk adjustor that is closely related to the one used by Medicare and the new state health insurance exchanges. Its DxCG risk adjustor uses diagnostic cost groups and Rx groups. Like the ACG predictive model, DxCG depends on claims data.

The difference between risk adjustment and the broader kind of predictive modeling lies in the data inputs. Whereas both approaches use diagnostic codes, for example, risk adjustment excludes prior costs and utilization of services, which might reward inefficient providers. Predictive analytics, on the other hand, embraces prior costs and a wide range of other variables that might play a role in future health outcomes and utilization of resources.

# Financial Risk

Beyond measuring the efficiency of individual providers, healthcare organizations that aspire to take financial risk must be able to project the costs that their patient population is likely to incur. Predictive analytics can be a big help to these organizations, but they must also recognize the limitations of these tools.

Take inpatient care, which accounts for a large portion of health costs. The positive predictive value of a predictive modeling application might be as high as 80 percent, but only for high-risk patients. Applied to people with moderate health risks, the same predictor might have a lower positive predictive value. Predictive analytics can forecast which patients will go to the ED with good accuracy in some cases. But because of the unpredictable nature of some ED visits, which may be related to car accidents or various types of trauma, the algorithm does not predict ED visits as well as hospitalizations.[20] Similarly, it is more difficult to predict an acute illness than to forecast the onset or exacerbation of some chronic diseases.

The more data on a person that is available to predictive analytics, the more accurate its forecast will be. Here again, a big data approach can be valuable. For example, one population health management software vendor claims that, by casting a wide net for relevant patient data, its application can predict 70 percent of the variability in the cost of caring for Medicare patients. By comparison, traditional models account for only 30 percent to 40 percent of that variability, says Anil Jain, MD, senior vice president and chief medical officer of IBM Watson Health.[21]

This model predicts costs better than conventional approaches do because it utilizes more extensive data than the demographic and diagnostic data typically used in predictive modeling. For example, its inputs include medications and procedures across the full longitudinal care process, including ambulatory and inpatient data. Thus, it is possible to gauge the likelihood that a particular patient will generate high costs in the following year. To calculate that probability, an organization must have data on a variety of risk factors, including information on the individual's prior costs and utilization of services, current health status, diagnoses, lab results, and medications; it would also help to know something about the non-clinical factors that are discussed later in this chapter. Applying an algorithm to those variables yields a risk score for each patient, based on individual characteristics, and an average score can be computed from that.

The organization benchmarks its average risk score against national standards or its historical costs. If its average cost to care for a patient is $1,000 per year, for example, it multiplies that amount times the number of patients and their average risk score to predict the amount that it will spend in the next year. The organization can then decide whether the capitation payment it is being offered is sufficient to cover its expected costs.

Each risk contract that an organization holds covers a separate population. So providers have to use the predictive modeling approach just described for people insured by each health plan with which they have risk contracts. (Bundled payments, though they also involve risk, require different calculations based on episodes of care.)

# Six ways to leverage predictive modeling

1. *Risk stratification:* Classify patients as low-, medium-, or high-risk. Use that information to allocate resources at a population-wide level, identify high-risk patients, alert providers and care managers about those patients, and design interventions to prevent other people from becoming higher-risk.

2. *Prescriptive analytics:* Use another layer of analytics as a clinical decision-support tool that translates predictions into recommendations on how to improve outcomes. Support the recommendations with evidence gleaned from the actual patient data, care guidelines, and peer-reviewed studies.

3. *Workflow automation:* Couple predictive modeling with automation tools that enable providers to reach out to patients with care gaps and allow care managers to engage more patients in various ways, ranging from high-touch case management to web-based education and coaching.

4. *Readmission prevention:* Use preventive modeling to identify which patients are most likely to be readmitted. Intervene with these patients so that they receive the support they need to avoid readmission.

5. *Provider attribution and risk adjustment:* Apply risk adjustment to benchmark the performance of individual providers, sites, and your whole organization in comparison to others. Use risk adjustment to measure variations in care, improve quality, and show payers how your organization ranks in utilization and quality.

6. *Financial risk calculations:* Employ predictive modeling to calculate how much care delivery will likely cost for your population in the coming year. Use these figures to determine whether the organization will lose or make money under proposed risk contracts.

The health risks of individuals are always changing, of course, and a few outliers could have catastrophic costs in the next year. Large organizations have a better ability to withstand the financial consequences of these catastrophes than small ones do. Provider organizations typically obtain stop-loss insurance to cushion them in the event of unexpected losses — a definite possibility in these risk contracts.

Predictive modeling can help organizations factor in these outliers by proactively identifying some of them so that appropriate interventions can be offered. By tracking these catastrophic cases over time, an organization can get a sense of which patients are likely to hit the stop-loss limit, which might be $100,000. It can then provide extra resources to ensure those patients receive appropriate care. Though it is impossible to forecast all catastrophic events, focusing intensively on those that are most likely to occur can have strongly positive results for the patients, their providers, and the bottom line.

# Data Sources

To do the most effective predictive modeling, organizations must have access to multiple sources of data that describe the health status of individuals and populations as completely and as currently as possible. Moreover, the information must be very timely to be actionable for care management.

"The more data you have, the better able you are to predict outcomes," Patrick Gordon, executive director of the Colorado Beacon Consortium, said in a publication of that organization. "Access to more actionable data within a process driven by clinical judgment and shared patient decision-making improves the ability of a practice team to proactively align resources with patient needs."[22]

Nevertheless, the data available for predictive modeling today has some serious deficiencies. Claims data is neither timely nor precise and requires extensive edits and cleansing; clinical data is usually limited to a single organization and is occasionally plagued by data quality issues; and patient-reported data, except for that from patient satisfaction surveys, has been largely missing until now. Until the information that healthcare organizations can apply to predictive modeling improves, it will be more useful for some purposes, such as risk stratification of populations, than for others, such as predicting the health risks of individuals with a high degree of accuracy.

Nevertheless, some healthcare systems are beginning to combine claims and clinical data in ways that enable them to use predictive analytics more effectively. And as risk-bearing organizations seek to engage patients in their own care, they are beginning to recognize the importance of patient-reported data.

## Claims data

Claims data usually lags the provision of services by one to three months, but it offers the broadest view of the healthcare services that patients have received and the prescriptions they've filled. In the view of Jonathan Weiner, a professor of health policy at Johns Hopkins University, ACOs and other entities that manage population health will be heavily dependent on claims data well into the next decade.[23] But that is starting to change as an increasing number of healthcare organizations adopt software that integrates claims and clinical data.

For purposes of calculating the financial costs and risks of a particular patient population, there is no substitute for claims information. The clinical data available to a healthcare organization is generally limited to the care provided within that enterprise, but everybody who provides services to insured patients submits claims.

Some health plans make claims data available to providers and/or ACOs. Other healthcare organizations that are also self-insured employers have begun the journey toward population health management by using the claims data for their own employees. But unless an organization includes a health plan — such as Kaiser Permanente, HealthPartners, or Geisinger — it is unlikely to have access to complete claims or encounter data for most or all of its patient population.

The analytic tools now available to healthcare providers are mainly those that insurers have historically applied to claims. Today, when clinical data is combined with claims, it must be integrated into that framework. But some vendors are moving beyond that approach, and eventually, predictive modeling will become more clinically oriented, with claims data used to round out the picture.

## Clinical data

The spread of electronic health records in recent years has led to a massive growth in the amount of digitized clinical data. But much of this data is unstructured, making it unavailable to predictive modeling and other analytic tools. Moreover, because patients receive health care from multiple providers, clinical data generated by one organization may not be sufficient to describe what has happened to a patient or to that person's current health status. Health information exchange is improving, but still has a long way to go.

According to a HIMSS Analytics white paper on analytics, the data challenges to healthcare organizations include the ones in this list:

- Getting data into the system in a structured way, whether it is collected on paper or comes from another source, such as prescription fill data from pharmacies.

- Extracting data from source formats and combining them into a usable aggregated database.

- Missing data elements required for analysis. In some cases, this occurs because providers fail to enter data in the correct fields. Data may also be unobtainable if providers cannot exchange information electronically or if the data is housed in multiple databases within an enterprise.[24]

Even if an organization has an enterprise data warehouse (EDW), it might find that it takes too long to aggregate and normalize the data for the predictive analytics that are used in care management. A healthcare system might solve this problem by building a registry within the EDW and making sure that the registry receives updates on clinical data, such as lab results, within 24 hours of its becoming available. In an organization that includes multiple inpatient and ambulatory EHRs, one solution is to create a registry that receives data directly from the organization's or the ACO's internal health information exchange.[25] Another promising approach, as noted in Chapter 6, is to form a data lake using a Hadoop software framework, which can produce reports and update registries in less than a day.

## Patient-reported data

To increase the accuracy of predictive analytics and risk stratification, it is essential to obtain information on how patients regard their own health status, their non-clinical risk factors, and the obstacles to managing their own health. Some of this data can be collected during visits to their providers, but much of it changes continually and must be gathered between visits or after discharge from the hospital. Consequently, organizations must provide ways for patients to report this data themselves on a regular basis.

The importance of patient-reported data cannot be overestimated. For example, a particular patient might be considered at moderate risk based on clinical data such as slightly elevated blood pressure and obesity. But that patient's propensity to become seriously ill is much greater if one considers the person's lifestyle, socioeconomic status, and ability to obtain healthy food. The chance of a recently discharged patient being readmitted, similarly, will be higher if that person has no one to take care of him or her at home, is depressed, or cannot afford the copayments for prescription drugs.

Among the types of patient surveys that have been developed for collecting information pertinent to health risks are health risk assessments (HRAs), patient activation surveys, and functional status surveys. HRAs, which are used mostly by large, self-insured employers, ask people about a wide range of health and lifestyle factors. Activation instruments measure a patient's knowledge, skills, and confidence in managing his or her own health care. Functional status surveys, which some providers use to measure outcomes after hospitalizations or post-acute care, ask patients how they're feeling and how well they're functioning. Both generic and condition-specific instruments are available for this purpose.[26]

The healthcare providers that have begun using HRAs are applying them in a different way than employers do. Whereas employers tend to use HRAs in wellness and health coaching programs, healthcare organizations use these tools to collect outcomes data, to improve the patient experience, and to guide post-discharge care. Functional status surveys are often included in these HRAs. For example, some providers use the 12-question short-form survey known as the SF-12 functional status instrument with patients recovering from knee surgery.

## Broadening the data palette

As mentioned earlier in this chapter, non-clinical factors that affect health status and the ability to access medical help can be important in patient outcomes. Data on the social determinants of health (SDH), which we explore in Chapter 13, is therefore relevant to predictive modeling.

The challenge is how to find this data and convert it into computable form. Not much of it is available in the structured fields of EHRs, although some applications include fields for living status, marital status, and employment status. The Institute of Medicine (IOM) has said EHR vendors should be required to include additional data on educational attainment, financial resource strain, stress, depression, physical activity, social isolation, intimate partner violence, and neighborhood median household income.[27]

Some of this information can be culled from unstructured portions of EHRs, using natural language processing (see Chapter 14). In addition, some care management systems prompt care coordinators to ask patients about their living arrangements, and instruments are available to measure a person's depression. A patient's zip code can enable researchers to scan U.S. Census databases for the median household income and the median educational attainment in that person's neighborhood. And the Centers for Disease Control and Prevention (CDC) has released a quantity of data that can be useful in searching for social determinants of health.

# Conclusion

Predictive analytics are emerging as must-have tools for any organization that wants to do population health management. These analytics cover a wide range of applications, including those that forecast patients' future health, classify them by their current health status, predict hospitalizations and readmissions, and adjust providers' performance evaluations by their case mix. In addition, predictive modeling is being used extensively to help organizations calculate the likely cost of caring for a particular population. This function is an increasingly important one as more and more organizations take financial risk for care.

Predictive modeling has some serious limitations. The biggest challenges have to do with the available data. Claims and clinical data both have their own issues, and patient-reported data — which could form a much fuller picture of a patient's situation — is still quite limited. But predictive analytics are already invaluable tools in the new healthcare delivery models. As the data improves and new algorithms are devised, the value of these tools will increase further, but only if they're connected to workflow automation solutions that make their insights actionable.

Predictive analytics, as discussed earlier in this chapter, are as important to managing within a budget as they are to producing better patient outcomes and improving an organization's quality scores. But, along with other population health management IT solutions, they do not fit comfortably into traditional notions of return on investment (ROI), because it is difficult to measure the impact of costs that are avoided across a health system. As we discuss in the next chapter, organizations need to change their definition of ROI as they move into the era of value-based reimbursement.

As healthcare organizations and clinicians are rewarded for meeting quality targets while also finding ways to rein in costs, it's important that organizations invest in the technologies required for success. Here's how organizations can realize ROI in a value-based reimbursement environment.

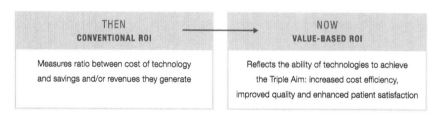

| THEN | NOW |
| --- | --- |
| **CONVENTIONAL ROI** | **VALUE-BASED ROI** |
| Measures ratio between cost of technology and savings and/or revenues they generate | Reflects the ability of technologies to achieve the Triple Aim: increased cost efficiency, improved quality and enhanced patient satisfaction |

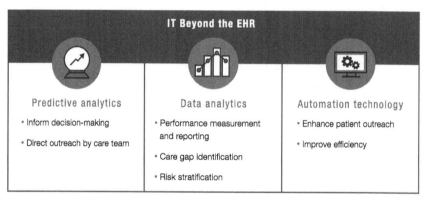

### IT Beyond the EHR

**Predictive analytics**

- Inform decision-making
- Direct outreach by care team

**Data analytics**

- Performance measurement and reporting
- Care gap identification
- Risk stratification

**Automation technology**

- Enhance patient outreach
- Improve efficiency

**INCREASE REVENUE**

- Better efficiency results in **increased capacity** to handle more patients
- **Fewer care gaps** result in more fee-for-service revenue
- Patient outreach and improved care quality result in **pay-for-performance rewards**

**INCREASE SAVINGS**

- **Health cost savings** that increase retained revenue under risk contracts
- **Operational savings** that can be reinvested in care management
- Healthier patients **reduce future unnecessary healthcare costs**

# 8

# Automation Solutions and the ROI of Change

- *Introduction:* How organizations can achieve ROI in a value-based reimbursement environment.
- *Financial environment:* As financial pressures increase on healthcare organizations, new payment models require a different kind of health IT infrastructure.
- *The new return on investment:* ROI from population health management IT, based on improved quality and efficiency, is becoming important with the emergence of new healthcare payment models.
- *Automated population health management:* Automation tools can manage population health, avoiding manual methods that are expensive and time-consuming.
- *How automation produces ROI:* Patient outreach, analytics, care management, patient engagement, and transitions of care can all be performed efficiently at a population-wide level with the help of automation and analytic solutions.
- *How to calculate ROI:* The ROI from using three automation tools is calculated for a hypothetical group of 200 physicians.

As the U.S. healthcare system shifts toward a value-based reimbursement model, healthcare organizations need to adjust their thinking about the concept of return on investment (ROI).

Conventional ROI measures the ratio between the cost of new equipment, software, or staff and the savings and/or revenues they generate. But in a world where providers are rewarded for meeting quality targets and/or are at financial risk for medical costs, the definition of ROI has to change. It should reflect the ability of technological solutions to increase staff efficiency and contain healthcare costs.

Analytic and automation tools can be used to manage population health, and they're now indispensable in helping providers obtain higher value-based payments. The best solutions designed for population health management offer four types of ROI:

- Health cost savings that increase provider-retained revenue under risk contracts

- Bigger pay-for-performance rewards because of patient outreach and higher quality care

- Increased fee-for-service revenues from patient visits to fill care gaps

- Operational savings that can be reinvested in care management

In this chapter, we discuss how healthcare organizations should measure health IT return on investment in the new environment, with examples of how specific healthcare providers approach this issue. We conclude with a hypothetical scenario that shows how ROI can be calculated.

Hospitals and healthcare organizations have faced an increasingly adverse financial environment in the past few years. Hospitals' operating margins dropped steeply from 2012 to 2013 as the absorption of physician practices and outlays for health IT drove up their costs.[1] Although their margins recovered with cost-cutting in 2014,[2] healthcare reform and value-based reimbursement have created new challenges.

The Affordable Care Act (ACA) has proved to be a mixed blessing for healthcare organizations so far. Fewer of the uninsured are signing up for coverage through the state insurance exchanges than expected.[3] Only thirty-one states have expanded Medicaid.[4] High deductibles in many health plans have discouraged some insured people from seeking care.[5] And some insurance companies are keeping costs down in the exchange plans by selectively contracting with lower-cost providers.[6]

Meanwhile, Medicare and Medicaid payments continue to cover only part of care delivery costs.[7] The amount of hospital expenses that go to bad debt and charity care continues to rise.[8] And the ability of hospitals to bargain with commercial payers depends largely on their market clout — a key reason for the new wave of consolidation among healthcare providers.[9] Independent physicians have little bargaining power; their average reimbursement from private plans is expected to continue declining because of the recent mergers of several national insurers.[10]

Healthcare organizations also must bear the growing costs that result from unfunded government mandates. These include investments in health IT to meet Meaningful Use requirements that, for hospitals and large physician practices, can be in the multi-million-dollar range.[11] The industry-wide conversion to ICD-10 diagnostic codes — while not catastrophic — has also been quite expensive when software and training costs and productivity losses are included.[12]

The Centers for Medicare and Medicaid Services (CMS) is reducing payments to hospitals that have excessive readmission rates.[13] Many hospitals are being penalized financially under Medicare's value-based payment program if their costs are too high or if they miss quality targets.[14] Starting in 2015, groups of 100 or more eligible professionals became subject to CMS's value-based modifier. This pay-for-performance program will be applied to groups of ten or more physicians in 2016 and to all physicians in 2017.[15]

Starting in 2019, as noted earlier, CMS will start paying physicians in traditional Medicare either under the new Merit-Based Incentive Payment System (MIPS) or through alternative payment models (APMs) such as accountable care organizations (ACOs) and patient-centered medical homes (PCMHs). MIPS will score doctors on quality, resource use, meaningful use of EHRs, and practice improvement activities.[16]

## Transition to value-based payments

The introduction of the value-based modifier, MIPS and APMs are part of a larger trend in the industry: the move to value-based reimbursement. Though fee-for-service still dominates, healthcare providers can expect to see value-based payment methods account for a progressively larger amount of their revenue in coming years.

Value-based reimbursement started 15 years ago with the introduction of pay-for-performance programs. Under these programs, health plans offer financial incentives to physicians for meeting their targets on a number of quality measures.[17] To reach these targets, practices must regularly measure their performance — a nearly impossible task without the use of information technology, including the EHR and other types of applications.

Several years ago, the patient-centered medical home movement began to gain traction. (See Chapter 3.) As payers started to see the potential of this approach for lowering costs, they began to reward physician practices for gaining PCMH recognition. The National Committee for Quality Assurance (NCQA), which recognizes the bulk of medical homes, requires that practices show their mastery of 26 elements in six categories for the highest level of PCMH recognition. The majority of those criteria involve the use of health IT in one way or another.[18]

Meanwhile, both CMS and private payers are encouraging the development of ACOs, networks of hospitals and practices that take responsibility for the cost and quality of care. There are now more than 700 public and private ACOs. Some of these organizations participate in the Medicare Shared Savings Program (MSSP), which allows them to either share savings only or to take financial risk from CMS. Many ACOs have shared savings or risk contracts with commercial insurers in addition to CMS programs. (See Chapter 4.)[19]

The MSSP requires ACOs to meet quality goals on 33 measures.[20] Because of this and because they must coordinate care among disparate providers, ACOs are heavily dependent on health IT. As we explain later, they must also use specialized solutions to manage population health, which is especially important if they're taking assuming risk.

Bundled payments, which are budgets for episodes of care, are also growing in importance. CMS in 2013 launched a bundled payment demonstration project that currently has over 1,600 participants.[21] Meanwhile, many healthcare organizations are entering or considering entering bundled-payment agreements with private payers.[22] Typically, these arrangements involve hospitalization and post-acute care for a specified period, although some providers are also experimenting with payment bundling for episodes of chronic care. Again, health IT is indispensable, not only for communications between hospitals and other providers but also for tracking services and dividing payments.

At this point, most healthcare organizations recognize that the payment system is changing nationally and that they must prepare for value-based reimbursement, regardless of their market's present dynamics. They know they cannot do it without health IT. But the transition to value-based payment may still take years to reach the tipping point where more revenue will be tied to value than to volume, and providers must be sure that they will see a return on their investment in PHM software. So their chief financial officers ask, "How do we measure ROI?" The answer depends on the kinds of IT tools they acquire and how those tools can help them achieve their strategic goals.

## The new return on investment

The evidence of "hard" ROI from legacy healthcare IT is mixed,[23,24] and the "soft" return from quality improvement has been difficult to prove. But when new applications for population health management (PHM) are combined with existing clinical data, the case that health IT can generate ROI is much stronger.

Clinical applications have been typically designed for traditional fee-for-service sick care, not for PHM.[25] For a practice to become a patient-centered medical home or function effectively within an ACO, or for a healthcare organization to form a well-coordinated, high-quality ACO, it needs ancillary applications that can use clinical and claims data to manage population health. By automating the process of ensuring that all patients receive the right care at the right time, these tools can help organizations increase their value-based reimbursement, thereby achieving ROI.

Even in a fee-for-service environment, some ROI can be expected from the use of patient outreach applications that spur patients to make appointments for needed preventive and chronic care. But most of the ROI from PHM solutions emerges in the business models that reward higher quality and efficiency. These rewards include pay-for-performance (P4P) incentives, PCMH care coordination payments, ACO shared-savings and risk contracts, bundled payments, and the potential upside of Medicare's value-based modifiers.

According to the Health Information Management and Systems Society (HIMSS), health IT can create these five kinds of value:

- *Satisfaction:* The satisfaction level of patients, providers, staff, and others
- *Treatment/clinical:* Patient safety, quality of care, and efficiency
- *Electronic information/data:* The use of evidence-based guidelines, data sharing, population health, and quality reporting
- *Prevention/patient education:* Improved disease surveillance and patient compliance with therapies
- *Savings:* The savings from improvements such as reduced days in accounts receivable, patient wait times, and emergency department admissions[26]

In HIMSS's schema, value extends far beyond the hard ROI of immediate savings and revenue increases. The value created by health IT benefits not only providers but also patients, payers, and the community — in other words, those who determine what providers are worth and what they should be paid. If value-based reimbursement is framed in these terms, health IT solutions for population health management (PHM) hold the key to ROI in the new healthcare environment.

# Automated Population Health Management

Population health management, as stated earlier, requires healthcare organizations to optimize the health of their patients. Rather than focus mainly on diagnosis and treatment, providers must also try to prevent patients from getting sick or sicker. They must do this as efficiently as possible to conserve the limited amount of healthcare resources.

To manage population health, a provider organization must ensure that all its patients receive appropriate preventive and chronic care. Not all patients visit their providers on a timely basis or adhere to their care plans, however, so organizations engaged in PHM have to reach out to noncompliant patients between visits. They must also monitor their patients' health, engage them in self-care, and give them educational materials about their conditions. They have to stratify their populations by health risk and provide care management to their highest-risk patients. And they must supply clinical decision support to their providers so that they know which patients need preventive and/or chronic care when they visit the office.

It is too expensive and time-consuming for any healthcare organization to do all this work manually. For example, many organizations have hired care managers to manage severely ill patients. These care managers may not be able to serve all the people who need their help, because they must spend much time doing routine tasks like searching for patient data and trying to contact patients.

The addition of care managers and other health professionals required to do population health management substantially increases the operational costs in patient-centered medical homes. For example, a 2015 study found that the incremental costs associated with PCMHs in two states varied from $7,691 to $9,658 per full-time equivalent (FTE) primary care provider per month. The average estimated cost per member per month for a panel of 2,000 patients was $3.85 in Utah and $4.83 in Colorado.[27]

In a 2013 study, researchers interviewed nine administrators of primary care practices, seven of which included at least one PCMH. Based on the results of those interviews and other data, they calculated that a PCMH requires 4.25 FTE staff members per FTE physician, 1.57 staffers more than the average primary care doctor does in a non-PCMH practice. Most of this difference represents the hiring of nurse care managers. The incremental cost of this proposed infrastructure is $4.68 per member per month.[28]

Healthcare systems and group practices cannot afford this many care managers, so they must consider ways to automate the process. Based on time-and-motion studies at Prevea Health, a multispecialty group in Green Bay, Wisconsin, automation enables care managers to manage two to three times as many patients as they can with manual methods. Routine tasks such as chart prep and patient follow-up communications take less time when they're automated, the internal studies show.

Automation software can enable organizations to reach the entire patient population on a periodic or as-needed basis, whether or not patients seek care. It can provide care managers with near-real-time information on patient health needs that allows them to prioritize their interventions. And it can provide timely alerts to providers about patient care gaps so that they can be addressed during office visits.

The ROI of automation tools comes from multiple sources. Among other things, these applications can be used to

- Message patients to make office appointments for necessary care
- Streamline operations, reducing the cost of labor
- Enable care managers to work with additional patients
- Improve the patient experience, helping organizations retain patients and increase market share
- Improve healthcare quality and reduce costs, enabling providers to qualify for higher value-based reimbursement

The literature on the ROI of these automation tools is slim. However, evidence shows that the patient-centered medical home — which relies on health IT as the basis of care coordination and quality improvement — has helped some healthcare organizations cut the cost of care. For example, the Patient-Centered Primary Care Collaborative (PCPCC) recently released an analysis of 30 peer reviewed, industry, and government studies on the impact of the PCMH. Most of the studies showed that PCMHs were associated with reductions in cost and utilization. (See Chapter 3.)[29]

Today, the majority of medical homes receive pay-for-performance incentives from health plans, and nearly half of them share in the savings they create.[30] The extent of those financial returns has not been quantified, but the shared savings of ACOs — many of which are built on the foundation of PCMHs — in the Medicare Shared Savings Program (MSSP) have been reported.

In the first year of the MSSP, for example, savings exceeded $380 million, and nearly half of the participating ACOs had lower expenditures than predicted. Of those 54 ACOs, 29 received $126 million in shared savings.[31] The next year, 86 of 330 ACOs received $341 million of the savings they generated for Medicare.[32]

# How Automation Produces ROI

Technology-driven automation makes PHM cost-effective by reducing the amount of work required to care continuously for a patient population. Among the areas where automation is recommended are patient outreach, analytics, care management, patient engagement, and transitions of care. This section holds a brief summary of each of these areas.

## Patient outreach

Population health management requires a healthcare organization to maintain regular contact with all of its patients, whether or not they visit their providers. To do this kind of outreach efficiently and in a way that results in better health outcomes, organizations need several kinds of automation tools. First, they must have patient registries that list all patients, their health problems, and what has been done for them. Combined with software that stratifies the patients by health risk and shows their care gaps, these registries can be used to trigger automated messaging to patients who need preventive and/or chronic care.

Research has shown that these kinds of outreach programs raise the percentage of patients who visit doctors to obtain the recommended care. Besides improving the health of the population — which can garner value-based incentives — such tools also drive increases in fee-for-service revenue when patients visit their providers.

Prevea Health, a 180-physician multispecialty group in Green Bay, Wisconsin, has made good use of these tools. Since 2009, Prevea has built patient-centered medical homes in 15 primary care sites that include

50 providers and 17 care managers who care for 29,000 patients. But the group found that its medical homes could not manage population health effectively without automation.

Prevea automated the processes of identifying gaps in care and performing patient outreach. Patients who needed care received automated messages asking them to make appointments to see their providers. As a result, appointments for preventive and chronic care soared. According to a peer-reviewed study, patients with diabetes who received automated messages were three times as likely to visit their physicians and have an HbA1c test as non-contacted patients. And twice as many patients with hypertension who received this intervention had both a visit and a systolic blood pressure reading recorded in Prevea's EHR.[33]

Prevea has not done a formal analysis of its ROI from using automated outreach to bring in additional patients for follow-up care. But Bon Secours Virginia Medical Group did such a study and found that automated messaging generated $7 million in revenues from follow-up visits. Those 40,000 visits created an ROI of 16:1 on the group's technology investment.[34]

## Analytics

To use health IT in population health management, an organization must first develop the capability to collect, aggregate, and normalize the data on its patient population. After it has accomplished that task, it needs analytic and other tools to make the information actionable. Among these tools are applications for risk stratification, care-gap identification, care planning, and care management. These solutions can be used for multiple purposes, including automated patient messaging, alerting providers, setting priorities for care managers, engaging patients, and evaluating provider and organizational performance.

Bon Secours Virginia Medical Group in Richmond, Virginia, a group practice with 475 providers — nearly half of them in primary care — has used analytics in conjunction with other health IT solutions in its PHM program. As a result of deploying all these tools, Bon Secours has seen a 6:1 return on investment.[35]

Bon Secours aggregated data from its clinical information systems and other sources into a population-wide registry that enabled it to implement multiple quality-improvement programs simultaneously. Besides stratifying the population by health risk, the registry allowed care teams to drill down to the data they needed about cohorts and individual patients. This enabled them to monitor their patients' health status and deliver timely, automated interventions.

Bon Secours' ACO participates in the MSSP and has value-based contracts with CIGNA and Anthem. Under the ACO's shared savings agreement with CIGNA, Bon Secours netted $800,000 for its 2014 performance.[36]

# Care management

A growing number of group practices have staff members who are dedicated to providing team-based primary care. But these care managers find it difficult to serve all their high-risk patients. Automated solutions can make the difference between success and failure in this all-important area.

One organization that has made significant progress in automating care management is Northeast Georgia Physicians Group (NGPG). Using a grant from the Center for Medicare and Medicaid Innovation (CMMI),[37] the 270-provider group combined a patient registry and automated messaging with a care management program for high-risk individuals.

Focusing first on out-of-control diabetic patients, NGPG assigned a nurse care manager to each one and gave the nurses the authority to make certain clinical decisions, such as adjusting medications or dosages. In 120 days, NGPG decreased the HbA1c levels of its nearly 7,000 uncontrolled diabetics by an average of 1.6 points. More than half the patients achieved significant reductions in A1c levels.

The group used the same automated solutions to engage the patients who visited the ED most frequently. With care managers contacting these patients to determine the reasons for their visits, NGPG was able to decrease their trips to the ED significantly within just three months.

Although NGPG did not measure its ROI directly, it is clear that the ability to prevent diabetic complications and keep people out of the ER can save money for the healthcare system. And when payers save money, they will share it with providers under value-based contracts.

# Patient engagement

The most potent tool in the population health management tool kit is not a piece of software. It is the patient, whose health behavior often holds the key to his or her future health status. But automation solutions can help care managers identify, reach, and motivate patients to become active participants in their own health care and make measurable improvements in their conditions.

The power of patient engagement has been demonstrated by North Mississippi Medical Center, a 650-bed facility in Tupelo, Mississippi, and a winner of the Malcolm Baldrige National Quality Award. In 2012, this organization's ambulatory group, North Mississippi Medical Clinics, Inc. (NMMCI), decided to initiate contact with patients prior to office visits and to get them involved in taking better care of themselves between visits.

NMMCI had an advanced EHR, but that system lacked the population health management tools required to make a difference in patient outcomes. In addition, the patient registry it had been using for years tracked only the patients a physician had seen in the previous 30 days.

After putting a more robust, population-wide registry in place, NMMCI initiated a pilot project aimed at improving the outcomes for 76 patients with diabetes who had high HbA1c levels, defined as a value of 9 or greater. The group used analytics with their registry to identify these patients and alert care managers so that they could intervene with them prior to office visits.

After the nurses had their work lists, they called the patients and encouraged them to get their lab tests done before seeing their providers. The care managers were also able to educate these patients face-to-face after they had seen their providers. Finally, they sent automated messages to the patients to thank them for their visits and urge them to call back if they had any questions about their plan of care.

The results of this campaign were positive. Of the 76 patients who had HbA1c levels >9.0, 31 (41 percent) dropped to below 9. And of the 45 patients still considered high risk, 39 received education on how to manage their diabetes more effectively.

# Transitions of care

Many hospitals and healthcare systems are trying to reduce readmissions to avoid CMS penalties.[38] Hospitals are also paying increased attention to patient satisfaction, which can affect both their reimbursement and their marketing effectiveness. Scores on the Hospital Consumer Assessment of Healthcare Providers and Systems (HCAHPS), the government's 26-item patient experience survey, are being posted on Hospital Compare, a CMS website for Medicare beneficiaries.[39] And HCAHPS scores are factored into CMS's value-based purchasing program, which can result in financial bonuses or penalties for hospitals.[40]

Hospitals are also concerned about the patient experience in their emergency departments. When people are satisfied with their ED experience, they're more likely to use the hospital for any procedures or tests they may need in the future. Many hospitals use the Press Ganey Patient Satisfaction survey to find out how well their EDs are doing.

Automation tools can be used to boost patient experience ratings while reducing the likelihood of readmission. One such application sends automated messages to patients within 24 hours after discharge from the hospital or ED. The messages ask the patients to complete a short assessment of their experience. They are asked how they are feeling and whether they understand their discharge instructions, have questions about their medications, and have made an appointment to see their primary care doctor. If they have questions, a care manager contacts them later.

Riverside Health System in Newport News, Virginia, has used this system in the ED at Riverside Regional Medical Center (RRMC) since 2012.[41] In the first year, RRMC raised its ED's overall Press Ganey score from 58 percent to 63 percent and increased its patient recommendation score from 60 percent to 64 percent. At the same time, it improved the quality of care by providing additional support to patients who needed it. Riverside Health System has introduced the solution in the EDs of three other hospitals and plans to launch it in RRMC's inpatient units to boost its HCAHPS scores.

Prevea Health has also applied automation to transitions of care with the help of its two partner hospitals: St. Mary's Hospital Medical Center and St. Vincent's Hospital. Using an automation tool to identify at-risk patients who have just been discharged, Prevea has its care managers contact those patients within 24 to 72 hours after they leave the hospital. The care managers make sure that the patients understand their medications and their care instructions. This extra attention helps smooth care transitions and prevent readmissions.

# How to Calculate ROI

We have calculated that a hypothetical group of 200 physicians can expect to derive from using its population health management solutions. This ROI comes from a combination of fee-for-service revenue, pay-for-performance incentives, and savings that represent increased revenues under risk contracts. There are also operational savings, but these are redirected into improved care management that supports the other categories of ROI.

Here is a brief description of the PHM solutions used in this analysis: First, proactive patient outreach software uses a population-wide registry and evidence-based clinical protocols to identify care gaps, send automated messages to all patients, and track the results of the contacts.

Other analytics are applied to the registry, allowing users to drill down to individuals and subpopulations and identify opportunities for care improvement. Clinical analytics also make it easy to gather data and report on quality measures for value-based payment programs.

Care-management software stratifies populations by health risk and identifies high-risk patients. This solution also gives care managers tools to execute focused interventions that lower risks and improve outcomes. In addition, care managers can use the tools to view care gaps before, during, and after a patient's visit to his or her provider. Care managers can also target outreach campaigns to subpopulations that need help, such as diabetic patients who have not received an A1c test in the past six months.

## Patient outreach: Additional visit revenues

The hypothetical physicians group, divided evenly between primary care doctors and specialists, is caring for about 200,000 active patients. Twenty percent of the population, or 40,000 patients, are covered by insurance contracts that include pay-for-performance (P4P) incentives. Another 15 percent, or 30,000 patients, are covered by risk contracts.

About 45 percent of the fee-for-service population, or 76,500 patients, have not received all recommended care. Automated messaging can successfully contact 80 percent of the patients with care gaps. Of those people, 20 percent, or 12,240, will make appointments with their provider to receive necessary services, and 15 percent, or 11,475, will return for follow-up visits.

At an average office charge of $85, those visits to fill care gaps generate $2,015,775 in additional revenue for the group. That includes $1,040,400 in revenue from initial visits to help patients adhere to their care plans, and $975,375 from follow-up encounters.

## Pay-for-performance: Maximizing incentives

The care management tools drive automated messaging to the entire population, across the gamut from healthy people to those with advanced illnesses. In a P4P population of 40,000 patients, care managers would have to make 247,200 phone calls to reach 80 percent of the patients. At an average 1.5 minutes per call, that task would require 6,180 hours. By not having to make those calls, care managers would be freed to work closely with patients at risk of complications, improving the group's P4P scores.

Let's assume that, by using manual methods of care management, the group was able to qualify for 25 percent of available P4P incentives. At an average rate of $1.50 per member per month (PMPM), the practice would receive just $165,000 of an incentive pool of $660,000 for the year. But if the increased productivity of care managers could help raise that percentage to 95 percent, the group would get $627,000, representing additional P4P revenue of $462,000. If the incentive were raised to $2.00 PMPM in the second year, the extra income would be $616,000; if it rose to $2.50 PMPM, the group would receive an extra $770,000.

## Risk contracts: Lowering overall costs

As in the P4P example, automated messaging would also give care managers additional time to work with high-risk patients covered by value-based contracts. Assuming that 30,000 patients were covered under these agreements, 185,400 calls would be required to reach 80 percent of them. At 1.5 minutes per call, the automated messaging would save the nurses 4,635 hours that they could use in care management.

Based on the average costs of care delivery, we calculate that this population would generate medical expenses of about $165 million a year. If a care management program powered by automation tools could save only 0.5 percent more than could be achieved through manual efforts, that increment would represent a cost decrease of $825,000. Under a financial risk contract, that additional money drops straight to the group's bottom line.

## The bottom line

Looking at the three sources of ROI for the 200-doctor group, we project that the use of PHM automation tools would produce annual revenues of $2,015,775 from fee-for-service visits, $462,000 from P4P, and $825,000 from at-risk contracts. Those amounts add up to $3.3 million, many times the cost of the software for a group of this size.

The staff efficiencies created by automation can also be measured. In the scenario we describe, the group would save 10,815 hours that could otherwise be spent contacting patients. That's equivalent to the annual work of 5.6 full-time care managers. However, no organization would assign nurses to do nothing but dial patients all day long. What happens in groups without automation tools is that most patients simply do not hear from their providers between visits.

The time savings created by automation could result in a hard ROI from lowering the number of care managers. But an organization that is trying to maximize its value-based reimbursement would be wiser to reinvest the time savings in greater productivity for its care managers. By enabling them to intervene with more patients, the organization can achieve ROI by providing more value to payers.

# Conclusion

The transition to value-based payment requires a new kind of thinking that equates waste reduction and quality improvement with income. This new attitude must also be applied to thinking about return on investment. The investments that used to produce revenue — and that still do, in many cases — will not necessarily be the ones that will lead to financial success in this new world.

What will generate ROI are investments in information technology that help organizations work with more patients across whole populations — not just the highest risk patients — to produce better health outcomes. The care manager is an essential part of this approach, but any population health management initiative that relies on manual methods is doomed to failure. Organizations need electronic tools that automate routine outreach tasks, and they need analytics that automate the process of risk stratification, care gap identification, and performance measurement. An infrastructure that uses the latest advances in data warehousing and cognitive computing can extend these gains. With these tools in hand, healthcare organizations can move forward confidently to claim their share of value-based reimbursement.

The key to creating ROI — and to managing population health — is care coordination, or planned care. The next chapter shows how automation tools can help providers coordinate care for an entire patient population at an affordable cost.

# Section 3

## Implementing Change

# CARE COORDINATION THROUGH INFORMATION TECHNOLOGY

Care coordination is critical to success in both clinically integrated networks (CINs) and patient-centered medical homes (PCMHs). The right technology is critical to optimal coordination.

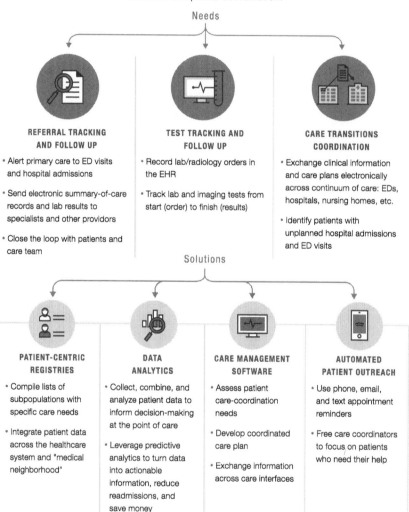

## Needs

### REFERRAL TRACKING AND FOLLOW UP

* Alert primary care to ED visits and hospital admissions
* Send electronic summary-of-care records and lab results to specialists and other providers
* Close the loop with patients and care team

### TEST TRACKING AND FOLLOW UP

* Record lab/radiology orders in the EHR
* Track lab and imaging tests from start (order) to finish (results)

### CARE TRANSITIONS COORDINATION

* Exchange clinical information and care plans electronically across continuum of care: EDs, hospitals, nursing homes, etc.
* Identify patients with unplanned hospital admissions and ED visits

## Solutions

### PATIENT-CENTRIC REGISTRIES

* Compile lists of subpopulations with specific care needs
* Integrate patient data across the healthcare system and "medical neighborhood"

### DATA ANALYTICS

* Collect, combine, and analyze patient data to inform decision-making at the point of care
* Leverage predictive analytics to turn data into actionable information, reduce readmissions, and save money

### CARE MANAGEMENT SOFTWARE

* Assess patient care-coordination needs
* Develop coordinated care plan
* Exchange information across care interfaces

### AUTOMATED PATIENT OUTREACH

* Use phone, email, and text appointment reminders
* Free care coordinators to focus on patients who need their help

# 9

# Care Coordination

- *Introduction:* Care coordination, which is vital to both ACOs and patient-centered medical homes (PCMHs), has made progress in U.S. health care — although it can achieve its full potential only through information technology.
- *Defining care coordination:* Care coordination can be defined in many different ways. But above all, care coordination is planned care.
- *Early examples from the PGP demonstration:* Medicare's Physician Group Practice (PGP) demonstration, the precursor of its ACO shared-savings program, provides important lessons on care coordination from leading group practices.
- *Patient-centered medical home:* Designed to rebuild primary care and improve care coordination, the PCMH has proved its value. However, many practices find the approach too expensive without automation. The latest PCMH criteria require a health IT infrastructure that can support the necessary automation tools.
- *Technology use in care coordination:* Current EHRs are often not sufficient for care coordination, and other health IT tools must be deployed, including registries, care management software, and automated patient outreach tools.
- *Continuum of care:* For the PCMH to coordinate care across the continuum, the electronic exchange of clinical data is key. Medical homes should use an array of health IT solutions that can help them facilitate care coordination throughout the medical neighborhood.

Despite the recent slowdown in the growth of health costs, the United States still spends far more than other advanced countries do and has less to show for it.[1] Consequently, the government and private payers remain focused on the Triple Aim of reducing the cost of health care, improving population health, and enhancing the patient experience.

The two leading models for transforming health care to achieve these goals are the patient-centered medical home (PCMH) and the accountable care organization (ACO). Care coordination is a fundamental requirement of both approaches,[2] but it has a long way to go before it achieves its potential.

Even within large health care organizations, care coordination is often poor.[3] In the fragmented medical communities where most care is delivered, coordination among unrelated heath care providers is rudimentary or nonexistent. And, whereas both secure email and patient portals have been around for some time, they have hardly begun to address the coordination of information across health care entities.

What this situation leads to is tremendous waste, suboptimal outcomes of care, and higher-than-necessary costs. It has been estimated, for example, that 10 percent of direct care costs could be saved if the patients with the most poorly coordinated care were better managed.[4] On the patient side, they are left frustrated and without the assistance to improve their quality of life.

The challenges of care coordination reflect the fragmentation of the system and the counterproductive financial incentives of heathcare providers. Among the main barriers to better coordination are the tendency of many patients to seek care from multiple providers without having a personal physician engage them as they move across care settings;[5] poor communication between ED physicians and ambulatory-care providers;[6] slow or no communication between inpatient and outpatient providers;[7] inadequate exchange of information between referring doctors and specialists;[8] lack of financial incentives for care coordination;[9] insufficient staff in primary care offices to do care coordination;[10] and suboptimal use of health information technology.[11]

Although the better use of technology would not be sufficient to overcome all the obstacles, it is a vital component of care coordination. A study on the development of the patient-centered medical home states:

> Data-driven tools must enable population-based decision-making, facilitate patient tracking, and provide the data to ensure that practices are meeting their clinical goals for patients. Physicians, care coordinators, and their teams must be empowered with tools that allow them to track patients as they interact with other elements of the healthcare system and to monitor their clinical progress over time.[12]

Another paper on the role of health IT in quality improvement points out:

> Clinical processes must evolve so as to improve care and be more responsive to patients' needs, and HIT's capabilities must evolve along with them. HIT has particular potential in such areas as coordination of care, workflow efficiency and use of teams, clinical decision support, and population health management — all areas offering glimpses of both the potential and the challenges associated with improved HIT use.[13]

This chapter explains what care coordination is and describes some of the lessons that can be derived from heath care organizations that are leaders in building systems of planned care. In addition, we show how the latest information technology is being used to support care coordination.

# Defining Care Coordination

In discussions of care coordination, one may hear it described as the process of guiding patients through the system, of managing the care of patients with chronic diseases, or of trying to help very sick patients stay out of the hospital. Actually, it is all these things and more. The Agency for Healthcare Research and Quality (AHRQ) offers this definition:

> Care coordination is the deliberate organization of patient care activities between two or more participants (including the patient) involved in a patient's care to facilitate the appropriate delivery of healthcare services. Organizing care involves the marshaling of personnel and other resources needed to carry out all required patient care activities, and is often managed by the exchange of information among participants responsible for different aspects of care.[14]

The key phrase in this description is "deliberate organization." Whatever its specific application, coordinated care is planned care. And *planned* means something that goes beyond a particular doctor's orders or treatment plans. This is planning that may involve multiple providers, care-team members, and, of course, the patient.

These are the components of care coordination, according to AHRQ:

- Essential care tasks
- Assessment of a patient's care coordination needs

- Development of a coordinated care plan
- Identification of team members responsible for coordination
- Information exchange across care interfaces
- Interventions that support care coordination
- Monitoring and adjustment of care
- Evaluation of outcomes, including identification of care coordination issues[15]

In addition, AHRQ identifies the key concepts associated with care coordination:

- Collaborative relationships among heath care professionals
- Multidisciplinary care teams who contribute specialized knowledge in non-hierarchical relationships
- Continuity of care across clinicians and care settings
- Chronic disease management, which often uses nurse case managers to help patients follow treatment plans and cope with their conditions
- Case management, which depends on a case manager who closely follows high-risk patients
- Care management, which applies "systems, science, incentives, and information to improve medical practice and help patients manage medical conditions more effectively."

# The Physician Group Practice Demonstration

Most of the advances in care coordination have been achieved in group-model HMOs, like Kaiser Permanente and Group Health Cooperative, and in big multispecialty groups such as the Marshfield Clinic in Marshfield, Wisconsin, and the Geisinger Clinic in Danville, Pennsylvania. A glance at the approach taken by Geisinger in CMS's Physician Group Practice (PGP) Demonstration is illuminating in this regard.[16]

The Geisinger Clinic is part of a health system that includes the 367-bed Geisinger Medical Center and two other hospitals. The medical group employs about 640 physicians in 41 practice sites.

Geisinger already had disease-management programs in place when it joined the PGP demonstration. A key concept of disease management is that it requires care planning and close coordination among providers across the spectrum of care. The group wanted to expand those programs and extend them to Medicare patients. Among the conditions its programs addressed were asthma, chronic kidney disease, chronic obstructive pulmonary disease, heart failure, diabetes, hypertension, osteoporosis, and smoking cessation. Additionally, Geisinger introduced a case-management program for high-risk, complex patients.

In the PGP pilot, Geisinger sought to reduce hospital admissions and readmissions through disease and case management, enhanced use of its EHR, and an advanced medical home model known as ProvenHealth Navigator. Specifically, Geisinger emphasized patient-centered, team-based care across the continuum, transitions of care coordination, readmission risk screening, and telephonic care management and/or device-based remote monitoring for heart failure patients. It also redesigned its systems of care to reflect evidence-based guidelines.[17]

Technology was central to Geisinger's approach. For example, the group utilized patient registries in conjunction with its EHR to identify and resolve patients' care gaps. These registries were used to initiate interventions such as referrals to specialists, laboratory test orders, and secure emails to ensure that patients received needed preventive and chronic care. The alerting of patients about pneumococcal and influenza immunizations was particularly successful.

The lessons learned from the PGP Demonstration have been carried forward in various public and private efforts to encourage providers and health systems to build strong care coordination capabilities for PHM and value-based care.

# The Patient-Centered Medical Home

The patient-centered medical home, an approach designed to rebuild primary care and improve care coordination, has become a major focus of healthcare reform. (See Chapter 3.) The National Committee for Quality Assurance (NCQA) has provided PCMH recognition to over 10,000 practice sites encompassing over 48,000 clinicians, and more practices continue to apply for recognition.[18]

Coordinated, planned care is a key feature of medical homes. According to a report from the Patient-Centered Primary Care Collaborative (PCPCC), "In studies of the medical home, care coordination has emerged as one of the key pillars of programs that have demonstrated improved outcomes and lowered costs."[19]

But unless a medical home is part of a large group or a heathcare system, it typically encounters difficulties in paying for care coordinators, as we noted in Chapter 8. Today's fee-for-service heathcare system does not compensate providers for most activities outside of face-to-face encounters with clinicians.

Some care coordination costs are related to workflow. For example, Greenhouse Internists, a five-physician practice in Philadelphia that participated in a medical home pilot, hired a nurse educator to help patients manage their chronic conditions. The educator used the medical assistants in the practice to reach as many patients as possible. The project ran into difficulties, partly because of the complexity of changing workflow and also because data from the patients' action plans had to be entered manually into the group's EHR. The practice spent $7,500 to create a special electronic form for this purpose.

Greenhouse's doctors felt the self-management project was helping some patients, but less than 30 percent of the diabetic patients who visited the office set self-management goals, and few people entered home measurements of blood pressure or glucose levels on the practice website, as requested. Moreover, the practice's investment in care coordination would not have been possible without the extra reimbursement it received for being in the medical-home pilot.[20]

Insurance companies have been willing to foot the bill in pilots, and some are paying doctors extra for providing medical homes. Governmental entities are also encouraging the model. As noted in Chapter 3, Medicare is participating in multiple medical home projects, and the majority of state Medicaid programs are also involved in PCMH demonstrations.

Additionally, Medicare's Chronic Care Management program, launched in 2015, is designed to pay physicians for coordinating care for Medicare patients between visits. (See the accompanying sidebar.) And the 2015 MACRA legislation includes explicit financial incentives for practices that demonstrate evidence of clinical practice transformation, such as care coordination.

## Technology solutions

One way to meet the challenge posed by such staffing needs is to use information technology wherever possible to automate care coordination and care management. For example, University of North Carolina (UNC) Health

Care, a large multispecialty practice, has received NCQA recognition as a Level 3 medical home. The group uses an EHR, a patient registry, a patient health survey, and care management software to improve the health of its population.

UNC's care management application (called Visit Planner) provides care-team members with automated prompts to assess patient needs. It also coordinates and identifies team-member roles throughout a patient visit.

Groups that have automated certain care-management functions, such as patient outreach, have obtained a return on investment by generating additional visits for needed chronic and preventive care. As a result, one study indicates, patients are more likely to receive recommended care.

Using data from Prevea Health, a large multispecialty group in Green Bay, Wisconsin, researchers found that patients who received automated telephone messages were more likely to have both a chronic-care office visit and an appropriate test than patients who were not contacted. Compared to a control group of non-contacted patients, about three times as many diabetic patients who were successfully contacted had both a visit and an HbA1c test. And twice as many patients with hypertension who received this intervention had both a visit and a systolic blood pressure reading recorded in Prevea's EHR.[21]

Another benefit of automating care management is that it eliminates much of the routine work, giving care managers and care coordinators time to provide services to more of the patients who need their help. Although this strategy doesn't reduce the cost of labor, it can increase a practice's value-based reimbursement by raising quality scores and preventing complications that generate higher health costs.

## NCQA criteria

The health IT infrastructure required for this kind of automation is imbedded in NCQA's 2014 PCMH recognition criteria. Among other things, these guidelines require the use of health IT in care coordination and care transitions, as follows:

- *Test tracking and follow up:* Providers must record lab and radiology orders in the EHR and incorporate the majority of lab results in structured data fields. NCQA also requires applicants to track lab and imaging tests from the time they're ordered until results are available. One method is to flag orders not accompanied by results in the EHR.

- *Referral tracking and follow up:* Providers must send an electronic summary-of-care record to other providers in more than 50 percent of referrals. The referring doctor must also give the consultant or specialist a range of information, including lab results and the current care plan, which can be transferred from the electronic record. A critical factor is the ability to track referrals until the consultant's report is available — a difficult objective to achieve without the use of an EHR.

- *Coordinate care transitions:* Providers must exchange key clinical information electronically with other care providers, including hospitals, ERs, extended care facilities, and nursing homes. Providers must have the ability to identify patients with unplanned hospital admissions and emergency department visits, to share clinical information with admitting hospitals and EDs, and to consistently obtain patient discharge summaries from the hospital and other facilities.[22]

---

# Medicare to reward physicians for care coordination

To counter the financial disincentives for care coordination, the Centers for Medicare and Medicaid Services (CMS) in January 2015 began paying physicians to coordinate care for patients who have two or more chronic conditions and are in the Medicare fee-for-service program.[23] Two-thirds of Medicare beneficiaries have two or more chronic diseases, and 70 percent of Medicare patients are in the fee-for-service program.[24]

In return for a care coordination fee of about $42 per patient per month, physicians must assess patients' medical, psychological, and social needs; check whether they are taking medications as prescribed; monitor the care provided by other doctors; and ensure smooth transitions of care when patients move from a hospital to their home or a nursing home. These tasks are to be performed *between* patient visits by physicians or, more likely, by other members of the care team, such as care managers, care coordinators, and certified medical assistants. Care team members may have non-face-to-face communications with patients or may intervene on behalf of patients through communications with other providers.

Patients can ask their physicians to join the program, or their doctors can invite them to participate. Those who do must sign a consent agreement. They also have to pay 20 percent of the fee for those services, or approximately $8.00 per month.

Additionally, the NCQA guidelines require patients to have electronic access to their health records and include criteria related to team-based care and population health management that would be impossible to meet without health IT tools. For example, care teams must support all patients in self-management, self-efficacy, and behavior change and must identify which patients need interventions from care managers.

# Technology Use in Care Coordination

As heath care organizations form ACOs and medical homes, they have to coordinate care effectively across populations and care settings. A consensus report on combining these two care-delivery models observes that care coordination will be the linchpin of heathcare transformation:

> The effective coordination of a patient's healthcare services is a key component of high-quality, efficient care. It provides value to patients, professionals, and the healthcare system by improving the quality, appropriateness, timeliness, and efficiency of decision-making and care activities, thereby affecting the experience, quality, and cost of health care.[25]

The consensus report also emphasizes the role of health IT in care coordination while asserting that the current EHR is insufficient for this purpose.

> Anchoring the EHR in the traditional visit-based care delivery model limits the potential of the medical home to generate paradigm-shifting care delivery transformation and the positive outcomes it promises. Health IT requires new functional capabilities, such as multiple team member access and permissions, care management workflow support, integrated personal health records, registry functionalities, clinical decision support, measurement of quality and efficiency, and robust reporting.[26]

Most of the technologies required to achieve these goals are already available; but some of them, such as interoperable systems that allow communications across disparate EHRs and other applications, are still emerging. Among the reasons why the existing technologies are not being properly deployed in most cases are these:

- EHRs are not designed to do population health management or care coordination.

- Registries tend to be focused on patients with particular conditions rather than on entire populations.

- Care management workflow support is still a relatively new concept, but one that more and more groups are embracing.

- Health information systems within and across health systems and community providers cannot "speak" to one another, thereby hampering timely communications related to new information about patients.

## Key building blocks

As noted in Chapter 1, various forms of information technology, including registries, care-management software, and automated patient-outreach tools, have all been deployed successfully, in conjunction with EHRs, to manage patient populations.

The automated stratification of patients into health-risk categories is especially important to groups seeking to do population health management. For example, UNC Health Care uses a health-risk assessment (HRA) survey to find out how sick each of its patients with diabetes is. Then it uses an advanced patient registry and evidence-based algorithms to drive team-based care for each of those patients, depending on the severity of his or her condition.

Many practices use electronic registries to supplement their EHRs. These registries compile lists of subpopulations that need particular kinds of preventive and chronic care, such as annual mammograms for women over 40 or HbA1c tests at particular intervals for diabetic patients. The continuously updated data in the registries comes from EHRs, practice management systems, or a combination of the two. Evidence-based clinical protocols, which can be customized by physician practices, trigger alerts in the registries. When a registry is linked to an outbound messaging system, patients are notified by automated telephone, email, or text messages to contact their physicians for appointments. Some registries can also send actionable data to care teams prior to patient visits.[27]

The use of technology to automate patient education and to prompt certain actions can improve compliance, health behavior, and self-management of chronic diseases. Promoting this idea, a 2007 AHRQ report on the use of information technology in primary care noted:

An example of automation to support better individual patient care would be the automatic generation of patient education handouts (including and utilizing patient-specific data and information). Once an action is determined to be appropriate for better care, the health IT system should produce the action based on patient data, in many cases without even requiring provider interaction. An example would be the production of a mailing list for all diabetic patients who have not had an eye exam in the last year.[28]

Today, one group practice that has been especially successful in using technology to automate population health management is Northeast Georgia Physicians Group (NGPG), the largest multispecialty practice in its region. As part of an initiative to have all its primary care sites recognized as patient-centered medical homes, NGPG in 2012 adopted several automation tools to scale up care coordination and care management to its entire population. These included an application that combined a registry and continuous care gap identification with automated messaging to alert patients who needed to be seen for preventive and/or chronic care. In addition, NGPG used a reporting tool that not only measured organizational performance but also allowed care managers to spot patients who needed help in managing their chronic conditions. Another automation program gave the care managers additional tools to risk-stratify patients and to develop personalized care interventions for those who required them.[29]

The initial results were promising. In the six months between January and July 2013, NGPG tested the outreach and care management applications in 10 sites. The care managers used them on a daily basis to track and target 860 diabetic patients who had an HbA1c > 9. By the end of the study period, NGPG had helped 412 of those patients lower that value to less than 9 percent. Including all participants, the patients' A1c values declined by an average of 1.3 percentage points.

Orlando Health, a major heathcare system in Orlando, Florida, has deployed the same set of applications that NGPG uses to improve population health management in a clinically integrated network of physicians. Having recognized that the network's multiple EHRs were inadequate for the task, Orlando Health combined them with the automation tools for patient outreach, reporting, and care management.

Before acquiring these tools, the healthcare system was struggling with the NCQA requirements for gaining recognition of its primary care sites as patient-centered medical homes. It was very time-consuming to create custom reports for care management manually, and the data was often incomplete and out of date. By being able to generate reports from a registry in near-real-time themselves, the care managers gained an indispensable tool for targeting the patients who most needed their help. Automated messaging to subgroups of patients with care gaps also reduced the care managers' routine tasks, allowing them to spend more time with patients. These tools enabled Orlando Health to scale up its population health management efforts without adding care managers to the 15 it already had.[30]

The overall lesson to be drawn from the efforts to improve care coordination is that it is difficult to make significant progress without the use of information technology. The identification of patients with particular conditions, health risk assessments, the ability to send care gap alerts to providers, the care management of chronically ill patients, tailored patient education, and persistent reminders to patients to get the care they need — all these interventions require some degree of automation to be performed in a timely, consistent, cost-effective manner.

## Continuum of care

The Patient-Centered Primary Care Collaborative (PCPCC) views the patient-centered medical home as the hub of the medical neighborhood. That ecosystem includes both heath care providers (primary care doctors, specialists, behavioral health providers, hospitals, home health agencies, and long-term-care facilities, for example) and community organizations that encourage healthy living, wellness, and safe environments (YMCAs, schools, faith-based organizations, employers, and public health agencies, to name a few).[31]

For primary care practices to coordinate care and manage population health effectively within this medical neighborhood, they must have a health IT infrastructure, the PCPCC notes. The key health IT tools required for this approach include EHRs, patient registries, health information exchanges (HIEs), tools for risk stratification, automated outreach and referral tracking, patient portals, telehealth applications, and remote patient monitoring systems.

HIEs can facilitate care coordination where they are available. In addition, an increasing number of organizations are starting to exchange clinical summaries via the Direct Project's secure messaging protocol.

New automation tools can also help providers improve transitions of care across the medical neighborhood. For example, some organizations use an application that messages patients shortly after a hospital discharge. The patients are asked whether they have questions about their discharge instructions or medications. This tool can be used to automatically transfer patients to a care-team member or can trigger outbound calls from their physician or primary care practice.

Online tools can also facilitate referrals. For example, MyHealth Access Network, a government-funded initiative that operates a health information exchange based in Tulsa, Oklahoma, has successfully used information technology to promote closed-loop referrals between primary care doctors and specialists. In a 2012 case study, the Office of the National Coordinator for Health IT (ONC) said that MyHealth's referral approach resulted in patients receiving specialty review 2.5 times faster than patients whose doctors used the traditional referral approach. Online, closed-loop referrals also reduced unnecessary specialty consults by 24 percent.[32]

# Conclusion

The interventions explored in this chapter are all necessary but not sufficient to attain the Triple Aim.[33] U.S. health care is still in the early stages of organizing itself so that, for example, providers communicate easily with each other about patient care across care settings and between organizations. Patients are also just beginning to gain access to their own medical records and communicate online with their physicians.[34]

Nevertheless, the recent advances in health IT and further developments in this vital field will continue to support and enhance care coordination as it expands across the spectrum of care. As reimbursement methods change to support coordinated care, we can look forward to a proliferation of new IT tools that will help turn the vision of affordable, high-quality health care for all into a reality.

Another key component of heathcare transformation that is just starting to be applied in a rigorous way is the Lean approach to process improvement. The next chapter shows how some organizations are starting to use Lean thinking and IT-driven automation to improve care management.

The Lean approach to continuous quality improvement can be coupled with IT-driven automation to help care teams become more productive and efficient.

Lean thinking requires active participation by people at all levels within an organization, and involves:

**1** WORKFLOW ANALYSES TO IDENTIFY WASTE

**2** RAPID EXPERIMENTATION TO REDESIGN WORKFLOWS

**3** IMPLEMENTATION/SOCIALIZATION OF SUCCESSFUL SOLUTIONS

## Lean Care Management + Health IT

PEOPLE

PROCESSES

TECHNOLOGY

Volume
**HEALTHCARE NOW**
(fee-for-service)

Value
**HEALTHCARE IN THE FUTURE**
(pay-for-performance)

### Lean Thinking
**ENABLES...**

- Value defined from the customer's perspective
- Maximized workflow efficiency
- Identification of ways to improve processes and eliminate waste

### Automation Tools
**FACILITATE...**

- Risk stratification
- Pre-visit planning
- Care coordination
- Patient outreach
- Care management tasks

### Care Teams
**BECOME...**

- More productive
- More efficient
- More effective
- More valuable
- More patient-centered
- More highly satisfied

# 10

# Lean Care Management

- *Introduction:* Care teams have been shown to help high-performing practices raise their capacity and productivity while improving quality and care coordination. The Lean approach to continuous quality improvement, coupled with IT-driven automation, may provide the missing ingredients to make the care-team model an economic winner.

- *A Lean foundation in health care:* The key concepts of Lean thinking — including value stream mapping, continuous flow, and continuous improvement — can be applied to health care. A Lean care management approach is now starting to gain traction among leading-edge groups.

- *High-performing practices:* These practices exhibit many elements of the Lean approach, including the use of "level-loading" (the balancing of throughput to meet demand just in time) of work across care teams, the reduction of non-value-added work steps, the "voice of the customer (patient)," and rapid experiments with solutions to improve processes. Using Lean techniques, these practices allow team members to utilize the full range of their abilities and skills.

- *Lean care management:* No one-size-fits-all approach will work for every group. But pre-visit planning and care coordination, along with workflow mapping and reengineering, help some practices increase efficiency and reduce waste.

- *Automation in Lean processes:* Incorporating health IT into Lean processes can enable care teams to manage entire populations. Automation tools for risk stratification, patient outreach, and care management can leverage the capabilities of care managers and enable physicians and all care-team members to work at the top of their licenses — in other words, letting them focus on the work that their professional licenses and training allow them to do, rather than on tasks requiring less skill.

Primary care practices must be reengineered to achieve the Triple Aim of improving the experience of care, improving population health, and reducing the cost of care. As new value-based payment and delivery models continue to expand, practices have strong incentives to take on the necessary reengineering. In addition, shortages of generalist physicians in many areas of the country, coupled with increasing patient demand, offer additional pressure to redesign the current fee-for-service primary care model.

One promising alternative to the traditional model involves the use of care teams that include a variety of clinical and non-clinical staff members. By sharing responsibility for care among team members, high-performing practices have been able to increase their capacity and productivity. A growing body of evidence also shows that this model can improve quality and care coordination.[1]

Launching the team care model can be culturally and financially challenging as healthcare organizations traverse the path from volume-based payment (fee-for-service) to value-based payment (population-based quality performance and cost savings). Effective care coordination can require additional staff and technology that few small practices can afford.[2] Strategic leaders recognize that investing in team-based care today is imperative for success tomorrow as value-based payment becomes more dominant.

Practices managing population health typically need additional RNs to serve as care managers for patients with complex chronic diseases. In addition, family medicine societies and the National Committee for Quality Assurance (NCQA) have recommended that behavioral health specialists be integrated into the patient-centered medical home (PCMH), an increasingly prevalent model that emphasizes team-based care.[3] And it is not unusual for high-performing practices to include pharmacists, nutritionists, diabetes educators, health coaches, and social workers.[4]

Not all these kinds of professionals are included on all care teams. Nevertheless, based on the literature and interviews with practice administrators, researchers have calculated that a PCMH care team has an average staffing ratio of 4.25 staff per full-time primary care physician. By comparison, the staffing ratio in the typical primary care practice is 2.68:1.[5]

Some health plans pay care coordination fees or incentivize practices that have been recognized as PCMHs.[6] Value-based reimbursement may also be available in the form of shared-savings and risk contracts with a quality component.[7] To the extent that primary care practices can deliver that kind of value while also increasing their own efficiency, they should do well in the emerging world of value-based reimbursement. In many cases, that should justify the extra overhead that fully capable care teams add to practices.

Most practices are now using manual methods of care management that do not achieve the labor-saving potential of health IT. And, unless they have a systematic approach to process improvement, they often are not as efficient as they could be in engaging everyone in their patient panels.

To maximize efficiency and achieve the Triple Aim, primary care providers should consider two emerging trends: *IT-driven automation* and *continuous quality improvement* based on Lean and Six Sigma principles. These approaches, while common in other industries, have only recently begun to gain traction in health care. And they are already showing promise as healthcare organizations transition from the model of the physician who has sole responsibility for providing care to the care-team model in which many healthcare tasks are delegated to non-physicians.

Lean thinking goes back decades to the Toyota production model. Later associated with Six Sigma, which focuses on reducing defects and variations in processes, Lean is a continuous quality improvement method that relies on motivating frontline workers to reduce cycle time (the time required to complete a defined process) through waste elimination. A growing number of healthcare organizations have fully adopted Lean principles to improve quality and reduce waste by reengineering workflows, and many other providers are getting started.

Automation is not required in order to apply Lean in health care. But automation tools and other types of health IT can be powerful adjuncts to the transformation of health care based on the Lean approach. Health IT solutions can be used to automate many routine tasks of care management, increasing the productivity of care teams.

For example, it is inefficient for a healthcare organization to have care managers call every patient with gaps in recommended care. Automated phone, texting, or email messaging could reach the vast majority of these patients, significantly reducing the amount of staff time that must be devoted to this task. As a result, the organization could employ fewer care managers or could deploy its existing ones more effectively to help high-risk patients.

The combination of Lean with automation can boost care teams' productivity and can eliminate much of the waste in health care. This chapter explains the basic tenets of this approach.

# A Lean Foundation in Health Care

The Toyota Production System, which began in the 1950s, was originally called *just-in-time production* and was later rebranded as *Lean*. After Toyota used this manufacturing approach to catch up to, and later surpass, the U.S. automakers, many other companies began to emulate its methods.[8]

This list describes the key concepts of Lean thinking:

- *Value:* Define value from the customer's perspective. Products should be designed for and with customers, should suit the purpose, and should be set at the right price.

- *Value stream:* Each step in production must produce value for the customer, eliminating all sources of waste. (See Table 10-1 for the types of waste to be targeted in primary care.)

- *Flow:* The system must flow continuously and without interruption. Flow depends on materials being delivered, as and when they are needed, to the quality required.

- *Pull:* The process must be flexible, producing what customers need when they need it.

- *Perfection:* The aim is perfection. Lean thinking creates an environment of continuous improvement, emphasizing suggestions from workers and learning from previous mistakes.[9]

Several Lean principles are applicable to health care. First, workflow is analyzed and broken down into a series of steps so that any failure in the process can be easily identified. Second, problems are addressed immediately through rapid experimentation with proposed solutions. Third, those ideas that succeed are spread throughout the organization. Fourth and most important, people at all levels of the organization are expected to contribute suggestions for improvement and to participate in testing these "countermeasures" to solve problems.[10]

Gaining the cooperation of frontline staff is not easy or natural in many organizations, especially in health care. Health care is organized along hierarchical lines that can be difficult to break down. In both physician practices and hospitals, physicians stand at the top of the clinical pyramid, with all other clinical staff deferring to them. Non-clinical staff report to administrators and practice managers and also defer to physicians in doctor-owned practices.

| Type of Waste | Lean Definition | Sample Solutions |
|---|---|---|
| Defects | Errors resulting from omissions, inaccurate information, or mistakes. Errors often require rework and can cause harm. | Use algorithms to evaluate patient care gaps against evidence-based guidelines, and take action to close them with automated patient communications and provider alerts. |
| Overproduction | Providing more services than needed, including redundant services. | Query an integrated patient registry before ordering tests and services for patients. |
| Waiting | Idle time for the customer or staff member while waiting for needed information, action, or resources. | Build in same-day appointment slots to improve access; redesign the visit-preparation process with daily huddles and new roles for care-team members while rooming patients. |
| Not fully utilized | Unused talent, creativity, and skills. | Train medical assistants to do health coaching; delegate or automate non-clinical tasks to maximize the use of clinical team members' specialized skills. |
| Transportation | Moving people, equipment, and supplies, which takes valuable time and resources. | Do lab testing in the office rather than send patients to another location. |
| Inventory | The supply of resources waiting to be consumed by customer demand. | Survey patients to determine the best days, times, and locations to hold group education sessions so that supply matches demand. |
| Motion | The movement of people or resources while performing tasks. | Colocate physicians and medical assistants in practice units to eliminate extra steps (walking, messaging) to communicate; utilize automated reporting and alerts to minimize computer clicks and research time. |
| Excess processing | Redundant or otherwise non-value-added activities. | Ask patients to update existing information instead of completing new profiles at every visit. |

**Table 10-1:** *"Leaning Out" Eight Types of Waste in Primary Care*

Lean thinking requires that these hierarchies be flattened for the purposes of quality improvement. Management must give employees the freedom to critique existing processes and to suggest ways to improve them. Physicians, too, must be willing to delegate tasks to care teams and to let them find ways to improve the workflow and add value to the process.

Even without the addition of Lean, physicians may find it hard to accept the idea of delegating some of their duties to care teams in patient-centered medical homes. In a paper evaluating the national medical home demonstration project of the American Academy of Family Physicians (AAFP), the authors noted:

> We found that changing roles was perhaps most difficult for physicians, who believed deeply that primary care doctoring was based on a strong, trusting relationship between a patient and a physician. Sharing that relationship with other practice staff members was, for many, a significant challenge to their identity as physicians.[11]

There are other cultural changes that practices must make as they transition from a physician-dominated model to a care-team model. In an appendix to the study just cited, the researchers note that the leaders of one practice in the demonstration project ran into challenges when they tried to use their registry in population health management, "largely due to difficulty in reassigning roles and responsibilities to the existing mix of staff."[12]

Because change is so difficult, healthcare leaders at the organization, physician, and care-team levels must present a united front and make it clear that this is the direction in which the organization plans to go. Change management also requires champions at multiple levels who have the authority to remove barriers and influence change. "The champion should be someone who is easily accessible and at least one level higher than the leaders of the primary processes being changed when an improvement is cross-functional," say Lean experts who coauthored a paper on the subject for IBM Watson Health.[13]

Engaging frontline employees to be involved in process improvement poses another cultural challenge, but when leadership is persistent, the effort pays off: The Illinois-based Christie Clinic, for example, worked on incorporating Lean concepts for several years before its efforts bore fruit. The organization has divided its 800 employees, including 160 providers, into 71 site-based teams that work on process improvement. In a two-year period, these teams made 2,000 improvement suggestions, and most of those have been implemented.[14]

In a research paper from the Institute for Health Technology Transformation, Christie Clinic CEO Alan Gleghorn said that the key to applying Lean in his organization was to create an environment where it was safe for frontline employees to propose process improvements. They also had to be told that this was expected of them as part of their jobs, he added.[15]

The first big application of Lean principles to ambulatory care occurred around 2000. That was when the Boston-based Institute for Healthcare Improvement (IHI) launched a three-year initiative to redesign primary care at 40 practice sites across the country. The program aimed to remove barriers to patient access, reduce waste and inefficiency, and improve patient-doctor communications, among other goals. Open access scheduling, team care, non-visit care via phone and email, and practice huddles to plan daily work were all part of the game plan.[16]

Clinical staff received new roles and enhanced responsibilities, and the care-team approach necessitated the addition of staff in many practices. But doctors had more time to spend with patients, the patients were happier, and the practices ran more smoothly.

Many aspects of the IHI program were later incorporated into the PCMH approach, which got off the ground in 2006, when the AAFP started its demonstration project. Meanwhile, a number of healthcare organizations were already experimenting with Lean thinking. The better-known healthcare systems that have embedded Lean to-date include ThedaCare, Virginia Mason Medical Center, Group Health Cooperative, and Cleveland Clinic.[17]

ThedaCare, a Wisconsin organization that also participated in the IHI project, has founded the ThedaCare Center for Healthcare Value (TCHV), which disseminates its knowledge of Lean and brings together members of TCHV's Healthcare Value Network to exchange insights. The Healthcare Value Network now includes more than 60 member organizations.[18]

Similarly, the Virginia Mason Institute has disseminated its knowledge of continuous quality improvement and Lean methods to many other healthcare organizations.[19]

# High-Performing Practices

Several studies of high-performing primary care practices have examined the characteristics that enable them to deliver high-quality care efficiently. Though none of these studies looks at these practices through the lens of Lean principles, many of them have absorbed Lean thinking into their approaches.

Other practices — notably, those that have studied the Virginia Mason and ThedaCare models — are consciously embedding Lean into process improvement.

The high-performing practices discussed in these studies all use care teams. Those teams not only improve care delivery but also provide the environment required for the implementation of Lean processes. Before examining how the Lean approach can be applied to care management, let's take a look at how care teams transform primary care.

## Performing at top of license

The care-team approach requires that practices think about how best to use each team member to provide better care with less waste. A cardinal principle is to enable care-team members to work at the top level of their training, experience, and ability. For example, physicians should not do clerical work that does not require their level of knowledge. Nurses should be empowered to do as much as possible within the limits of their licensure. And lower-level employees can also be trained to perform important functions for the care team.

A study funded by the Robert Wood Johnson Foundation, for example, found that many high performing groups train medical assistants (MAs) to do pre-visit chart reviews, identify patients with gaps in care, and contact them via calls or letters. Some MAs who received extra training also act as health coaches for patients with chronic conditions. And MAs in some groups lead daily huddles of care teams to plan the day's activities. Using MAs for these kinds of tasks has been shown to improve rates of preventive services and outcomes of care.

RNs in these practices provide intensive support for high-risk patients with chronic diseases, follow up on patients discharged from the hospital, and coordinate complex specialty care. They also work with patients who have multiple conditions and medications.

In this model, physicians, physician assistants, and nurse practitioners can perform their indispensable diagnostic and treatment functions while other team members prepare patients for their visits and help them with their care plans afterward.[20]

Another study finds that the common characteristics of high-performing practices are proactive planned care, shared clerical tasks, improved communication, and improved team functioning.

The 23 study sites built their capacity to serve patients by giving nurses and other non-physician clinicians partial responsibility for delivering care. For example, at North Shore Physicians Group in the Boston area, MAs perform an expanded range of functions during the rooming process. These include reviewing medications, setting agendas, completing forms, and closing care gaps. MAs review health monitoring reminders, give immunizations, and book appointments for mammograms and DXA scans for osteoporosis.

Clinica Family Health Services, based in Lafayette, Colorado, has created standing orders so that RNs can diagnose and treat simple problems such as strep infections, ear infections, and urinary tract infections on their own. Non-professional health coaches provide patient education and counseling to help patients with chronic conditions set goals and formulate action plans.[21]

## Care-coordination approaches

Three different approaches to team-based care in primary care practices have been described and are often used together:[22] the top-of-license model; the enhanced traditional model, in which nurses, MAs, and front-office staff are organized to support the physician in nontraditional ways; and the care coordinator model, which is designed for population health management.

In the latter approach, the care team includes a care coordinator, usually a nurse, who works for multiple providers. The care coordinator's main tasks are to coordinate patient transitions in care and to manage high-risk patients. The coordinator also coaches patients who manage their own conditions poorly.

The nurses on the care team perform a number of high-level functions, including identifying care gaps, administering EKGs and immunizations, assessing cognitive capabilities and mobility, and supporting patients between visits.

This care-coordination approach helped increase one practice's mammography screening rates from 37 percent to 70 percent and increase the blood pressure control of its diabetic patients from 39 percent to 72 percent over a three-year period. But the practice had to reduce the number and role of care coordinators because of financial difficulty in supporting the model with no extra reimbursement from payers.[23]

# Lean Care Management

There is no one-size-fits-all method on how to create an optimal care team or design the workflows that enable the team to deliver the best care with maximum efficiency. Practices vary by specialty, size, resource, payer mix, and the composition of the patient population. The use of information technology and automation can vary dramatically from one practice to another. And the medical neighborhoods in which practices operate — including whether they are part of a healthcare system — also influence the way care teams function.[24]

All of this only begins to explain the nuances that must be considered when one sets out to improve the care-management processes in a particular practice. For example, many high-performing practices use pre-visit planning and pretesting to avoid inefficient visits that do not meet the needs of the patient. A care coordinator might contact an out-of-control diabetic patient who is overdue for a visit and ask that person to make an appointment. In addition, the care coordinator might arrange for the patient to have an HbA1c test before the visit so that the physician can discuss the results with the patient.

This kind of pre-visit planning has been shown to reduce the total amount of work, save time, and improve care.[25] But some providers may feel that the approach is not patient-centric, because it requires the patient to go to a reference lab before his or her visit. Other doctors expect that they might have to order other tests during the encounter; so rather than ask the patient to travel to the lab twice, they prefer to order the tests at the end of the visit.

What this scenario underlines is the need for continuous quality improvement by care teams trained in Lean principles. Some groups are taking this approach and are finding that it helps them optimize workflows in their own, unique environments.

In a study of 23 high-performing groups, the researchers observed that the practice from the ThedaCare Clinic in Oshkosh, Wisconsin, had raised its clinical and operational performance from last to first place among ThedaCare's 22 primary care clinics.

The group attributed this turnaround to systematic workflow planning using Lean techniques. These methods included identification and elimination of waste through value stream mapping and process standardization. Clinic site director Kathy Markofski reported, "The team maps out the workflow of a patient visit. We identify wait times, do a root cause analysis, develop countermeasures, and then quickly reassess with data."[26]

At the Cleveland Clinic, "the physician and clinical staff meet weekly to review data and refine their workflows," the study notes. They look at what went well and what did not go well and then consider the changes they need to make to improve the workflows.

Practices that follow Lean principles can benefit from a quality management committee or a similar entity to supervise the quality improvement process and ensure that the group is meeting the quality metrics specified in its payer contracts. But this committee should not do the actual work of process improvement.

"They can educate people about what the measures are, and they can be the ones to pull together the quarterly or monthly meetings and share the data so everyone has a common 'line of sight,' which is also a Lean principle," says Karen Handmaker, vice president of population health strategies for IBM Watson Health. "But the work is done on the front line, and the care teams build it up from the bottom."

# Checklist for Lean care management

✔ Make care team transformation a strategic objective with assigned leadership and visible executive support.

✔ Create an environment that supports continuous quality improvement.

✔ Form multidisciplinary care teams to share the work of care management.

✔ Map clinical and administrative processes and engage staff in suggesting how they could be improved.

✔ Identify and eliminate waste through value-stream mapping and process standardization.

✔ Reengineer processes to allow all care-team members to perform at the top of their licenses.

✔ Make pre- and post-visit care planning part of the clinical process.

✔ Introduce a quality management committee to supervise the quality improvement process and track progress and results.

✔ Use automation tools and other technology solutions to reduce waste and improve efficiency — but only after analyzing and reengineering workflows.

# Automation in Lean Processes

As mentioned earlier in this chapter, Lean does not require health information technology. One of the earliest and most effective parts of Lean manufacturing, for instance, was the kanban cards used to control and replenish inventory.[27] Kanban "signals" have also been used to improve patient flow in practices. For example, a flag or other marker may be placed outside of an exam room to indicate when a room is empty and medical staff, equipment, and supplies are ready and available for the next patient. That step can reduce the amount of time patients spend waiting in exam rooms, which provides no value for the patient or the clinic.[28]

While simple techniques such as this one can improve workflow and increase value, applying health IT and automation tools within a Lean context can also help organizations manage population health more efficiently.

The majority of primary care practices now have electronic health records (EHRs), which generate data that can be used to improve the quality of care. However, EHRs were not designed as the basis for Lean process improvement.

For example, ThedaCare found that its EHR could not produce a single plan of care for the multiple physicians, nurses, and other professionals who care for patients across the continuum of care, including primary care, specialty care, and the hospital. As a result, multidisciplinary care teams could not use the EHR to coordinate care. Eventually, ThedaCare and its vendor reprogrammed the software to accommodate the single care plan.[29]

Aside from some control chart and kanban applications, not many off-the-shelf programs are designed specifically for the Lean approach in health care, experts say.[30] Some population health management solutions, though, could be adapted to the Lean approach.

Automation tools, for instance, can play an important role in Lean process improvement. These tools cannot fix a broken process; but after a practice has analyzed and reengineered its workflows, it can consider where automation fits in and how it can improve care management processes further. By delegating routine tasks to automation tools, care teams can provide appropriate forms of care management to most of the patient population while improving their ability to help patients who need human assistance.

# Basic automation tools

The first step in this process is to use an analytic application that stratifies the patient population by health risk. For example, a population might be broken down into low-, medium-, and high-risk individuals. This becomes the basis for deciding which automated workflow and communication tools to use with each population segment. The risk-stratification analytics should be applied to a combination of clinical, claims, and, where available, patient-generated data to see a wide-angled view of patients' health status. Health risk assessment surveys can also be helpful in evaluating patients' health behavior.

Automation tools can be used to link workflows to each other, as shown in the figure below. For example, a patient-centric registry provides a wide range of data on all patients, including their health conditions, the services provided to them, and their due dates for particular preventive or chronic care services. Using embedded protocols for recommended care, reports can be run on registry data to reveal patient care gaps. The program can then send alerts explaining to providers that patients need certain kinds of care, such as mammography or diabetic eye exams, when they next visit the office. Another kind of automation tool uses the same registry data and protocols to generate automated messages to patients who need preventive or chronic care. These messages ask them to make appointments with their providers.

A different type of population health application produces work lists that enable care coordinators to prioritize their management of high-risk patients. Rather than have to wade through electronic charts and look at each patient's lab results, recent ED visits, and other relevant data, the care managers can instantly see which patients are at the greatest risk of complications and/or hospitalization. This type of automation can save a great deal of time and can help the care managers attend to the sickest patients proactively.

A basic assumption of population health management is that many of the patients who have serious health risks are "below the waterline": that is, they haven't yet developed the condition or the exacerbation that will generate high health costs. To manage population health properly, organizations must target not only high-risk patients but also those with low and medium risks. The organizations must also initiate patient engagement campaigns to improve the health of those with various chronic conditions and keep healthy patients healthy.

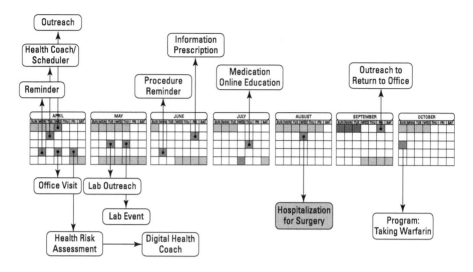

This is an area where automation excels: Technology and mobile healthcare applications can simultaneously launch hundreds of educational campaigns and other interventions aimed at people in different subcategories. Of course, some patients need human interventions as well, so automation is only part of the mix. If used correctly, automation becomes a member of the care team to which certain tasks are delegated.

# Automation in practice

Integrating automation tools has helped a number of healthcare organizations improve their care management processes and achieve better patient outcomes. Though it is still less common for clinics to combine automation with Lean principles of continuous quality improvement, early evidence indicates that this would be an even more effective method to increase efficiency and cut waste than automation alone.

With that qualification, here are a few examples of how organizations have used automation tools to improve their ability to manage population health:

✔ North Mississippi Medical Clinics (NMMCI), a branch of North Mississippi Medical Center in

Tupelo, Mississippi, operates a regional network of 38 primary and specialty-care clinics. To improve its care management, NMMCI purchased a patient registry and automation applications that it interfaced with its EHR.[31]

Care managers used the registry to identify patients who had poorly controlled diabetes. An automation tool generated work lists showing all preventive services and lab tests required for patients in that category who were scheduled to visit in the next two days. The care managers communicated via email and messaged the patients and encouraged them to complete any necessary lab work before their visits. Workflows were automated and standardized so that no patients slipped between the cracks.

As a result of this campaign, 31 of the 76 patients who originally had HbA1c levels >9 dropped below that level. Most of the other at-risk patients received specific education on how to manage their diabetes more effectively through automated email campaigns.

✔ Prevea Health, a 180-doctor, multispecialty group in Green Bay, Wisconsin, needed a way to reach out to chronic disease patients who had care gaps but did not make appointments to see their providers. Care management processes were largely manual, making it quite difficult to engage all these patients regularly.

Prevea acquired a population health management solution that included a registry and related technology. Through an interface, the group's EHR populated the registry automatically with demographic and clinical information. Using embedded clinical protocols, a program linked to the registry triggered automated messaging to patients who had care gaps in the areas of diabetes and hypertension. Those patients who were contacted made office appointments at two to three times the rate of non-contacted patients.[32]

The key lesson of Prevea's experience is that the ability to identify patients with care gaps must be coupled with automated outreach capabilities to improve compliance.

✔ Bon Secours Virginia Medical Group (BSVMG), a hospital-owned, multispecialty group with more than 100 locations in and around Richmond, Virginia, has used a care-team approach and the patient-centered medical home model to prepare for value-based reimbursement.

BSVMG uses an outside registry connected to its EHR for risk stratification and other applications for identifying patient care gaps. In addition, its population health management solution suggests appropriate interventions for subpopulations of patients. Because these interventions can be automated, care teams are able to communicate with many patients at one time and to implement multiple quality improvement programs simultaneously. An analytic application is also being deployed to measure the performance of providers, sites, and the entire practice.

Partly as a result of the process improvements enabled by automation, BSVMG has been able to succeed in its performance-based contracts with commercial payers. Under a contract with a single health plan, the group expected to generate annual savings of $4 million that it will share in. Meanwhile, the increased visits by patients with care gaps have generated more than $7 million in incremental revenue.

Overall, the experience of these and other groups has shown that automation tools can increase the effectiveness and efficiency of care management. In addition, the automation of workflows guarantees that organizations will be able to reach most of the targeted patients who need preventive or chronic care or other services.

## Top-of-license approach

Earlier in this chapter, we discuss a care-team model that assigns to every care-team member the work that matches his or her training and expertise. Automation can be part of this *top-of-license* approach. The goal is to assign patients to the appropriate staff members or to automation-only capabilities. With the help of risk stratification, the care team can decide which approach will work best for each individual. A healthy patient might need only automated reminders to maintain wellness and receive recommended preventive services. A patient who is at risk of developing a chronic condition might receive automated interventions as well as health coaching from medical assistants (MAs) or other non-clinical coaches. Nurses and MAs work with patients who have chronic conditions to prevent disease progression and avoid unnecessary complications. And nurse care managers have responsibility for managing high-risk patients with multiple conditions.

## Downstream value

The team-based, population health management approach discussed in this chapter confers financial advantages in a value-based reimbursement system. Whether an organization has pay-for-performance, shared-savings, or risk contracts, the ability to improve outcomes and lower costs will result in a better bottom line. And health IT is a key component of that capability.

According to the Health Information Management and Systems Society (HIMSS), health IT can create five kinds of value:

- *Satisfaction:* The satisfaction level of patients, providers, staff, and others
- *Treatment/clinical:* Patient safety, quality of care, and efficiency
- *Electronic information/data:* The use of evidence-based guidelines, data sharing, population health, and quality reporting
- *Prevention/patient education:* Improved disease surveillance and patient compliance with therapies
- *Savings:* From improvements such as reduced days in accounts receivable, patient wait times, and emergency department admissions[33]

By eliminating waste and improving care processes, the health-IT-enabled Lean approach can provide even more downstream value to payers and accountable care organizations (ACOs). Better ambulatory-care management leads to lower rates of ED visits, hospital admissions, and readmissions. Care-delivery transformation enables primary care physicians to provide more comprehensive care and limit referrals to specialists. And, as mentioned earlier in this chapter, the efficient use of care teams also increases practice capacity so that providers can see more patients.

Automation tools enable care managers to do more and manage patients better. Practices can use these tools to stratify and reach their entire populations, not just those who visit their care providers, which is what population health management is all about. And these tools can help care-team members practice at the top of their licenses by taking over time-consuming, routine tasks.

# Conclusion

The transformation of healthcare delivery requires high-performance care teams. But care teams that include care coordinators and other ancillary professionals are likely to be too expensive for many primary care practices because many important services of care-team members are not reimbursed under most contracts, although this situation is starting to change.

Value-based reimbursement can justify the higher overhead expense if practices can produce real savings. But to move the needle on cost and quality, practices need to undertake a kind of population health management that's impossible to do using manual methods. Automation tools can enable practices to meet this challenge while making them more efficient.

Automation alone, however, cannot fix broken processes or create new ones. One proven way to do that is to use the Lean approach to continuous quality improvement. Lean thinking, coupled with automation tools, can make care teams more efficient and productive while helping practices deliver value to patients and payers.

Leading healthcare organizations are moving in this direction. They will be among the organizations best suited to succeed in the world of value-based reimbursement.

Automation tools can also enable organizations to engage the majority of their patients in improving their own health. As we explain in the next chapter, patient engagement — a basic tenet of population health management — can achieve only modest success unless providers use all the technology tools at their disposal to reach patients and persuade them to change their health behavior.

### THE HOLY GRAIL OF POPULATION HEALTH MANAGEMENT

The key to managing the health of a population is getting individuals engaged in their own health and healthcare. The more people can do to help themselves—while also maintaining close contact with their providers and care teams—the more likely they are to have better outcomes.

### ASSESS AND ADDRESS SOCIAL DETERMINANTS OF HEALTH THROUGH:

#### Provider-Patient Relationship

- Shared decision-making
- Continuous contact between healthcare organizations and their patients

#### Engagement Strategies

- Based on population data and risk stratification
- Tailored to subgroups of the patient population
- Delivered through multiple modalities

### How to Engage Patients in Their Health

### INCREASE PATIENT KNOWLEDGE AND CONFIDENCE, THROUGH:

| CARE MANAGEMENT | PATIENT EDUCATION | TELEHEALTH |
|---|---|---|
| Collaborative care planning and automated communications | Cloud-based educational materials as well as self-management and community based services | Remote patient monitoring |
| **MOBILE HEALTH APPS** | **PERSONAL HEALTH RECORDS** | **SOCIAL MEDIA** |
| Health and wellness promoted via smartphones and tablets | Patient portals that share EHR data and permit easy communication between patients and providers/ care teams | Patients with specific conditions referred to online communities providing education and support |

# 11

# Patient Engagement

- *Introduction:* Patient engagement is essential to improving health outcomes and is therefore an integral part of population health management. Visits to physicians alone are not enough to sustain patient engagement, but the physician-patient relationship is critical to success in this area.

- *How to engage patients:* Patient activation is a formidable challenge. Increasing patients' knowledge of their conditions and building confidence in their ability to change are key factors. Low health literacy, cultural and language differences, and poverty are major barriers to patient engagement.

- *Care management:* The automation of patient outreach can help healthcare organizations engage the majority of people in their populations. By combining automation with tools for risk stratification and identification of care gaps, the organizations can also deliver tailored interventions to patients.

- *Patient education:* With a large percentage of people going online for health information, it's natural to use automated, web-based educational materials to teach them more about their conditions. When combined with health coaching and other online communications, this approach can be a powerful tool to increase patient engagement.

- *Telehealth:* Remote patient monitoring and other forms of telehealth can also help patients get more involved in their own care while keeping clinicians apprised of their health status. Numerous studies show the clinical benefits of telemedicine.

- *Mobile health apps:* The proliferation of smartphones and tablet computers offers new routes for practices to increase patient engagement through apps that promote wellness and better control of chronic conditions.

- *Personal health record (PHR):* The PHR has long been viewed as a potentially powerful tool for involving patients in their own care. But so far, PHRs have had fairly low uptake, even by patients with chronic conditions. Physicians must start sharing EHR data with patients and use PHRs in other ways to get patients onboard.

- *Social media:* Social media have had a huge impact on consumers, and the majority of physicians use them in clinical care. But for the most part, physicians are using these media to obtain information on medical studies and communicate with other healthcare professionals, not with patients.

As the healthcare industry starts to reengineer care delivery to accommodate new reimbursement models, providers on the front lines of change recognize the need for population health management and for increasing patients' engagement in their own care. These two approaches are inextricably bound together, because it is impossible to manage the health of a population without getting patients more involved in self-management and the modification of their own risk factors. This chapter discusses the fundamentals of patient engagement and shows how automation tools and web-based care management can facilitate this key process.

Studies demonstrate that patient engagement is essential to improving health outcomes and that the lack of such engagement is a major contributor to preventable deaths. In fact, it is estimated that 40 percent of deaths in the United States are caused by modifiable behavioral issues, such as smoking and obesity. People with chronic diseases take only 50 percent of the prescribed doses of medications, on average. Fifty percent of patients do not follow referral advice, and 75 percent do not keep follow-up appointments.[1]

Many patients are unaware of their risk factors because they have not received recommended screening tests. For example, when a group of 4,000 people were screened for high cholesterol, a government study found, only 40 percent of those who had this condition were aware of it. Even among people who knew they had high cholesterol, only 14.5 percent were taking cholesterol-lowering drugs, and just 6.8 percent had reduced their levels below the goal of 200 mg/dl.[2]

In a study on the impact of eliminating copayments on drugs prescribed to heart-attack survivors, the authors noted that rates of adherence to these medications — including statins, beta blockers, ACE inhibitors, and ARBs — ranged from 36 percent to 49 percent.[3] In an accompanying editorial, Lee Goldman, MD, and Arnold M. Epstein, MD, commented, "Perhaps the most sobering findings were both the low baseline adherence and the small improvement in adherence in what should have been a highly motivated group of patients after myocardial infarction."[4]

High deductible health plans, including those accompanied by health savings accounts, can also affect medication compliance. A study of consumer-directed plans that included high deductibles found that medication compliance among consumer-directed plan members with chronic conditions fell during the first year of enrollment, compared to similar enrollees in PPO plans.[5]

Visits to physicians alone are insufficient to address the overall compliance problem. "Sporadic contact (such as every six months) with a healthcare provider is often inadequate to maintain and reinforce complicated lifestyle modifications and pharmacologic regimens," noted Thomas Pearson in a paper on the prevention of cardiovascular disease.[6]

One goal of population health management is to maintain continuous contact with patients and to address modifiable health behaviors that may lead to or exacerbate chronic diseases.[7] To be effective, population health management should include a variety of interventions — some of them automated — to keep patients engaged and help them manage their own care between visits.

# The Physician-Patient Relationship

As important as continuous contact is, the key to patient engagement is the physician-patient relationship. When a doctor advises a patient to quit smoking, for example, the chance of that person doing so increases by 30 percent.[8] So, it can be inferred that all patient outreach and educational efforts must be performed on behalf of the patient's physician in order to have a strong likelihood of success.

Shared decision-making between physicians and patients also increases the probability of improved outcomes,[9] so that must be part of the engagement formula. Although patients vary in their desire to be involved in decision-making, one recent study showed that most people want to participate in major medical decisions.[10]

Shared decision-making is a key part of the patient-centered medical home (PCMH), which has been embraced by more and more physician practices and healthcare organizations in recent years. In the PCMH, every patient has a personal physician who takes responsibility for the patient's care and coordinates referrals across care settings. In addition, the patient is considered part of the care team, and the patient and his or her family can participate in quality improvement at the practice level.[11]

Both in the PCMH and the chronic-care model of disease management, patient engagement is critical. But as every physician knows, it is difficult to motivate many patients to participate in their own health care. What follows are some findings of the research on the psychology of patient activation and the interventions that have been shown to engage patients.

# How to Engage Patients

Patient engagement is crucial to improving population health because patients with chronic diseases — the individuals who generate 75 percent of health costs — must manage their own conditions most of the time. Care management can help them do that, but they still face a tough challenge, as patient activation expert Judith Hibbard explained:

> Patients with chronic diseases often must follow complex treatment regimens, monitor their conditions, make lifestyle changes, and make decisions about when they need to seek care and when they can handle a problem on their own. Effectively functioning in the role of self-manager, particularly when living with one or more chronic illnesses, requires a high level of knowledge, skill, and confidence.[12]

When patients have the knowledge, skill, and confidence to help manage their own health, Hibbard observed, they do better. "A growing body of evidence shows that patients who are engaged, active participants in their own care have better health outcomes and measurable cost savings," she pointed out.[13]

But it is not easy to activate some patients, either because they are depressed or because they don't believe they are up to the task (or both). According to a report from the Center for Advancing Health, for example, only 30 percent of seniors feel they have the motivation and the skills to participate fully in their own care.[14]

Hibbard and her colleagues characterized patient activation as a developmental process that they broke down into four stages:[15]

- Believing that the patient's role in care is important
- Having the confidence and the knowledge necessary to take action
- Actually taking action to maintain and improve one's health
- Staying the course even under the stress of adverse life conditions

In a 2004 study, Hibbard's team looked at whether changes in patient activation led to changes in health behavior in a cohort of people between 50 and 70 years old. The intervention group attended weekly workshops that covered topics related to self-management of care and coping with social isolation. Compared with the control group, the intervention group became more activated initially, but the difference faded after six months. However, individuals in both groups who became more activated had a positive change in a variety of self-management behaviors.[16]

## Activation models

How to activate patients to change poor health behavior — which can worsen chronic conditions or cause patients to get sick — has been the subject of considerable research. Here are a few of the approaches that have been tried:

- *Transtheoretical model:* In this approach, care managers or coaches increase awareness of the need for change. Then they motivate patients to make changes and help them make concrete action plans. Later, they assist patients with problem-solving and social support, and reinforce maintenance of health behavior changes. The key is to help patients change their self-concept and have them see how social norms support improvements in their health behavior.[17]

- *Social cognitive theory:* The underlying concept of this model is that the more you believe you can do something, the more likely you are to do it. Care managers try to help patients build confidence in their ability to improve health behavior and avoid unhealthy behavior even in stressful conditions. This approach addresses both the psychosocial dynamics influencing healthy behavior and methods for promoting behavior change.[18]

- *Health belief model:* Proponents of this approach argue that many people will change their health behavior if they believe it will help them avoid a negative health outcome. Techniques include defining risk, consequences of risk, and benefits of change; identification of barriers and tips to overcome them; promotion of action through information and reminders; and confidence building through training, guidance, and reinforcement.[19]

- *Behavioral economics*: Advocates of behavioral economics note that patients are "predictably irrational" in their decision-making. For example, they may prefer the short-term rewards of overeating or lounging around to the long-term rewards of being more fit and perhaps living longer because of eating more wisely and exercising. Providing these patients with little "nudges" in the form of rewards or penalties for good or bad health behavior may change the individual's calculus, these theorists say.[20]

## Obstacles to patient engagement

There are many barriers to patient engagement that go beyond the willingness of patients to take responsibility for self-care or to follow doctors' orders. These include the social and economic environments in which patients must function, cultural factors, the lack of health literacy in a large portion of the population, knowledge deficits, and poor access to health care. (See Chapter 13.)

For example, a recent study shows a large disparity in patient activation between Hispanic immigrants and white people born in the United States. Some of this disparity — between not only Hispanics and whites but also African-Americans and whites — has to do with social and economic differences, the study found. But in the case of Hispanics, cultural and language barriers also play an important role in the disparity.[21]

The lack of health literacy is a major obstacle across the U.S. population. More than 90 million adults have *low health literacy,* which means they have difficulty understanding and using health information.[22] Educational materials often are not written at a level that people can easily grasp and make use of — a situation that is exacerbated when a patient's primary language is not English.

Finally, many people simply lack good access to health care. They may not have a regular primary care physician; and even if they do have one, it may be difficult to secure an appointment, take time off from work, or find transportation to see the doctor. Additionally, some patients cannot afford the tests or medications that their physician orders, especially if they have a high deductible health plan or lack insurance.

Population health management cannot overcome all these obstacles to patient engagement. But the automation of care management and care coordination can significantly improve the odds that the majority of patients can be actively engaged in managing their own care. The rest of this chapter shows how this can be done in several domains, including care management, patient education, and interventions that utilize a variety of new technologies.

# Care Management

Most physicians do not have enough time to keep track of all their patients, let alone reach out to them between visits. Moreover, many lower-level clinical tasks can be performed by non-physicians or can be automated. So in any organization focused on population health, a care team does the day-to-day work of caring for and engaging the patient.

In some healthcare organizations, care managers focus mainly on telephonic management of high-risk patients who may be admitted to the hospital or go the emergency department unless their urgent needs are met. This is an important task of the care team, but it is only one component of population health management. Of the patients who generate the highest costs in a given year, less than 30 percent would have been included in that category in the preceding year.[23] So an organization that hopes to improve the quality and lower the cost of care must pay attention to its entire population.

Maintaining continuous contact with every patient in a practice, however, is a task that exceeds the capability of even the largest healthcare organizations if they use only manual processes. Care managers are expensive, and the number of patients they can coach is limited. To expand the care managers' reach and the influence of physicians on their patients, some degree of automation is required.

## Patient outreach

For example, many patients have gaps in their preventive and chronic care. In some cases, this happens because the patient hasn't visited the practice in a long time. In other cases, the patient hasn't been informed of needed services during office visits or has not complied with the physician's recommendations.

Some practices try to contact patients with care gaps between visits. But, even if a practice has a good system for identifying these patients, manual outreach is prohibitively costly in terms of staff time and phone and mailing costs. So, this is usually a hit-or-miss process, and it is not scalable to larger groups.

New automation tools can facilitate this part of the patient engagement process and ensure outreach to all patients who need services. Using data extracted from a practice management system or an electronic health record, these solutions build patient registries and use clinical protocols to trigger messaging to patients who have an existing care gap and need to make an appointment with a physician. Frequently, this messaging results in patients reconnecting with their physicians after a long absence.

A study at Prevea Health, a large, multispecialty group in Green Bay, Wisconsin, showed that automated outreach to noncompliant patients with diabetes or hypertension increases the likelihood that those patients will make office visits and get the care they need. The study concluded, "An automated identification and outreach program can be an effective means to supplement existing practice patterns to ensure that patients with chronic conditions in need of care receive the necessary treatment."[24]

## Risk stratification

As mentioned earlier in this chapter, the majority of high-cost patients today had a much lower risk of generating high costs a year ago. So organizations that want to embrace population health management must adopt techniques to identify patients who are likely to become high risk and to prioritize care management of those patients. (See Chapter 6.)

Some health insurers are giving accountable care organizations predictive modeling software — similar to the programs their actuaries use — to accomplish that task.[25] But it is also possible to do risk stratification — while also increasing patient engagement — by asking patients to complete online health risk assessments (HRAs), just as many employers and health plans do.[26] Though patients resist filling out long forms, practices can break up HRAs into smaller, bite-size chunks about specific areas of a patient's health behavior, such as diet, exercise, or smoking.

Healthways, a health promotion company based in Franklin, Tennessee, has developed and validated another survey instrument called the Gallup-Healthways Well-Being 5™. This instrument measures domains of well-being that go beyond the traditional HRA categories. The Well-Being 5 yields information about an individual's sense of purpose in life, social interactions and support structures, financial situation and hardships, perceived involvement in the community, health behaviors, health status, and substance abuse. The factors that don't pertain directly to physical health may nevertheless be among the social determinants of health, which we discuss in Chapter 13.[27]

HRAs and Well-Being 5 surveys enable organizations to classify patients by their health conditions, health behaviors, and functional status. This helps providers spot patients who may become high risk and gives them data for analyzing their patient population. In addition, some HRAs measure stages of patient activation — something that Hibbard recommends. "This would enable early intervention with patients who lack the skills to self-manage before they inevitably move to a higher health-risk group," she noted in a *Health Affairs* paper.[28]

It's important to remember, however, that HRAs or any other type of patient-entered data can supply only part of the information needed for accurate risk stratification. Analytics that use claims data and clinical data are needed to round out the picture for each patient.

## Patient education

The research on patient activation shows that patients feel more confident about managing their health conditions when they have more knowledge about them. Today, many patients go online for this information. According to the Pew Research Center, 72 percent of adult Internet users said they had sought answers to their health questions online in the past year, and 35 percent said they had gone online to figure out what medical condition they or another person might have.[29]

Online patient-education materials may be multimedia and interactive — a big improvement over the paper handouts that many practices still use. When patients view some of these programs, they can ask questions and receive answers online. One vendor of online education services even allows physicians to see whether patients have reviewed the materials they were asked to read or view. Such materials are available for both postsurgical care and the care of chronic conditions.[30]

When combined with automated patient communications, these online educational materials can be powerful tools to motivate patients. Physicians can put in a standing order for particular education pieces to be directed automatically to patients at various points in the care process. Such an approach relieves the burden on practice staff of ensuring that patients receive the proper information at the appropriate time.

Health coaching has also been shown to improve patient outcomes, and some evidence shows that online coaching has similar results.[31–33] The latest digital coaching tools, which start with health risk assessments, can help patients improve their health behaviors by losing weight, eating better, or exercising more, for example.[34]

To have the desired effect, these automated education and health coaching tools must be tailored to the target population. They must be not only condition specific but also written in consumer-friendly language. They must be designed to address health literacy and language barriers, or else they will fail.

## Telemedicine

The use of remote patient monitoring and alerting in chronic disease management dates back to the late 1990s.[35] Since then, telemonitoring devices have become more sophisticated and less expensive, and the ability to transmit data has grown exponentially. The main obstacle to faster growth of telemonitoring is the healthcare reimbursement system, which still does not compensate physicians for non-visit care in most cases. That barrier, too, is expected to disappear, as value-based care becomes the new paradigm. CMS has already made a start in this direction by reimbursing physicians for reviewing remote monitoring data as part of its chronic care management program.[36]

Telemonitoring helps care teams extend their reach, and it engages patients in their own care. It has also been shown to improve outcomes when combined with active care management. According to one study of telemonitoring in diabetes care, for instance, "prompting follow-up procedures, computerized insulin therapy adjustment using home glucose records, remote feedback, and counseling have documented benefits in improving diabetes-related outcomes."[37]

The benefits of telemedicine have been known for some time. In 2007, the Agency for Healthcare Research and Quality (AHRQ) surveyed the literature on the impact of what it called "consumer health informatics [CHI] applications," which would now be called telemedicine, or telehealth.[38] The majority of the studies evaluated interactive, web-based applications or web-based, tailored educational applications. Fifteen percent of the studies looked at computer-generated, tailored feedback applications, and 8 percent evaluated interactive computer programs and personal monitoring devices.

The meta-analysis found that the CHI interventions improved self-management, knowledge of health conditions, adherence to treatments, and health behavior. Some of the studies evaluated clinical outcomes for cancer, diabetes, mental health, diet, exercise and physical activity, asthma, COPD, breast cancer, Alzheimer's disease, arthritis, asthma, back pain, aphasia, COPD, HIV/AIDS, headache, obesity, and pain. "Over 80 percent of studies found significant influence of CHI applications on at least one clinical outcome," the report concluded.

Subsequent studies have confirmed the benefits of telemedicine. A 2008 study by the Veterans Health Administration (VHA) found that the VHA's telemedicine program reduced hospital bed days by 25 percent and hospital admissions by 19 percent for a cohort of 17,000 participating patients.[39] A 2012 study of telemedicine in a California care coordination program found that it reduced mortality rates for patients with congestive heart failure by 57 percent over three years.[40] And a four-year, 500-patient study by the Geisinger Health Plan showed that remote monitoring of heart failure patients reduced 30-day readmissions by 44 percent and produced a return on investment of more than 3:1.[41]

# Mobile health apps

In recent years, the number of people using smartphones, tablets, and other web-connected mobile devices has exploded. According to the Pew Research Center, 68 percent of U.S. adults now own smartphones, and 45 percent have tablet computers.[42]

The rise of mobile communications has been accompanied by rapid growth in the number of health-related applications designed for mobile devices. Though many of these are intended for professionals, the bulk of them are aimed at consumers. These applications range from symptom checkers and apps that measure vital signs to programs that help users find "quality"-evaluated doctors and hospitals.[43] The latest iPhones and iPads also have video chat features that physicians can use to examine patients remotely.[44]

The mobile health apps that have the greatest potential in population health management are those linked to care management. In a 2011 study, for example, a mobile, web-based self-management patient coaching system was shown to help patients with diabetes reduce their HbA1c levels more than a control group that received usual care.[45] Another study showed that mobile alerts to diabetic patients using glucometers with smartphones were as effective in lowering HbA1c as an Internet-based glucose monitoring system.[46]

## Personal health records

The value of personal health records has been debated and continues to be uncertain. But in large healthcare organizations like Kaiser Permanente and Group Health Cooperative, where PHRs are linked to EHRs, millions of patients are using PHRs to view parts of their medical records, see lab results, request prescription refills, schedule appointments, and email their physicians.[47] Patients at the Palo Alto Medical Foundation who had PHRs indicated that these tools made them feel like part of the medical team and kept them in closer touch with their providers.[48]

In a study of the use of health IT in patient-centered medical homes, David W. Bates and Asaf Bitton noted that PHRs can increase patient engagement and self-efficacy, but that they have a low acceptance rate by patients, especially those who are chronically ill. One reason, they said, is that current PHRs have serious limitations; for example, many do not include clinical data from EHRs and other sources.[49]

To remedy these defects, they argued, physicians must overcome their reluctance to share EHR data with patients, and interfaces must be improved to make it easy for patients to upload clinical data. In addition, PHRs should have the capability to communicate online with care teams and track vital signs such as weight, blood pressure, and blood sugar. There should also be a mechanism for care managers to provide feedback when a patient's indicators are worrisome, the authors said.

Another study maintained that the potential of PHRs will not be realized until they integrate a wide range of patient data that goes beyond the EHR in a particular practice or organization. In addition, the authors said, such integrated PHRs must include a range of tools to help consumers apply the data to self-management.

According to these experts, the data elements within a PHR alone are not sufficient to realize improvements that can be considered transformative. Significant value will be realized only when PHRs incorporate systems, tools, and other resources that leverage the data in the record and enable consumers to play a more active role in their health and health care.[50]

## Social media

Social media such as Facebook, Twitter, and LinkedIn are having a huge impact on consumers. Some people spend more time on social media than they do on all other Internet sites combined. From a logical viewpoint, it would seem that patient engagement strategies should include the use of social media.

But physicians and their patients use different social media, and doctors are not eager to communicate with patients via Facebook or Twitter.

A 2012 survey showed that a quarter of physicians used social media daily in their clinical work. Sixty-one percent of respondents did so at least once a week, and 58 percent found social media were beneficial and improved patient care.[51]

Another study discovered that 67 percent of doctors employ social media for professional purposes, but their top destinations are professional sites and LinkedIn. The majority of doctors use Facebook in their personal lives, but only 15 percent use it in health care. And, while a third of physicians have received invitations to "friend" their patients, 75 percent of those doctors declined to do so.[52]

The biggest reason for physicians to avoid using Facebook and Twitter for professional purposes is the fear of breaching patient confidentiality online. In addition, some doctors are afraid of learning information about patients that the patient has chosen not to disclose, such as recreational drug use. And many doctors prefer to keep their personal and professional lives separate.[53]

Nevertheless, physicians and care teams can refer patients with specific conditions to online communities such as PatientsLikeMe that provide education and mutual support to people with those conditions. That would certainly increase patient engagement. But before they do so, doctors would be well advised to check out these sites to make sure that they're providing reliable, objective information.

# Conclusion

Patient engagement is vital to quality improvement, better patient outcomes, and population health management. Some observers even regard it as the "holy grail" of PHM. To improve patient engagement, organizations must reach out to every patient, using the techniques that have been shown to motivate patients to participate in their own health care.

Care teams provide the non-visit, continuous care that is essential to population health management. They are also responsible for promoting patient engagement between visits. But care managers who use manual processes cannot intervene with every patient. That effort requires the use of health information and communication tools that automate the process so that care managers can devote themselves to the patients who need the most attention.

Besides automating care management, the latest technologies enable organizations to analyze population data and stratify patients by health risk. Based on that information, they can design engagement strategies tailored to particular subgroups of patients.

Other new technologies, ranging from telemonitoring and mobile health to PHRs and social media, can be employed to increase patient engagement. But to be effective, they must be linked with provider-led care management, and they must invoke the power and influence of the doctor-patient relationship.

By combining all these techniques, healthcare organizations can provide truly patient-centered care. When patients are fully engaged in their own health care, they will have better outcomes, and the growth in health costs will start to abate.

An important aspect of patient engagement is the challenge of post-discharge care. Hospitals have recently become quite focused on this kind of care because of Medicare's penalties for preventable readmissions. The next chapter takes a close look at the implications of post-discharge care, the challenges to ensuring that patients receive proper follow up, and the role that information technology can play in making that happen.

# USING AUTOMATION TO IMPROVE POST-DISCHARGE CARE

IT automation tools can help minimize the breaks in patient communication and monitoring that can lead to readmissions.

## Problems

### HIGH HOSPITAL
### READMISSION RATES

- Gaps in care transitions
- Inadequate patient and caregiver education
- Poor handovers

## Solutions

### IT AUTOMATION
### TOOLS

- Improved communication between in patient and out patient care teams
- Use risk stratification of patients to prevent (re)admission
- Multi-modal post-discharge communication with patients
- Patient education and engagement

## Results

### IMPROVED QUALITY
### OF CARE

- Increased patient satisfaction
- Reduced hospital readmission rates
- Better outcomes
- Lowered health care costs
- Improved provider/ care team satisfaction

# 12

# Automated Post-Discharge Care

- *Introduction:* Readmissions, which affect nearly a fifth of Medicare patients discharged from the hospital, are more numerous than they should be because of the fragmentation of our healthcare system. Multiple government programs have been established to address this problem.
- *Gaps in care transitions:* Among the reasons for preventable readmissions are poor preparation of patients in the hospital, poor handovers to ambulatory care providers, and a lack of hospital follow-up after discharge.
- *Best practices:* Academic experts have identified several approaches that can reduce readmissions. Examined here are the Institute for Healthcare Improvement's (IHI's) recommendations; the Coleman Care Transitions Intervention (CTI); and the Naylor Transitional Care Model.
- *Automation:* Though these approaches have proved successful with some patients and subpopulations, they cannot be applied to all discharged patients, because they rely on one-to-one case management. To reduce readmissions further, healthcare organizations should employ automated methods of following up with patients and making sure their needs are met.

Readmissions are a major problem in U.S. health care. Nearly one in five Medicare patients discharged from the hospital returns there within 30 days,[1] and roughly 75 percent of those readmissions are considered preventable.[2]

**185**

Medicare pays about $17 billion annually for 2.5 million rehospitalizations of its beneficiaries, and other payers spend roughly the same amount every year for all readmissions of non-Medicare patients.[3]

The immediate cause of a readmission is usually a rapid deterioration in the patient's condition, related to the patient's primary diagnosis and/or comorbidities. But in a broader sense, it can be attributed to systemic failures that begin in the hospital and continue in the fragmented healthcare settings that patients move through after discharge.

In a typical scenario, patients receive inadequate preparation for discharge; the handover from the hospital to the outpatient provider is poorly handled; and patients and their family caregivers are left to cope on their own with medical issues that they do not understand.[4] In fact, only about half of discharged patients follow up with their primary care physicians after they leave the hospital, and those who do not are much more likely to be readmitted than those who do see a doctor.[5]

# New Government Incentives

Until recently, some hospitals held the attitude that their responsibility for care ended when the patient walked (or was wheeled) out the door. Other facilities have used a variety of techniques to reduce readmissions, with mixed results. But new government incentives, plus a rising awareness of the need to improve patient safety, are forcing hospitals to place an increased emphasis on discharge planning and post-acute care.

Front and center are the regulations from the Centers for Medicare and Medicaid Services (CMS) on preventable readmissions. Since October 1, 2012, hospitals with excessive readmissions (rehospitalizations that are significantly higher than the national average) have lost a percentage of their Medicare reimbursement across the board. In fiscal year 2013, the decrease was up to 1 percent of reimbursement; the maximum penalty increased to 2 percent in 2014 and to 3 percent in 2015.[6]

In the first year of this program, CMS examined 30-day readmission rates for patients with heart failure, acute myocardial infarction, and pneumonia — three of the leading conditions for which patients are readmitted. Since 2015, CMS has also scrutinized readmissions for an acute exacerbation of chronic obstructive pulmonary disease (COPD), elective total hip arthroplasty, and total knee arthroplasty.[7]

This program has already had a measurable effect. In 2013, the 30-day readmission rate for Medicare dropped to 17.5 percent from the historical rate of 19 percent. That drop represented about 150,000 fewer readmissions than expected.[8]

CMS has also launched other programs that might contribute to lower readmission rates. To begin with, the agency is spending $500 million — or half of the $1 billion earmarked in the Affordable Care Act for improving patient safety — to help hospitals and their community partners decrease readmissions over a five-year period ending in 2016. Through the government-sponsored Partnership for Patients, CMS is paying these community-based organizations a set amount per discharge for managing Medicare beneficiaries at high risk for readmission.[9]

Two other CMS initiatives authorized by the health reform law are also designed to cut readmissions: bundled payments and accountable care organizations (ACOs).

Under CMS's bundled-payment demonstration, which started in April 2013, providers may choose among four different options. These choices include retrospective bundled payments to hospitals, physicians, and other providers for acute care only; hospital care plus post-acute care for a specified period; and post-acute care only. The fourth option involves a lump-sum prospective payment for hospital care plus readmissions that occur during the 30 days after discharge.[10]

The Medicare Shared Savings Program (MSSP) for ACOs, which began in 2012, is also expected to have an effect. ACOs have a strong incentive to cut readmissions in order to generate savings that they can share.[11]

Nevertheless, it's difficult for healthcare organizations to decrease readmissions significantly in our fragmented, uncoordinated healthcare system. While most of the levers of improvement are known, reengineering inpatient processes and engaging patients and outpatient providers remains challenging.

Fortunately, new applications of health information technology now offer inexpensive ways to automate post-acute-care processes. These solutions, which are discussed later in this chapter, can raise the effectiveness of care managers, improve the communications between inpatient and outpatient providers, and make it easier for patients and caregivers to absorb and apply the knowledge required for the self-management of complex conditions.

# Gaps in Care Transitions

The literature on care transition problems shows five main areas that contribute to preventable readmissions:

- Poor preparation for discharge
- Patients' low health literacy and comprehension
- Failure or inability of patients to see physicians for follow up after discharge
- Lack of hospital follow up
- Lack of communication between inpatient and outpatient providers

Readmissions occur, by definition, after a patient's initial hospitalization. Yet the foundation for post-acute care is laid during the hospital stay — and that preparation is often inadequate. "The hospital discharge process is characterized by fragmented, non-standardized, and haphazard care," noted Brian Jack, an expert on hospital reengineering, and his colleagues.[12]

Nurses and first-year residents are often placed in charge of discharges. These staffers have many other duties and may relegate discharges to a lower priority. Making matters worse, there are no clear lines of authority. As a result, the system sets up these individuals to fail and creates a dangerous situation for patients.

A prime safety issue cited by many experts is missing or inadequate *medication reconciliation* — checking on all medications that the patient is taking or have been prescribed at the time of discharge. The medications that patients received in the hospital are often discontinued at discharge, whereas the drugs they were taking before they were admitted may or may not be resumed. Dosages may also change.[13]

The Joint Commission, a national healthcare accreditation organization, has identified medication reconciliation as a key requirement for ensuring patient safety.[14] The Institute for Healthcare Improvement also cites medication reconciliation as an opportunity to reduce readmissions.[15] This is clearly an area where hospitals could contribute to lower rehospitalization rates.

## Poor educational techniques

Another challenge in care transition is that of ensuring that patients understand what will be required of them after discharge. In one study, for example, 78 percent of patients discharged from the ED did not understand their diagnoses, their ED treatments, their home care instructions, or the warning signs of when to return to the hospital.[16]

Providers are partly responsible for this lack of comprehension. Physicians or nurses may rush through their instructions and not encourage patients to ask questions. They may not use the proven *teach-back* method of having patients restate the instructions in their own words. And they may not realize that because of patients' cognitive issues, their family caregivers are the ones who need to receive the instructions.[17]

Another big — and underappreciated — problem is the low health literacy of the U.S. population. Roughly 90 million Americans — nearly half of the adult population — have low functional literacy.[18] "Such patients typically have difficulty reading and understanding medical instructions, medication labels, and appointment slips," according to one study.[19]

What this means is that both oral and written instructions must be couched in terms that someone with fairly little formal education can understand. It also means that many patients require post-discharge communications to ensure that they are adhering to their medication regimens, following up with their outpatient physicians, and looking for danger signs in their own conditions.

## Poor handovers

Another glaring deficiency in post-acute transitions of care is the inadequate communication between inpatient and outpatient providers. Here are a few statistics that underline the chaotic state of these communications:

- Direct communication between hospital physicians and primary care physicians occurs in only 3 to 20 percent of cases.
- Only 12 to 34 percent of doctors have received hospital discharge summaries by the time patients make their first post-discharge visits. The range rises to only 51 to 77 percent after four weeks, affecting the quality of care in about a quarter of follow-up visits.[20]
- Approximately 40 percent of patients have pending test results at the time of discharge, and 10 percent of those require action; yet, in the majority of cases, outpatient physicians are unaware of these results.[21]

Other studies have found that discharge summaries often fail to provide basic information about hospital visits. Some summaries never even reach the primary care doctors who are caring for discharged patients.[22]

Though ambulatory-care physicians may be shooting in the dark when they see a recently discharged patient, at least they may know something about the patient's history, and they can find out what medications the patient is on. All of that works to the patient's advantage. But many discharged patients do not or cannot make an appointment to see a doctor within a week of discharge. A patient who is at high risk of complications and deterioration should be seen within 24 hours, but often this doesn't happen.

# Best Practices

A great deal of research has been done on the best methods for reducing readmissions. In this section, we focus on the Institute for Healthcare Improvement's (IHI's) recommendations as well as on the Coleman Care Transitions Intervention model and the Naylor Transitional Care model.

Other resources for healthcare organizations include the BOOST program of the Society of Hospital Medicine;[23] the Care Transitions Performance Measurement Set of the Physician Consortium for Performance Improvement;[24] and the Transitions of Care Consensus Policy Statement of the American College of Physicians and five other specialty societies.[25]

## IHI's patient-centered approach

IHI, a Boston-based nonprofit organization that has led two transitions-of-care initiatives, recommends that healthcare organizations create "cross-continuum" teams that involve all community stakeholders. It advises institutions to use a patient-centered approach that looks at post-discharge care through a patient's eyes (which is a Lean principle, as described in Chapter 10). By doing *deep dives* into several patient histories to find out why the patients were readmitted, IHI says, it is possible to understand where the entire process falls short and begin to fix it.[26]

Specifically, IHI recommends these actions:

- Focus on the patient's journey over time across care settings
- Make discharge preparations early
- Redesign health education materials using health literacy principles
- Provide intensive-care-management services for high-risk patients
- Ensure that patients have follow-up appointments with physicians
- Improve communications between inpatient and outpatient providers

The key changes that hospitals need to make, says IHI, are listed here:

- Enhanced assessment of post-discharge needs
- Effective teaching and learning by patients and/or caregivers
- Real-time handover communications
- Assurance of post-hospital follow up[27]

## Coleman Care Transitions Intervention

Eric Coleman, MD, MPH, a geriatrician at the University of Colorado Health Sciences Center, and his colleagues have created a Care Transitions Intervention (CTI) model that emphasizes the use of a transition coach.[28,29] Recognizing that patients and their caregivers are key parts of the post-discharge care team, the transition coach visits the patient in the hospital and again at home and makes three follow-up phone calls. The coach teaches the patients/caregivers, helps them develop self-management skills, and assesses their learning. Though some coaches are nurses, studies have shown that people with a wide variety of backgrounds can perform this function.

Overall, the CTI supports patients in four areas:

- Ensuring that patients and/or caregivers can manage their medications
- Giving patients personal health records to facilitate communications with providers and promote continuity of care
- Scheduling, preparing for, and completing follow-up visits with physicians
- Understanding danger signs for their conditions and knowing how to respond to them

A 2006 study showed that the CTI approach reduced the chances of rehospitalization by 40 to 50 percent.[30,31] More recently, researchers at Brown University found that the CTI cut 30-day readmissions of Medicare patients from 20 percent to under 13 percent.[32]

## Naylor Transitional Care Model

Mary Naylor, PhD, RN, and her colleagues at the University of Pennsylvania have developed another approach for decreasing readmissions: Their model involves care coordination by a transitional care nurse who generally has advanced practice training.[33]

Following evidence-based protocols, the nurse care manager visits the patient daily during the hospital stay; visits the patient at home during the first 24 hours after discharge and then weekly during the first month; telephones the patient weekly; implements a care plan that is continually reassessed in consultation with the patient, the caregiver, and the patient's primary care physician; and continues calling the patient monthly after the initial two-month period.

Randomized controlled trials have shown that the Naylor model reduces all-cause readmission rates, increases patient satisfaction, function, and quality of life; and decreases overall healthcare costs. In one study, the model reduced the number of readmissions at six months by 36 percent, and decreased costs by 39 percent.[34]

The literature on the efficacy of post-discharge phone calls has shown mixed results. But in one study, 19 percent of patients experienced medication-related issues that were resolved with post-discharge calls.[35] In another study, 35 percent of patients who received calls needed significant referral and aftercare instructions.[36] This evidence points to the need to reach out to the whole population of discharged patients while stratifying patients in order to increase the efficacy of these phone calls and of care management in general.

# Automation

The approaches outlined above have been shown to work with certain kinds of patients, and they can also be cost-effective with particular subpopulations. But, without the aid of automation, most organizations cannot afford to use these high-touch approaches to reach all patients who have been discharged from the hospital. Moreover, their approach to patient education is not as cost-effective as it could be, because it relies on one-to-one communication between patients or caregivers and coaches or nurses.

The existing models are also labor-intensive in other respects. The coaches and nurse case managers in the Coleman and Naylor models can handle only a limited number of patients. And, although human contact is essential in high-risk cases, automated approaches can perform many of the basic tasks required to support moderate-risk and low-risk patients during the post-discharge transition.

New automation tools can greatly facilitate the range of best practices designed to improve post-discharge care and reduce readmissions. Among the areas where automation can pay off in higher quality and lower costs are these:

- Risk stratification of patients
- Post-discharge communications with patients
- Patient education and engagement
- Closing provider communication loops

## Assessing patient risk

Some patients who are at high risk for readmission can be identified in the hospital. Certain conditions, such as congestive heart failure, make readmission likely; but in many cases, comorbidities are responsible for rehospitalization.[37] So some patients who are not obvious candidates for readmission may slip through the cracks. Other factors, such as adverse drug events because of poor or no medication reconciliation, can also lead to unexpected ER visits or readmissions.[38]

Ideally, hospitals should use predictive modeling to identify high-risk patients who are likely to be readmitted if they do not receive appropriate care after discharge. Utilized widely by managed care plans, predictive-modeling software analyzes hospital data, claims data on utilization and comorbidities, and patient surveys to stratify patients by risk level. (See Chapter 7.)

During the critical 24 to 72 hours after discharge, an automated phone assessment can be used to measure the satisfaction of discharged patients with their care while gathering data on their risk factors. This information allows a computer program to calculate a risk score. Based on that and on answers to condition-specific questions, alerts about high-risk patients can be transmitted to hospital care managers or triage nurses.

In addition, patients receiving automated calls may choose to be transferred to a hospital nurse help line or a call center if they prefer to speak to someone immediately about their concerns instead of receiving a subsequent callback. Those concerns may include worsening conditions, discharge or medication instruction questions, help with scheduling appointments, or other care-related matters.

If a patient has been identified in the hospital as high-risk, a nurse or transition coach should follow up with that patient at home or in the next care setting. Home telemonitoring may also be indicated, particularly for patients with heart failure. Signals from monitoring equipment alert care managers when the patient's condition deteriorates. But for low- or medium-risk patients, the automated-survey approach can establish whether the patient needs further professional assistance.

Moreover, the system can tell the hospital staff whether the patient has a follow-up appointment with a physician. And, if the system is connected with an outpatient registry, it can supplement hospital data with medical histories from integrated primary care systems.

## Patient education and engagement

Automation can also provide better, more consistent patient education that overcomes health literacy problems and ensures that patients understand the information they're receiving. This is an enormous opportunity to help patients increase their confidence and their ability to do self-management while reducing the amount of time and labor required to boost patients to that level.

Web-based, audiovisual educational materials are available, and some of them even provide feedback to providers so that they can see whether patients have viewed the materials.[39] In contrast, traditional programs lack the ability to test patients on what they've learned and make sure they're applying that knowledge to their own care. Digital coaching tools can fill this gap and help patients manage their conditions as much as they can on their own.[40]

## Connecting providers to each other

As the statistics cited earlier in this chapter show, the communication between hospital physicians and ambulatory-care doctors is generally subpar. There are a number of reasons for this, including a shortage of time, the difficulty of reaching outpatient providers, and the inherent problems of phone and fax communications.

The patient-outreach system just described can help close the communications loop in one significant respect: If ambulatory-care providers are using the same system to contact patients with preventive and chronic-care needs, that solution can also be used to notify primary care physicians and outpatient care managers when patients in their panels are admitted to the hospital and after they are discharged.

Some ACOs and health information exchanges perform the same service by linking their members with hospital admission/discharge/transfer (ADT) systems. The Office of the National Coordinator for Health IT (ONC) also explored ADT alerts in some of its 17 Beacon Communities.[41]

The Physician Consortium for Performance Improvement and an article in the *Journal of Hospital Medicine* both recommend providing a transition summary to primary care doctors within 24 hours rather than waiting for discharge summaries to be prepared and transmitted.[42,43] Such a summary, which could be communicated by phone, fax, or email, would include discharge diagnosis, medications, procedures, pending test results, follow-up arrangements, and suggested next steps.[44]

The use of EHRs could speed the delivery of these summaries; but hospitals and ambulatory-care practices frequently use different systems that are incompatible.[45] In the future, health information exchanges or new "plug-ins" for EHRs may overcome this barrier. Meanwhile, healthcare systems could investigate the use of the Direct Project secure messaging protocol to "push" information from one EHR to another.[46]

CMS is pushing interoperability among health IT systems very hard right now. In a January 2016 speech, CMS Acting Administrator Andy Slavitt said, "We are deadly serious about interoperability" and will not tolerate "information blocking."[47] Congress is also considering a bill that would punish EHR vendors for information blocking.[48] Private-sector organizations such as CareQuality and CommonWell Health Alliance, meanwhile, are trying to get vendors to cooperate on interoperability.[49] But after a long string of failures over the past decade, it appears that the best bet for achieving this goal is to develop new technologies such as Fast Healthcare Interoperability Resources (FHIR), which can be used to access discrete data in EHRs with the help of open APIs.[50]

# Conclusion

By reducing preventable readmissions, healthcare organizations could improve patient health and safety while responding to new government incentives and penalties. A patient-centered, automated approach is the most efficient and cost-effective way to make sure that all patients who have been discharged are properly taken care of. But such a model must be judiciously combined with high-touch care management to address the needs of high-risk patients appropriately.

Another important component of avoidable readmissions are social determinants of health, which play a key role in post-discharge care and the ability of patients to take care of themselves after they leave the hospital. The next chapter takes a comprehensive look at social and behavioral determinants of health and how integrated service delivery can improve patient outcomes.

**EXOGENOUS FACTORS LIKE THE COMMUNITIES WHERE PEOPLE WORK, THE HOMES WHERE THEY LIVE, CONDITIONS SUCH AS DEPRESSION, AND BEHAVIORAL INFLUENCES LIKE DRUG AND ALCOHOL ABUSE HAVE A LARGE IMPACT ON HEALTH VARIANCE.**

So does socioeconomic status, race, ethnicity, education, family structure, diet, exercise, employment, and environment.

### COMMUNITY SERVICES

To help patients, providers can connect with community services: behavioral health specialists, social workers, transportation coordinators, dietitians, pharmacists, and attorneys.

To manage population health, healthcare organizations must integrate the medical services they provide with the full range of social services each patient needs. Here's how:

### MEDICAL SERVICES

- Screen patients for social determinants

- Conduct comprehensive health assessments

- Connect patients to needed community and behavioral health services

### HEALTH IT

- Facilitate communication and care coordination between members of multidisciplinary teams

- Employ data analytics to collect actionable information on the clinical, social, behavioral, and functional-status dimensions of health

- Use cognitive computing/natural language processing to turn EHR progress notes and social worker case reports into actionable data

# 13

# Social and Behavioral Determinants of Health

- *Social determinants of health (SDH):* Including social and economic factors as well as physical environmental factors, SDH accounts for much more of the variations in individual health than health care does.
- *Behavioral health integration:* Though not technically part of SDH, behavioral health has a major impact on individuals and is impacted by SDH. It is increasingly being integrated with primary care. This trend will pick up steam now that patient-centered medical homes are moving in this direction.
- *SDH in health care:* SDH used to be the province of social services and public health, but healthcare organizations are starting to explore it as a way to reduce costs in a value-based care environment.
- *Approaches to SDH:* Models that address SDH range from having physicians target health behaviors to referrals of patients to community services to providing limited social support within a healthcare context such as home visits or care management. The integration of SDH into patient-centered medical homes has also been proposed.
- *Service delivery model:* A new approach is to fully integrate medical and behavioral care and social services within service delivery teams that can address the full range of a high-risk patient's needs. Patients and their caregivers must also be involved in these teams.

- *SDH data:* EHRs can provide some of the requisite SDH data, but may require natural language processing (NLP) to extract data from unstructured text. Advanced NLP can also pull SDH data from social service notes. Data is also available from numerous other sources.

- *Analytics tools:* SDH data can be stored in a data lake, and big data techniques can be applied to it to form a holistic picture of a patient/ client. That description can then be used to decide who should be on the patient's service delivery team. Other types of software can be used to determine the eligibility of patients for health insurance and various kinds of social benefits.

Effective patient engagement can improve health outcomes and lower costs, as discussed in Chapter 11. The automation of appropriate post-discharge care could take that further by using information technology to help the most vulnerable patients recover from hospitalizations. But to optimize population health and eliminate the 30 percent to 40 percent of healthcare costs that experts deem unnecessary, you have to look beyond the healthcare system to the fundamental drivers of health and disease.

Healthcare accounts for only 10 percent to 25 percent of the variance in individual health over time. The remaining variance is shaped by genetic factors (up to 30 percent), health behaviors (30 percent to 40 percent), social and economic factors (15 percent to 40 percent), and physical environmental factors (5 percent to 10 percent).[1] The latter two groups of factors, which together exert far greater influence on health than health care does, are collectively known as the "social determinants of health."

Behavioral health is not technically part of SDH, because it is a health condition rather than a cause of that disease. But social determinants of health have a major impact on mental health and on health behaviors such as alcohol and drug abuse and smoking. Though behavioral health traditionally has been segregated from medical care, it is being increasingly integrated into primary care. So, we include behavioral health in this chapter as an indispensable component of the nexus between health care and SDH.

So far in this book, we have discussed population health management in the context of patient populations. When we consider SDH, however, the focus shifts to the communities where people live, work, and play. Many of the factors that comprise SDH — such as employment, the availability of healthy food, and the physical environment where people live — are outside the control of physicians and hospitals. But healthcare organizations can work with community resources to help patients deal with SDH factors that affect their health and their access to care.

Except in community health centers, SDH has not been, until now, a major focus of health care. Healthcare providers do not know how to deal with SDH, and most of them assume that it is best handled by social service agencies, public health authorities, and other governmental bodies.

But this avoidance of SDH is starting to erode as the healthcare system shifts from volume-based to value-based reimbursement. As certain providers begin to assume financial risk for care, the importance of addressing aspects of SDH to improve population health and cut costs has become more evident. Meanwhile, hospitals seeking to lower readmissions and avoid Medicare penalties are starting to grasp the need for a holistic approach to post-discharge care.

There is also a growing recognition that the readmission reduction program fails to account for the SDH-related differences among the patient populations in various institutions. A recent study found, for example, that hospitals with high readmission rates are more likely to treat patients who have less education, are more disabled, and are more likely to suffer from depression than patients in hospitals with lower readmission rates. Altogether, the researchers found, population characteristics explain about half the differences in readmissions.[2]

Overall, SDH has a profound influence on how people live and die. It lies at the root of the health disparities between Caucasian people and racial minorities, between rich and poor individuals, between employed and unemployed people, and between well-educated and less-educated individuals. This is not just about the kind of health care that different groups receive — it is about the underlying factors that determine their health and longevity.

This chapter explains what social determinants of health are, how they influence individual health, and what healthcare organizations can do about them to improve population health. In addition, we explain how behavioral health affects physical health and why it should be integrated with primary care. Finally, we explore a new concept of service delivery that integrates health care with social services and the kind of information technology (IT) required to support that approach.

# SDH Impact on Health

The World Health Organization (WHO) defines SDH as "the conditions in which people are born, grow, live, work, and age, including the health system." The Centers for Disease Control and Prevention (CDC) describes SDH as "the complex, integrated, and overlapping social structures and economic systems that are responsible for most health inequities." These include "the social environment, the physical environment, health services, and structural and societal factors."[3]

More specifically, SDH encompasses socioeconomic status, race, ethnicity, education, family structure, diet, food security, physical activity, local economic development, employment, working conditions, financial resources, housing, location, recreational spaces, neighborhood crime, median neighborhood income, intimate partner violence, transportation, stress, social connections, social isolation, homelessness, and physical disabilities.[4, 5] The Institute of Medicine (IOM) also includes health behaviors such as alcohol and drug abuse and tobacco use in what it terms "social and behavioral health indicators."[6]

Socioeconomic status (SES) is important in this context because numerous studies have established the correlation between SES and health all over the world.[7] Race and ethnicity, too, are frequently related to health disparities. For example, a report from the California Department of Health showed that health outcomes are affected by education, employment status, gender identity, income, race and ethnicity, and sexual orientation.[8] And a recent Health Affairs study found that, whereas obesity and diabetes are on the rise among all U.S. residents, these diseases are most prevalent among African American and Hispanic American people.[9]

A relationship also exists between education and diet: Better-educated people tend to have better diets. One reason is that better-educated people are likely to have more money and easier access to supermarkets and other sources of healthy food than less-educated people do. Many low-income neighborhoods, one study pointed out, are "food deserts" that have fast-food restaurants but no place to buy fresh fruits and vegetables.[10]

Another paper noted that the working conditions in low-paid jobs — including work-family conflict, low job control, high work demands, and long hours — are generally worse than those in higher-paid positions. The predictable result: Individuals with more education and better-paying work have longer life expectancy than those at the other end of the scale.[11]

A national survey revealed that most physicians believe unmet social needs lead to worse health, and that patients' social needs are as important to address as their medical conditions. However, 80 percent of physicians surveyed were not confident in their capacity to deal with patients' social needs. Among the most glaring social needs that patients have, in their doctors' view, are fitness programs, nutritious food, and transportation assistance. Urban doctors' wish lists included employment assistance, adult education, and housing assistance.[12]

# Approaches to SDH

The first step in addressing SDH is to acknowledge just how huge and pervasive the impact of SDH is. No healthcare organization, even with the help of community resources, can resolve the root causes of SDH overall or for any individual patient. From the viewpoint of population health management, it would be a major accomplishment to help the 20 percent of people who generate 80 percent of healthcare costs to cope with some of their social determinants of health.

This group is the same one that chronic disease management and intensive case management have long targeted with limited success. A recent review paper found that healthcare-based models for supporting high-need, high-cost patients have had a relatively modest impact and that few have been widely adopted.[13] So perhaps broadening that approach to include SDH might have better results.

Several methods of dealing with SDH have been tried. (See Table 13-1 at the end of the chapter.) All these approaches have limitations, but collectively they suggest what a more successful SDH model should include. What follows is a brief look at how these different approaches have worked in practice and where they have fallen short.

## Model 1: Targeting health behaviors

In this approach, physicians and care teams try to induce patients to modify their health behavior. The aim is to get them to stop smoking, drink less, exercise more, and eat better. The influence of physician advice has been shown to be strong in this regard. But behavior change is hard, as we point out in Chapter 11. Physician office visits alone have a limited impact on compliance. Even with health coaching, motivating patients is a complex process, and there are numerous social, cultural, and personal obstacles to patient engagement.

| SDH Model | Base | Target | Integration[1] | Experience[2] |
|---|---|---|---|---|
| Providers target health behaviors | Ambulatory care clinic or hospital | Health behaviors in all patients | None | Universal |
| Referrals to community services | Ambulatory care clinic or hospital | SDH for all patients | None | CHCs, some physician practices |
| Limited social support within health care | Healthcare providers, care managers | Behavioral health, SDH for specific groups such as sick seniors or infants and parents | Partial | Pre- and post-natal home visit programs |
| Patient-centered medical home | Primary care practices, CHCs, health homes | SDH for all patients or those with chronic diseases | Partial | New York Medicaid program, Vermont Blueprint for Health |
| Holistic care management | Community health teams, ACOs, care management services | SDH for chronic disease patients, other high-risk individuals | Partial | Vermont Blueprint for Health, Montefiore, hot spot initiative in Camden, NJ |
| Service delivery teams | Full spectrum of healthcare and community services | SDH, behavioral health for all patients | Full | None |

[1]*The degree of integration between healthcare and community resources.*
[2]*Real-world examples. None exists for service delivery teams, which are still in the development stage.*

**Table 13-1** *Models for Addressing SDH*

Some researchers have pointed out that positive changes in health behavior not only require action by the individual but also require "that the environments in which people live, work, and play support healthier choices. Efforts focused solely on informing or encouraging individuals to modify behaviors, without taking into account their physical and social environments, often fail to reduce health inequalities."[14]

So, although physicians should certainly continue to urge patients to live healthier lives, targeting health behaviors directly is not the solution. Health reformers must cast a wider net to have a real impact on SDH.

# Model 2: Referral to community services

Community health centers (CHCs) care primarily for lower-income people, most of whom are indigent or are on Medicaid. Because these patients face formidable problems related to SDH, and because CHCs have a whole-person orientation, these clinics have long sought to address the social determinants of health.

A recent study of CHCs found that most of their SDH interventions originate as a response to an issue or a problem brought to the clinic's attention by patients, staff, or clinic leadership. CHCs try to deal with these issues, but they cannot do it alone, because they lack the necessary resources and skills. To make up for this lack, many of them create partnerships with agencies at the local, state, and federal levels, often using time-limited grants.[15]

Some CHCs have adopted the Chronic Care Model of disease management. This model urges providers to encourage patients to participate in relevant community programs. Collaboratives organized by the government with the Institute for Healthcare Improvement (IHI) have pushed forward such projects.[16]

CHCs address a broad range of SDH factors, including social welfare, parenting, assistance in obtaining long-term care, food security, shelter, employment counseling, and environmental health risk reduction. But in many cases, they do so by referring patients to other programs. Though this is certainly a step in the right direction, it does not integrate SDH with health care. From that viewpoint, it perpetuates the fragmentation of the healthcare and social services systems.

Nevertheless, we would be remiss not to mention the excellent work that some CHCs have done on their own. For example, Beaufort-Jasper-Hampton Comprehensive Health Services in Ridgeland, South Carolina, has inspected the homes of elderly patients for safety and to provide assistance in fall prevention; improved lunch programs at local schools; and provided substance abuse and behavioral health programs to help residents obtain and hold jobs. To help eradicate soil-borne parasitic worms in children, the CHC created an environmental health team that built cluster wells and installed bathrooms in low-income residents' homes, using funds from the local United Way and federal grants.[17]

## Model 3: Targeted social support within a healthcare framework

The Commonwealth Fund (CWF), a New York think tank that focuses on health care, suggests an integrated SDH approach to improve care for very sick and/or frail elderly patients. CWF proposes a framework consisting of these six components:

- Identify subgroups of patients with similar needs and challenges. Subgroup descriptions should consider patients' behavioral and social service needs, as well as their medical conditions.

- Shift the delivery of care for high-need patients from institutional settings to home and community settings whenever possible.

- Build the capacity to assess and actively manage social and behavioral health needs in addition to medical needs.

- Make it easier for patients, caregivers, and professionals to closely coordinate with one another. This includes taking advantage of digital options such as secure texting, email, telehealth, and social media to improve communication among health care, behavioral health, and social services.

- Design and deliver services that meet goals set collaboratively by patients, caregivers, and providers.

- Allocate resources based on their potential to have a positive impact on the quality of life of patients and caregivers. This will require a more flexible reimbursement system that allows provision of comprehensive services.[18]

This framework represents a huge step toward a new approach to SDH. Unlike other models that focus mainly on health care, the CWF model acknowledges that healthcare professionals must work with other kinds of professionals to help patients overcome the environmental and social barriers to health improvement.

While the CWF proposal focused on the care of very sick, elderly people, some principles of this model are being applied to other subpopulations. For example, the Nurse-Family Partnership Program has had success with prenatal and early childhood home visits by nurses. Its focus goes beyond health care, encompassing support for parents' economic self-sufficiency, the planning of subsequent pregnancies, enhancing educational and employment opportunities, and connecting families with social services.

Several studies have documented the effectiveness of this program in improving prenatal-health-related behaviors and pregnancy outcomes, while reducing child abuse and neglect and enabling informed family planning decisions. The program is even credited with increasing maternal employment.[19]

A number of similar programs here and abroad feature early childhood visits intended to improve parenting and childcare and to expose children to educational resources. Some of these programs have had a fair degree of success in improving pediatric health and building stable households.[20]

These approaches, like the Commonwealth Fund framework, are moving in the right direction. Although they are starting from a health-centric perspective and focus on only one segment of the population, they are demonstrating the impact of integrating community resources to improve health outcomes.

## Model 4: Patient-centered medical homes

In a 2013 commentary in the *Journal of the American Medical Association*, a trio of pediatricians argued: "The patient-centered medical home . . . offers an important opportunity to promote population health through systematically addressing the social determinants of health."[21]

Among the strategies that the authors advised medical homes to adopt was screening for social determinants during medical visits. Aside from asking about psychosocial issues such as substance abuse, maternal depression, and intimate partner violence, they suggested that medical homes could screen for unmet material needs related to food, employment, and education. The results could be used to increase physician referrals to (and family contact with) community resources, they said.

They also proposed that the medical home concept be broadened to include the colocation of community resources, such as the supplemental nutritional program for women, infants, and children (WIC); help with transportation problems; and streamlined community services for patients. Child educational programs such as Reach Out and Read could also be run out of medical homes, they noted. And PCMHs could form partnerships with law firms to help patients with their legal problems.

In its 2014 criteria for PCMH recognition, the National Committee for Quality Assurance (NCQA) included a number of requirements related to SDH. First, the NCQA mandated that behavioral health needs be addressed within the PCMH. (See the section below on that topic.) Also, the practice must give uninsured patients information about obtaining insurance coverage.

The PCMH must also do a comprehensive health assessment that includes gathering information on family/social/cultural characteristics of each patient. The practice must consider characteristics such as poverty, homelessness, unemployment, sexual orientation, gender, education, and social support. Mental health, substance and alcohol abuse, smoking, risky sexual practices, and dental care must also be taken into account.

In addition, the PCMH has to establish criteria for identifying patients who could benefit from care management. Along with the usual factors, these include social determinants of health. And in intervening with patients who need care management, the PCMH "assesses and addresses potential barriers to meeting goals," which could include SDH.[22]

The state of New York has taken a modest step in the same direction with its Health Homes program for Medicaid patients who have complex chronic conditions. Though this is a care management model rather than a patient-centered medical home, it performs the PCMH's function of coordinating care among multiple caregivers. It also addresses certain nonmedical needs. Working within a network of providers, health plans, and community-based organizations, care managers try to ensure that patients in the program receive whatever they need to stay healthy enough to avoid ER visits and hospitalizations.[23]

Health Homes is part of New York's Delivery System Reform Incentive Payment (DSRIP) program, which aims to use Medicaid as a lever to restructure the state's healthcare delivery system. The primary goal of this program, on which the state plans to spend up to $6.42 billion, is to reduce avoidable hospital use by 25% over five years.[24]

## Model 5: Holistic care management

Going one step beyond health homes, certain innovative programs seek to integrate health care with social services in a care management context. The shining example now is the Vermont Blueprint for Health.

Initiated by the state government as a way to improve outcomes and control costs for patients with chronic conditions, the Vermont Blueprint for Health gives PCMHs access to community health teams (CHTs) that consist of nurse coordinators, social workers, counselors, dietitians, health educators, and other professionals. The PCMHs and CHTs receive separate capitated payments with funding from Medicaid, Medicare, and Vermont's three major commercial insurers.

A study of the Vermont Blueprint for Health describes the collaboration between the medical homes and the community health teams this way:

- The staffing provided by the CHT augmented the medical home practice team, driving better integration of medical and nonmedical services and improving coordination with other community providers. Additionally, community-based self-management programs operated alongside PCMHs and CHTs to help patients address tobacco use, chronic pain, diabetes, and behavioral health.[25]

- The case control study shows that the PCMHs supported by CHTs reduced spending per patient by $482 over a two-year period in comparison to a control group of nonparticipating practices. (Though this amount might not seem like a lot, it adds up for a patient population: Nearly $500,000 would be saved for 1,000 patients.) Most of the savings came from lower costs for inpatient and outpatient hospital utilization. The study group maintained higher-quality scores than the control group on most measures.

Montefiore Medical Center in the Bronx, New York, has taken a similar approach within its healthcare system and ACO. Having long held risk contracts with payers, Montefiore has about 600 care managers, including nurses, social workers, and community-based educators. They use health data as well as data on other factors — such as drug abuse, mental health problems, and homelessness — to predict which people are mostly like to get sick. They enroll the highest-risk patients in educational programs, using nonclinical health coaches. They assign the patients to the best care manager for them, based on their psychosocial profiles. And, they link these people with social service and community organizations that can help them.[26]

Another care management approach is the hot spot initiative in Camden, New Jersey. Dr. Jeffrey Brenner, the founder of this initiative, identified the areas in the city that generated the highest health costs, finding that 1 percent of the population accounted for 30 percent of health spending. He figured out how to help some of these patients by providing intensive care management and connecting them with social services. For example, he got a social worker to help one patient apply for disability insurance. Brenner also persuaded the patient to enroll in Alcoholics Anonymous and to return to church, helping him turn his life around.[27]

Eventually, a grant from the Robert Wood Johnson Foundation (RWJF) enabled Brenner to ramp up his data gathering and to hire a few people, including a nurse practitioner and a social worker. By late 2010, his team had provided care for more than 300 people on his "super-utilizer" map. Though that number does not represent a lot of people, it represents a lot of money saved. The question is whether such an approach is scalable.

Besides the models we've described, we have one other model to explore. This approach goes far beyond any of the others in integrating health care with community services and in supporting that effort with the latest information technology. But before we get to that, you must understand the outsized role that behavioral health plays in the SDH jigsaw puzzle, as described next.

# Behavioral Health

Behavioral health conditions affect nearly 20 percent of Americans and cost $57 billion per year.[28] Individuals with behavioral health and substance abuse conditions cost 2.5 to 3.5 times more to care for than do patients who have none of these issues.[29] Annual medical costs for patients with chronic medical and behavioral health conditions were 46 percent higher than for those with chronic conditions alone.[30]

Depression leads the list of the five conditions that drive the biggest percentage of health costs, followed by obesity, arthritis, back/neck pain, and anxiety. Depression also accounts for higher employer costs than any other condition.[31] People with serious health problems often have comorbid mental health issues, and up to 70 percent of primary care visits are related to psychosocial issues.[32]

Despite these documented facts, behavioral health is still treated as something different and apart from physical health. Insurance companies hire behavioral health contractors who pay mental health professionals in a reimbursement system that is separate from the healthcare payment system.

Partly because of the lack of integration of behavioral health, only 41 percent of people with behavioral health problems receive treatment. Of those patients, 56 percent are treated in general medical settings, and

44 percent are treated by behavioral health professionals.[33] Primary care physicians who have received little training in dealing with these issues may find it difficult to counsel patients properly. But when they refer people to psychologists or psychiatrists, the patients often fail to follow up. In some cases, this is because of the social stigma of mental health counseling.

According to experts, behavioral health care is most effective when it is integrated with primary care. Separating the two leads to worse outcomes and higher costs, especially for patients with comorbid conditions.[34] In addition, because healthcare providers often lack the time, training, and staff to recognize these conditions, 60 percent to 70 percent of patients who present to ERs and primary care clinics leave without getting treatment for their behavioral health issues.[35]

A Commonwealth Fund brief noted, "Behavioral health integration is still rare, and the integration of substance abuse services [is] even rarer, in part because there's been little or no financial incentive or administrative advantage to bringing what are now standalone medical and behavioral health operations together."[36]

## Advantages of integration

Where integration has been tried, it has produced measurable benefits. For example, the IMPACT model (Improving Mood — Providing Access to Collaborative Treatment) integrates depression treatment into primary care and other medical care settings. It has been shown to be twice as effective as traditional depression care, according to a government website. "IMPACT improves physical and social functioning and patients' quality of life while reducing overall healthcare costs."[37]

The Agency for Healthcare Research and Quality (AHRQ) says the integration of behavioral health into primary care is "a key functionality required to hit the Triple Aim. Most care systems don't do it systematically (if at all), although a great many are trying."[38]

As mentioned earlier, NCQA added behavioral health integration to its 2014 criteria for patient-centered medical homes. Though NCQA doesn't require practices to hire psychologists or social workers, colocation is highly encouraged and PCMHs must support patients' behavioral health and "collaborate" with behavioral health professionals.[39]

The Patient-Centered Primary Care Collaborative (PCPCC), a private-sector organization that promotes medical homes, strongly endorses the integration of behavioral health into primary care, using practice teams that include mental health professionals. It cites the high prevalence of behavioral health problems in primary care, the high burden of those issues, the cost of unmet behavioral health needs, and the opportunity to achieve the Triple Aim as reasons for medical homes to move in this direction.[40]

PCPCC refers to studies that document the drop in costs associated with behavioral health integration. In one study, depression treatment in primary care for patients with diabetes resulted in a cost savings of $896 per patient over two years. Another study showed that depression treatment in primary care resulted in $3,300 lower total healthcare costs over 48 months, for a return of $6.50 on every dollar spent.[41]

The integration of behavioral health occurs along a spectrum of practice arrangements. A Millbank study noted that this begins with routine screening for behavioral health problems, coupled with close referral relationships between primary care and behavioral health professionals. In some sites, behavioral health providers are colocated with primary care doctors, but have separate practices and appointment scheduling systems. In the most integrated sites, practice teams that include behavioral health therapists share systems and care plans.[42]

Whichever approach is taken, it is clear that behavioral health is a key component of overall health. In the biopsychosocial model of disease, first described by Engel,[43] biological, psychological, and social factors all play a significant role in human functioning in the context of disease. So any model that seeks to improve health by mitigating the social determinants that contribute to disease must incorporate behavioral health as well as traditional medical care.

## Solving the SDH Puzzle

After behavioral health has been fully engaged, healthcare organizations that seek to address SDH must figure out how to work with social services and other community resources. But before that can happen, healthcare providers need to consider how social workers view the high-risk patients that they are trying to help, and vice versa. This is not easy, because the two sides have different perspectives.

For instance, Ronan Rooney, cofounder and chief technology officer of Cúram Software Ltd., recalls visiting a free clinic where he talked with a physician who was disturbed that a patient with severe diabetes had failed to keep a post-discharge office appointment and had ended up in the hospital again. It turned out that the patient had come to the clinic, but hadn't shown up until 5 p.m. for a 9 a.m. appointment. The office staff had told him it was too late, and he had returned home. He didn't return because it had taken him three hours to walk each way. Meanwhile, the hospital had given him only three days' worth of the medication he required, and he couldn't afford to buy more of it on his own. Therefore, he stopped taking the drug and ended up back in the ER, where he was admitted to the hospital.

"So, the root cause of this man's issues — and of the significant costs his care generated — had nothing to do with clinical or healthcare issues," Rooney said. "The patient lacked access to care, so he couldn't access the services he needed. After meeting him, the doc I spoke with contacted a number of pharmacies to find ones that had free programs with drug companies. She signed him up for the programs, and then found out and told him how to physically get to these pharmacies. As she told me, 'Ronan, this is not doctor work!'"

This story illustrates the difference between how healthcare providers and social workers look at a particular case: The provider would think about prescribing a medication, for example, and the social worker would try to figure how the client could locate and get to a pharmacy where he could buy the drug at a low cost. To provide truly effective care and support, these two kinds of professionals must communicate with one another and, equally important, view the facts through a filter that combines their perspectives into a holistic picture of the individual.

Rooney calls this a *person-centric* view. Though healthcare providers now claim to be committed to patient-centered care and social services do something similar, he notes that neither profession's definition truly describes what holistic care should look like. Neither type of professional can address the social determinants of health alone, because each of them misses some of the crucial dimensions of human beings.

Better communication is necessary but not sufficient. According to the previously cited Commonwealth Fund framework for helping sick elderly patients:

> Integrating medical, behavioral, and social services requires more than simply improving communication among the traditional siloed agencies and professionals. Multidisciplinary teams of clinicians, behaviorists, case managers, and patients working together can better tailor treatment plans to address medical needs by managing

behavioral health conditions such as severe depression and non-medical issues such as unstable housing.[44]

It is no surprise that patients are regarded as an essential part of these teams. This reflects the Triple Aim goal of improving the patient experience, as well as the dictum "nothing about me without me" that the IHI introduced to the patient-centered care discourse. Moreover, the patient or client brings a third, vital perspective to the team that is different from those of healthcare and social service professionals. The individual's need for food, shelter, and safety, for example, are more important to him or her than whether a program meets its objectives of improving quality and lowering healthcare spending. If a drug prescription that could keep a patient out of the hospital is too expensive, that person won't fill it. So, any model that seeks to deal with SDH must include the patient/client's perspective.

## Team-based approach

Because of life challenges and, in some cases, behavioral health issues, many patients find it difficult to access care and to navigate the healthcare system. They need a great deal of hand-holding and assistance, and they could also benefit from an approach that tries to meet both their medical and non-medical needs.

The SDH models described earlier in this chapter (and outlined in the table at the end of the chapter) are all healthcare-centric, to varying extents. But what is really needed to improve the efficacy of care is a more holistic, multidisciplinary, and adaptive approach that goes beyond those models. *Multidisciplinary* connotes not only healthcare professionals but also other kinds of experts. These professionals should be included in a service-delivery team that is broad enough and has the right mix of skills and experience to take on relevant aspects of SDH. Similar to the model proposed by the Commonwealth Fund but with more extensive capabilities, such a team would be able to address SDH for all types of high-risk patients.

Ideally, this team would be just big enough to deal with 12 to 15 high-risk people at a time. The team leader would typically be a primary care physician. Other team members might include a care coordinator, a nurse, a behavioral health specialist, a social worker, a transportation coordinator, a dietitian, a pharmacist, and an attorney. Together with each patient and his or her caregivers, they would devise a plan that meets the patient's needs and then carry it out.

A service delivery team need not be based in a single facility; in most cases, it would not be. But if the team members were drawn from multiple entities, they would require excellent channels of communication. The team would have to be able to adapt quickly to changing circumstances, because the health and social factors of these patients can change overnight. The team would also have to be able to intervene in a variety of care settings, ranging from a hospital or a long-term care facility to a physician practice or a patient's home.

"The practical solution is to have a model that is responsive," says Rooney, whose company specializes in providing software for SDH. "Ideally, it would be predictive, but it must at least be responsive, so that when something goes wrong, it can react and fix the problem. To do that, you need a team, because it isn't just one issue going on. If there's a family, they have to be involved, too. And there needs to be technology that can support the team in that new service delivery environment."

## Harnessing technology

It would be impossible to apply this strategy without data from a wide variety of sources and specialized analytic tools. To start with, a healthcare organization would have to use a risk stratification application to identify the high-risk patients. After that, it would need to classify patients by their functional abilities and other characteristics. For example, one couldn't use the same approach for elderly patients who are immobilized at home as for those who are still active.

To build a holistic description of the patient, an organization could start with information already available to healthcare providers. It could use structured and unstructured EHR data to compile SDH-related information such as social and family histories, drug and alcohol abuse, and smoking status. Some of this information might also be included in questionnaires that patients fill out when they go to physician offices, visit the ER, or are admitted to the hospital. Some providers and employers also administer health risk assessments that include this information.

Most of the data that would be useful in handling SDH is not present in EHRs in a structured form. For that reason, the IOM has called on the Office of the National Coordinator for Health IT (ONC) to require EHR vendors to expand their structured fields as a condition of product certification. Among the additional fields the IOM wants to see in EHRs are standard measures for educational attainment, financial resource strain, stress, depression, physical activity, social isolation, intimate partner violence, and neighborhood median household income.[45]

In addition to informing clinical care, the IOM says, this data could be linked to factors such as food insecurity and lack of housing. The IOM assumes that public health departments and community agencies would use this kind of data to address SDH, but so could the service delivery teams discussed here.

In the meantime, natural language processing has advanced to the point where it can reliably extract concepts from unstructured text. (See Chapter 14.) This form of cognitive computing could be applied to turn SDH-related concepts in EHR progress notes and social worker case reports into actionable, structured data.

## Other data sources

Because EHRs are healthcare-centric, the data in them is inadequate to describe all the dimensions of an individual. That would be true even if the government heeded the IOM's recommendations and required EHR vendors to add SDH data to their systems' discrete fields. To fully understand a person for analytic purposes, it is necessary to create a database that includes clinical, social, behavioral, and functional status dimensions.

Some of this information could come from social services, including data from the adult and child welfare and food stamp programs. Functional assessment surveys, while still uncommon in mainstream health care, are performed in long-term care facilities and eldercare home support programs. Some healthcare systems have also begun to query patients about their functional status. Here are some types of relevant data and where they might be obtained:

- **Health insurance:** Available from EHRs and administrative systems
- **Place of residence:** Available in administrative records
- **Distances to nearest primary care clinic, food stores, and so on:** Available from geographical information systems
- **Living situation (whether the person lives alone, for example):** Available from social service agencies and other public records
- **Physical disabilities:** Available from EHRs and disability insurance records

- **Employment status:** Available from unemployment insurance records
- **Environmental hazards, such as lead paint or mold in houses:** Available from city or county building reports
- **Air quality:** Available from weather reports
- **Diet and exercise:** Available from health risk assessments
- **Medication compliance:** Available from prescription fill records accessed via Surescripts

Using big data techniques, analytic tools can integrate and assess this data to build a picture of the individual in the context of his or her clinical, psychological, and socioeconomic factors. The next step is to identify the person's social network, including family members, friends, neighbors, and others who influence that individual. Finally, the team needs information on the person's care network, including healthcare providers, providers of home services, social workers, food banks, and other places where the person seeks help.

Based on all that data, a healthcare organization can form a service delivery team for that individual. If he or she has behavioral health issues, for example, the team would include a behavioral health provider. If the person has trouble getting to a physician's office, a transportation coordinator would be part of the team.

Assuming that team members are based in multiple locations, a web-based platform can be used to facilitate communication, including teleconferences. Because most of these professionals are already using their own systems, however, they often may not want to log on to another system. It is therefore imperative to design mobile apps and other channels that will make it easy for team members to communicate and receive actionable data about their patients and clients.

To analyze in near-real-time all disparate data from the systems just listed, it would be helpful to aggregate it in the kind of data lake described in Chapter 6. This scalable, flexible approach would allow the care team to respond quickly to changes in the patient's health status and personal circumstances.

Software also exists to help social workers and their clients navigate the social benefit system and obtain all the benefits they're entitled to. In addition, revenue cycle management applications that many hospitals use can identify patients who are eligible for Medicaid and/or community assistance programs. Newer applications, termed *support for medical assistance,* provide a more patient-oriented focus and can be combined with social assistance eligibility software.[46]

---

# Conclusion

Social and behavioral factors play a giant role in health. To a much greater extent than health care proper, these factors explain the variances in individual health over time. For chronically ill people, social determinants of health can determine how well they are able to manage their conditions. Though concerted efforts to engage patients can make a difference, their socioeconomic status, unemployment, living conditions, lack of access to good food and transportation, and/or abuse of alcohol or drugs may block efforts to improve their health.

Many high-risk, high-cost patients struggle with these problems. Though SDH is clearly a barrier to successful population health management, it also represents an opportunity. By forming holistic, multidisciplinary, adaptive teams, healthcare organizations and community organizations can improve both the lives and the health of these people.

Although this approach entails additional costs, using the service delivery team can yield substantial financial benefits in a value-based reimbursement environment. If patients who hit the ER several times a month can be properly assisted in both medical and non-medical ways, for example, they will need emergency care much less often, and some of the resultant savings will flow back to providers.

The innovations discussed in this chapter would not be feasible without the support of new forms of information technology that can integrate and analyze many different kinds of data quickly enough to be useful to care teams. The next chapter discusses how this cognitive computing approach can take population health management as a whole to the next level.

Cognitive computing systems can process massive amounts of data to understand, reason and learn from it, helping providers develop enhanced care plans.

## Types of Structured and Unstructured Data

| **CLAIMS** | **PATIENT-GENERATED** | **MONITORING** | **CLINICAL** | **MEDICAL LITERATURE** |
|---|---|---|---|---|
| • Medicare and commercial payer data | • Health risk and behavioral health assessments | • Vital-signs monitors<br>• Wearable sensor | • EHR data<br>• Genomic data<br>• Lab results | • Clinical trials<br>• Research |

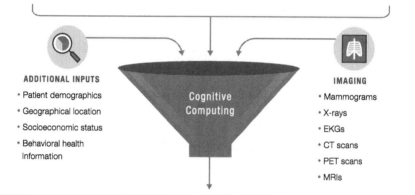

**ADDITIONAL INPUTS**
- Patient demographics
- Geographical location
- Socioeconomic status
- Behavioral health Information

**Cognitive Computing**

**IMAGING**
- Mammograms
- X-rays
- EKGs
- CT scans
- PET scans
- MRIs

## Cognitive Insights and Probablistic Recommendations

- Provides timely insights on populations and individuals

- Proactively identifies at-risk patient groups

- Predicts patient health needs and cost of care

- Uses natural language processing to convert unstructured data

- Supports personalized medicine and clinical decision-making

- Recommends interventions based on probability of success

- Improves patient engagement and communication across care settings (through the use of technologies like mobile health apps and wearable sensors)

# 14

# Cognitive Computing: The Future of Population Health Management

- *Cognitive computing 101:* The future of population health management (PHM) will be tied to the rise of cognitive computing, which uses massively parallel processing and artificial intelligence to convert unstructured data into structured data, search the medical literature, and find connections among myriad types of data. Clinicians can collaborate with cognitive computing systems, which learn from experience, to improve health care.

- *Natural language processing:* Cognitive computing has improved the capabilities of natural language processing (NLP) to the point where it can extract insights from unstructured data and correlate relevant studies for clinical decision support. This advanced form of NLP understands the context of language.

- *Beyond big data:* Cognitive computing is a next-generation big data approach that integrates knowledge-driven and data-driven decision support. It uses analytics to find valuable connections across many different kinds of data. It can also be used to compare patients who have particular characteristics with cohorts of similar patients to find out which therapies work best.

- *Population health management:* Cognitive computing can help healthcare organizations understand their populations better. It can provide insights into the non-healthcare factors that affect population health, such as demographics, geographical location, behavioral health, transportation, and socioeconomic status.

- *Genomic research:* As researchers make more progress in analyzing genomic data, cognitive computing will be able to tie markers for certain diseases to many environmental and personal factors that affect an individual's health. These analytics will guide physicians as they begin to provide precision medicine that varies with each patient.

- *Other kinds of data:* Cognitive computing will eventually merge advanced image and textual processing with visual reasoning abilities that can identify the relevant information in images. It has already led to innovative ways of using intensive care unit (ICU) data and is starting to integrate mobile monitoring data with electronic health records (EHRs) while giving feedback to patients.

- *Predictive modeling:* Cognitive computing will improve predictive modeling used in health risk stratification and financial risk management.

- *Patient engagement:* Personalized information and social support tailored by cognitive computing can help patients optimize their health. This technology can also use feedback from medical devices to support people in treating their own chronic diseases.

- *Care coordination:* Cognitive computing can help break down information silos, though it is not a cure for the lack of interoperability among systems. The ability to convert unstructured documents into structured data could improve communication across care settings.

To achieve the Triple Aim of an improved patient experience of care, improved population health, and lower per capita cost,[1] a healthcare organization must transform itself into an entity that is capable of population health management (PHM). Health IT is indispensable to achieving that goal. As we reiterate throughout this book, it is impossible to ensure that most patients receive recommended services and are engaged in their own care without using analytic and automation tools. And, as we note in Chapter 6, only a data infrastructure grounded in a big data approach can provide the flexibility, scalability, and comprehensiveness that PHM demands.

But the concepts that are now foundational to big data — handling the large volume and accelerating velocity of healthcare data, combining a wide variety of data types, and accounting for the inconsistency of the data, all within a flexible, scalable framework — are only scratching the surface of what today's ever more powerful computers and computer clusters can do with the right software. These new capabilities have given rise to an approach known as *cognitive computing*, which is expected to play a key role in the future of population health management.

Cognitive computing uses massively parallel processing and artificial intelligence to create a humanlike learning ability, combined with the ability to process millions of data points in seconds. Instead of being preprogrammed to provide particular answers to particular questions, a cognitive computing system draws deductions after searching large data sets, and it learns continuously from the feedback it receives about its conclusions. Though the current analytic approach applies one algorithm at a time, a cognitive computing system is a collection of overlapping, reasoning algorithms that can be expanded and updated.

The latest iteration of cognitive computing offers healthcare organizations a wide array of choices in areas ranging from clinical decision support and clinical quality improvement to medical research tools and analytics for managing population health. Here are some of the new directions explored in this chapter:

- *Natural language processing:* About 80 percent of the data in electronic health records (EHRs) is unstructured and therefore unavailable to analytic applications. Up to now, natural language processing has not been successful in recognizing concepts in unstructured text. Cognitive computing improves the accuracy of NLP by understanding language in context. As a result, it can convert unstructured data into structured data and extract insights from it. It can also use NLP to search the medical literature for information relevant to clinical decision-making at the point of care.

- *Genomic data:* Precision medicine is starting to become a real possibility as the cost of genomic sequencing drops. Genomic research generates massive amounts of data that requires big data solutions. Building on those solutions, cognitive computing will vastly increase the amount and types of data that can be combined with genomic information to support precision medicine. Eventually, it will enable physicians to use the results in everyday care.

- *Clinical quality improvement:* In some academic medical centers, cognitive computing systems are being used to improve clinical pathways. Quality improvement teams are starting to feed clinical data back into cognitive computing systems to upgrade those systems' algorithms. The next step is to combine these techniques with insights that cognitive computing gleans from the medical literature. This is already happening in oncology and will spread to other medical fields.

- *Understanding populations:* Big data techniques are being used to aggregate, normalize, and analyze multiple kinds of data and generate actionable reports for providers and care managers. However, many pieces are still missing from our understanding of population health. Cognitive computing can ingest and analyze data from many more sources than existing systems, including remote monitoring data and information on the social and behavioral determinants of health.

The health IT that will support future population health management (PHM) can be compared to a three-legged stool:

- **One leg is the kind of data infrastructure described earlier, which can aggregate and normalize different kinds of data to provide timely reports and answers to clinical questions.** Such an infrastructure must be flexible enough to answer a wide range of queries.

- **The second leg consists of analytic and automation tools that improve patient engagement and coordination across the continuum of care.** These applications can be used both to manage the care of high-risk patients and to engage all kinds of patients in their health care. One aim of these solutions is to ensure that all individuals receive recommended preventive and chronic care. This reduces the likelihood that they will be hospitalized or readmitted to the hospital.

- **Cognitive computing, the third leg, can expand the analytic abilities of current big data techniques while adding entirely new categories of data, including information from relevant studies.** In addition, cognitive computing can identify previously unknown connections among these different kinds of data. The learning ability of cognitive computing systems and their unparalleled speed and power can support personalized medicine and supply new insights into population health.

# Cognitive Computing 101

As we explain in Chapter 6, the big data approach is gaining traction in larger healthcare organizations because of its superior ability to deal with the volume, velocity, and variety of healthcare data. A recent review article noted:

> The increasing scale and availability of large quantities of health data require strategies for data management, data linkage, and data integration beyond the limits of many existing information systems, and substantial effort is underway to meet those needs. As our ability to make sense of that data improves, the value of the data will continue to increase. Health systems, genetics and genomics, population and public health: all areas of biomedicine stand to benefit from big data and the associated technologies.[2]

Following the publication of the first human genome sequence in 2003, the article pointed out, the rapidly expanding genomics field was the initial driver of big data techniques in health care. Since then, however, data scientists have pushed into other fields, and "the use of big data has now reached all areas of health care, biomedical research, and population health," the paper stated.

Cognitive computing, a branch of artificial intelligence, uses machine learning to expand big data techniques. For example, predictive analytics are typically based on algorithms that are trained through a "supervised learning" approach, in which the outcome is known ahead of time. That approach is fine when only certain kinds of data are being used. But when the algorithm encounters unknown data types and situations, as is frequently the case in health care, it may be unable to make a reliable prediction. That is where cognitive computing has the advantage — its algorithms can make predictions based on the data they have and test them in the real world. As the results are fed back into an algorithm, it is modified to reflect what it has learned. The algorithm becomes more and more accurate as it gains experience.

Another advantage of cognitive computing is its ability to link together many different kinds of data and analyze it in a particular context. This feature can help solve many IT challenges in health care and other industries. As a group of IBM researchers pointed out in a recent paper:

> Conventional programmatic computing, where you program a computer to process a known data set, is not adequate for managing

the volume and inconsistency in big data . . . . It requires cognitive computing, using data-centric, probabilistic approaches to data, where, after a fashion, the computer "thinks."[3]

# IBM Watson arrives

Cognitive computing arrived with a bang in 2011 when IBM Watson, a learning machine based on a new form of massively parallel processing, won the *Jeopardy!* game on national television.[4] Watson's software, which harnessed the power of a large computer cluster, used probabilistic algorithms to perform natural language processing that was able to understand language in the context in which it was spoken. Though Watson was trained in many different fields of knowledge, it learned far more than it had been taught as it prepared for the *Jeopardy!* game.

Immediately after that victory, which was the culmination of 10 years of research, IBM set out to apply the capabilities of Watson in a number of fields, including health care. Though other cognitive computing systems exist, Watson has had the most practical impact so far, and it is on this system that most of this chapter is based.

Recognizing that few companies could afford to purchase Watson outright, IBM made two critical decisions:

- It moved Watson to the cloud, where it could be accessed at any time, from anywhere.

- It "deconstructed" Watson into a group of services that customers could implement, along with application programming interfaces (APIs) that developers could use to write applications for Watson. Some of these developers work for IBM, but an increasing number of entrepreneurial firms are building the Watson ecosystem.

To create a cognitive computing application, a developer must first look at the kinds of questions that target users are likely to ask. The cognitive system must be seeded with a sufficient number of questions and answers to start the machine learning process. Typically, between 1,000 and 2,000 question/answer pairs seem to be the right number to start the process. After that, machine learning takes over as the application seeks data to answer questions and analyzes new data in light of its experience.[5]

A key component of cognitive computing in health care is natural language processing, which it uses to research topics in the medical literature and to search for relevant information locked up in unstructured data. To help clinicians make better decisions at the point of care, cognitive computing integrates knowledge-driven decision support, which draws data from existing knowledge such as journal articles and practice guidelines, with data-driven decision support, which looks for patterns in structured and unstructured healthcare data.

Among the unique features of cognitive computing is its ability to

- Comb through millions of documents in near-real-time to find particular facts or concepts.
- Use analytics to find useful or illuminating connections among many different kinds of data.
- Compare data sets to find matches or mismatches, which might include patients whose characteristics match those of particular cohorts or missing data in structured EHR fields, respectively.

Cognitive computing can help provider organizations manage population health. By searching text documents rapidly and converting unstructured data into structured concepts, it can help these organizations understand their populations and individual patients much better than they do now. As we discuss later, many non-healthcare factors contribute to health and disease, and cognitive computing can also help providers comprehend the roles that those factors play. After those factors are better understood, it will be easier to engage patients in their own care and improve their health behaviors.

# Natural Language Processing

Natural language processing (NLP, for short) has been around for 50 years, but it has not been widely adopted in health care. One reason is the uncertainty about whether its accuracy is sufficient for clinical applications. No matter how accurate NLP becomes, it will not be 100 percent accurate. For some purposes, however, the prevailing accuracy rate — which ranges from 70 percent to around 95 percent — is enough to make NLP highly useful.[6]

There are three types of traditional NLP approaches:

- A *rules-based* system, which searches for patterns in documents, works well for extracting simple measures, such as a blood pressure score or an ejection fraction, but is easy to confuse the system because of variations in terminology.

- A *grammar-based* NLP system considers how terms are used syntactically to map them to dictionaries of concepts, but it doesn't always identify matches.

- A *machine learning* system can learn patterns and excels at finding the most likely matches, but requires extensive training.[7]

Developers of speech recognition applications have tried to use rules-based systems to translate certain medical concepts into discrete data. But these systems have repeatedly stumbled over the issue of context.

For example, if a doctor orders a test to rule out a diagnosis, such as cancer, the word *cancer* refers not to a diagnosis but to the reason for the test. Yet NLP might not notice the difference. If a visit note says that a patient stopped smoking three days ago, that doesn't mean the person is a nonsmoker, though the program might interpret it that way.[8] Rules-based NLP programs also have difficulties with the "negation" problem. In this type of scenario, a physician may say that the patient does not have a symptom associated with a particular health condition, yet the application interprets that statement as a positive indication.[9]

A cognitive computing system combines the grammar-based and machine learning approaches into a flexible, comprehensive tool for searching unstructured text. It has the ability to understand what language means, including its nuances. It also has the computational power to search large amounts of text quickly to find matches of terms used in a query and rank them by confidence level. According to IBM, Watson's NLP accuracy rate is in the mid-90 percent range.

## Unstructured EHR data

The structured data in an EHR can provide the basic facts about a patient's health status and medical history, if the correct data has been entered in the appropriate fields. But the narrative of the patient's complaint, the care plan, and observations that don't fit into EHR templates are usually documented in free text, which is unstructured. In fact, some physicians simply dictate their findings, documenting nearly all their encounters as free text that is then transcribed by a person or a speech recognition program.

Unstructured documents contain many of the most important facts about a medical case, noted an IDC Health Insights paper:

> In many cases, unstructured text remains the best option for providers to capture the depth of detail required, for example, in a clinical

summary, or to preserve productivity by incorporating dictation and transcription into the workflow. Unstructured text records contain valuable narratives about a patient's health and about the reasoning behind healthcare decisions.[10]

That being the case, it is essential to make this unstructured data accessible to analytics. An advanced NLP system can mine unstructured data so that it can be analyzed along with structured EHR and claims data. "This powerful set of capabilities will serve as the basis for a new generation of information access and analysis systems that improve population health, discover factors for readmission, predict infection outbreaks, or improve quality measures," the IDC study pointed out.

Seton Healthcare Family, a Texas healthcare provider that operates 38 facilities serving 1.9 million people, has used a solution that combines NLP with predictive analytics to collect and analyze structured and unstructured data. In a study it conducted with IBM, Seton Healthcare Family developed a method to identify which patients with congestive heart failure were likely to be readmitted. Among the 18 top predictors were factors that are not usually documented in EHRs as structured data elements, including drug and alcohol use and living arrangement (whether the patient lives alone or not, for example).[11]

One large EHR vendor has incorporated IBM's NLP and content analysis software into its system. The EHR is able to convert unstructured notes into structured data for clinical decision support. It can also code some of this data for billing purposes.[12]

Carilion Roanoke Community Hospital in Roanoke, Virginia, has this kind of EHR, and the hospital used the EHR's NLP capability to "read" millions of notes. In the course of 18 months, the insights that Carilion extracted from the unstructured text enabled its clinicians to increase their ability to identify patients who had heart failure and had been previously undiagnosed.[13]

By analyzing unstructured data, cognitive computing can also find omissions in the structured record, such as diagnoses that have not been entered into a patient's problem list. Cleveland Clinic has leveraged Watson for this purpose, comparing physician and hospital admission notes with diagnoses listed in the EHR. "When the unstructured data is compared to the problem list from the EMR [electronic medical record], all too often omissions are identified," noted a recent book on cognitive computing.[14]

## Medical literature

Advanced forms of NLP can also be used to search the medical literature for evidence and insights that support clinical decision-making. Moreover, cognitive computing can integrate such knowledge-based analytics with data-driven analytics that look for patterns in real-world data.

This kind of approach reflects an ongoing change in how researchers are using EHR data in clinical decision support. Rather than simply trigger alerts about a person's allergies or medications, EHR data can now be used — in combination with insights from the literature — to provide support for how a physician thinks about diagnosis and treatment in individual cases.

This method starts with a statistical analysis that matches a particular patient with a large cohort of patients who have similar characteristics and were treated in various ways. By combining an analysis of those patients' outcomes with treatment guidelines based on studies that show the value of certain interventions for patients in clinical trials, the cognitive computing system can give physicians more information than they could find through a literature search alone. This combination of case-based and knowledge-based information "can be used for a range of decision support applications, including guideline adherence monitoring and personalized prognostic predictions."[15]

As in any approach based on machine learning, Watson requires extensive training within a particular medical specialty to reach this point. Oncologists at institutions such as Memorial Sloan Kettering and MD Anderson Cancer Center are already taking advantage of Watson's decision support capabilities.[16,17] In primary care, it will take longer to train Watson because of the large number of different health problems that primary care physicians encounter every day. But the cognitive computing system recently took a big leap forward by "attending" Cleveland Clinic's medical school and "learning" everything that the medical students were taught.[18]

# Data Types

Many diverse factors are converging to propel health care — including population health management — into the future. Genomic research is exploding; mobile health apps and devices are proliferating; imaging data is growing exponentially and becoming more liquid; social media is being scanned for clues to health behavior; and research on the social and behavioral determinants of health is revealing new opportunities for patient engagement.

Cognitive computing has the potential to harness all these factors in population health management. The research to support the integration of some kinds of data, such as genomic data and social media, is still in an early phase. In other areas, such as mobile health data, providers are not yet ready to use the information. But cognitive computing is already starting to analyze imaging data and will be ready to accommodate other kinds of data when it is available.

# Genomic data

Researchers have made impressive strides in analyzing genomic data, which requires a big data approach. A lot of number crunching is required in order to compare genotypes with the phenotypes of individual patients. Scientists do this to match particular patient characteristics and disease states with variations in the patient's DNA that make him or her different from other people.[19]

The significant drop in genomic sequencing costs, coupled with the widespread adoption of EHRs, has made this approach feasible, but it's still in an early phase. A more direct approach to harnessing genomic discoveries in clinical care has been embraced by a number of cancer centers. These institutions sequence cancer tumors and use cognitive computing to analyze the patient factors involved. They also employ the technology to search the literature for information about treatments for that particular type of cancer. Based on its analysis of all that data, IBM Watson has been asked to provide an additional source of input for expert discussions about how to treat particular patients.[20]

In the long run, as genomics begins to yield its secrets in fields other than cancer, cognitive computing will provide the key for translating those advances into approaches that doctors can use in everyday medicine. At the same time, genomics will become integrated with case-based and knowledge-based analytics to provide more personalized care and a deeper understanding of patient populations.

## Imaging data

NLP can extract meaning from unstructured text found in journal articles and EHR notes, but other kinds of unstructured data can also contribute to better medical decisions, including imaging data. A great deal of important information is available in X-rays, EKGs, mammograms, CT scans, PET scans, and MRI images.

Cognitive computing can use pattern recognition, coupled with clinical training, to "read" these images. Watson, for example, is being trained on a library of 30 million X-ray images. After the system is trained, it will be able to compare a patient's X-rays with clinically normal images to detect disparities. The radiologist can agree or disagree with its findings, but the computer can perform the readings much faster and with fewer errors than a radiologist who reads thousands of images a day.[21]

Moreover, cognitive computing can combine image readings with other data to monitor the results of specific interventions. For example, the system can tell how a cancer patient is doing by tracking the patient's tumor regression and can correlate that outcome with the patient's drug treatment, lifestyle, and, someday, genetic makeup. In addition, the system can compare the images with those of millions of similar patients to see how they differ and offer explanations for those variations.

Specifically, this is how IBM researchers described their plans for imaging data:

> We are developing a cognitive system with advanced textual, image processing, and visual reasoning abilities that is able to gather information from across an enterprise and identify important elements in the data to help clinicians in their decision-making processes.
> It is designed as a new layer above PACS [picture archiving and communication systems] and EHR management systems, which combines imaging data along with textual and structural patient data.[22]

## Monitoring data

Monitoring data comes from vital-signs monitors in hospitals and other healthcare facilities, as well as from home monitoring and mobile monitoring — including wearable sensors.

In hospitals, the automatic documentation of vital signs has begun to spread from ICUs to medical wards, allowing both real-time analysis and analysis of data over time. With training and feedback from clinical teams, cognitive computing can be used to provide more reliable alerts regarding certain conditions than traditional methods can. By combining the monitoring data with structured and unstructured clinical data, the system can also produce insights that improve the quality of care.

For example, a neonatal department in a Toronto hospital used cognitive computing to predict 24 hours in advance which babies might develop late-onset neonatal sepsis. The key to their success was the analysis of monitoring data streams over time.[23]

ICU data is normally thrown away after a day because there is so much of it. A 50-bed ICU, for instance, may generate a quarter of a terabyte of data per month. By storing this data in the cloud and analyzing it with the help of cognitive computing, clinicians could someday prevent complications such as adult sepsis, hospital-acquired infections, and respiratory, cardiac, and neurological events.[24]

Remote patient monitoring provides the other major opportunity here. Home monitoring is increasingly being used to track the vital signs of high-risk patients, such as those with congestive heart failure. The widespread use of smartphones, meanwhile, has created a universe of mobile health apps. Though most of these apps focus on fitness and wellness, some are used in tandem with specialized devices to measure health conditions such as diabetes (glucometers), hypertension (blood pressure monitors), and heart disease (electrocardiogram [ECG] strips and heart rhythm monitors).[25]

Most physicians are not reviewing this data yet, nor are they prescribing mobile health (mHealth) apps to patients. They would argue that they are not being paid for this activity (except in the Medicare Chronic Care Management program), that most mHealth apps haven't been validated, and that the amount of data that remote monitoring could generate would be overwhelming in any case. A reliable method of screening this data must be developed before mHealth will become a routine element of clinical care.[26]

Nevertheless, some companies are already delivering applications that can help patients understand their own monitoring data and improve their health. For example, Apple's HealthKit allows patients to collect their mobile monitoring data in one place, and some EHR vendors have integrated their platforms with HealthKit, allowing providers to give feedback to patients.[27]

## Non-healthcare data

As explained earlier, health care is just one of many factors that affects and determines a person's health. According to the World Health Organization, healthcare accounts for 10 percent to 25 percent of the variance in health over time. The remainder is related to genetic factors (up to 30 percent), health behaviors (30 percent to 40 percent), social and economic factors (15 percent to 40 percent), and environmental factors (5 percent to 10 percent).[28]

People with multiple health and social needs are high consumers of healthcare services. High-risk patients generate roughly 80 percent of healthcare costs. And social determinants such as homelessness, substance abuse, physical disability, and economic factors add massive costs to the healthcare system.[29]

There are many available sources of data on the social and behavioral determinants of health, some of which are discussed in Chapter 13. What all of this means and how it relates to clinical and genetic data has yet to be worked out in detail. But cognitive computing offers methods to integrate and analyze this information to help clinicians engage patients in their own health care. In addition, this wide-ranging assessment of health determinants can aid healthcare organizations in understanding their patient populations.

# Population Health Management

Cognitive computing brings a new dimension to population health management. Though the data lake approach described in Chapter 6 is essential for crunching administrative, clinical, claims, and patient-generated data quickly and efficiently, cognitive computing can add insights from many other sources, including the medical literature, genomic data, and social and behavioral information. Unifying all these disparate areas of knowledge can help healthcare organizations understand and manage population health.

For starters, cognitive computing brings a new power of statistical analysis to the task of describing and analyzing a specific patient population. Just as a cognitive computing system can be used to compare a patient's characteristics and the treatments the patient has received to those of many similar patients with the same health condition, such an approach can also be harnessed to compare a population or subpopulation to similar patient populations. Moreover, matching is not limited to how the population is constituted in demographic and disease categories. It can include myriad other factors that have been shown to be important in health.

These kinds of comparisons may indicate that a particular subpopulation — diabetic patients who are on Medicaid, live alone, and have poor diets because of limited access to fresh food, for example — may benefit from a particular kind of intervention that has worked in other places. Or cognitive computing may reveal that patients who have hypertension and who receive texted prompts to avoid salty foods have better outcomes than those who aren't prompted.

Some innovative healthcare systems are already starting to meld their clinical and administrative data with insights from geographical information systems. For example, Carolinas HealthCare System, based in Charlotte, North Carolina, began developing such a matrix a decade ago. Using census-based demographic data and geocoding software in conjunction with data on emergency room visits, the organization devised a method for "using information about patients' patterns of healthcare utilization and community-level data to identify areas where access to primary care services was limited and could be improved."[30]

This kind of data could be integrated with other attributes of patients who recently visited a healthcare system's emergency department to alert care managers that certain high-risk patients, for example, had no access to primary care or had disabilities that made it difficult to get to a clinic. These are the kinds of insights that a cognitive computing system could provide — in a more comprehensive, scalable way than any healthcare organization could do on its own — to support population health management.

## Predictive modeling

Cognitive computing can mine vast amounts of data and process that data in near-real-time, using algorithms that learn from experience. The sweet spot of cognitive computing is its ability to do this with a large number of different data streams and to correlate its insights from that data.

As explained in Chapters 6 and 7, predictive modeling is an essential part of the data infrastructure for PHM. Predictive modeling, in theory, should benefit from having more kinds of data available for analysis. So, cognitive computing should be able to improve the risk stratification of a population and the ability to predict the overall disease burden and health costs of that population. In addition, it could help care managers prioritize the patients who need help the most at any given time.

# Patient engagement

PHM cannot succeed without patient engagement. Although human contact is a necessary part of this strategy, especially for high-risk individuals, automation tools are required in order to scale patient engagement to entire populations. Cognitive computing takes automation to the next level while preserving the human touch.

For example, the Denver firm Welltok uses a Watson-based application, CafeWell Concierge, to provide personalized information and social support that helps individuals optimize their health. Designed for use by population health managers, health plans, and employers, CafeWell Concierge integrates large amounts of internal and external data. It uses natural language processing, machine learning, and analytics to provide personalized recommendations and answers to questions posed by health consumers.

Each CafeWell Concierge user receives an Intelligent Health Itinerary based on the user's health insurance benefits, health status, preferences, interests, demographics, and other factors. This document is a personalized action plan that includes resources, activities, health content, and condition-management programs. Users can also ask questions related to health and wellness. The cognitive application is trained to answer open-ended questions in seconds. It can also learn which rewards have the most effect in motivating individuals to change their health behaviors.[31]

Cognitive computing can also use feedback from medical devices to support people in treating their own chronic diseases. For example, IBM Watson Health has done some research with device manufacturer Medtronic on how patients with diabetes control their blood sugar levels. The initial investigation showed that, by running data from home glucometers through analytic models, it was possible to forecast that certain patients would likely become hypoglycemic a couple of hours before that occurred. If these patients could be alerted in real time and could do something about their risk factors, it would be more effective than having them show their doctor three months of data and try to remember what was going on when they last crashed.[32]

Mobile health apps and wearable sensors are the new frontier for patient engagement. By using Apple HealthKit, for example, health consumers can aggregate their mHealth data from multiple devices, and patients and care managers can receive insights about health problems from the cognitive analysis of the integrated data streams. The results can also be fed back into the Watson cloud so that it can learn which interventions produced positive results.[33]

One further step is required to make this mobile health data truly useful in population health management: A care manager who receives the HealthKit data analysis must be able to translate it into action. To do so, the care manager can use complementary applications that identify high-risk patients and help engage them in improving their health behavior. In addition, mobile data analyses can be used to inform automated online campaigns that educate and engage patients who have moderate chronic diseases or are healthy and need only preventive care. In fact, these campaigns could be conducted in a feedback loop with smartphone users.

## Care coordination

Cognitive computing does not magically make disparate healthcare applications interoperable. But it can break down information silos by aggregating and normalizing data from healthcare providers across care settings.

For example, a cognitive computing system that has access to multiple clinical information systems may discover that a patient who sees a primary care physician during flu season has already had a flu shot at a CVS pharmacy. Though claims data could supply the same connection, that information is much less timely than data that comes directly from provider information systems.

There are still many obstacles to gaining access to this data from all care settings. For example, post–acute-care facilities such as nursing homes and home care agencies use information systems that are far less capable of delivering discrete clinical data than are hospital or ambulatory care EHRs or pharmacy systems.[34] But cognitive computing's use of NLP to scan unstructured documents, coupled with its normalization of aggregated data, could supply the missing links.

## Workflow integration

If doctors and nurses have to leave their EHR workflow to obtain additional patient information or clinical decision support from a cognitive computing system, they are less likely to use it. So, the insights from cognitive computing must be available within the clinicians' workflow; the user interfaces must be intuitive and seamless; and clinicians should be able to get answers to their questions at the point of care.

Fortunately, there are already population health management solutions that can provide this kind of support within EHR workflow, along with automation tools that make the information actionable. When combined with the cognitive computing insights from structured and unstructured data culled from many different sources, these PHM solutions can present providers and care managers with reliable, timely analyses to support improved care delivery and patient engagement.

As mentioned earlier in this chapter, Watson's NLP capabilities and some of its analytics have been integrated with one of the leading EHRs. Besides enlarging the corpus of data available to clinicians, the integrated system is also being used to accelerate clinical trial recruitment. With the help of EHR data, Watson's clinical trial matching application allows physicians to identify patients during office visits who fit the criteria for particular studies. Since only 5 percent of cancer studies in the United States recruit sufficient participants, this solution could help drive medical research forward at a faster pace.[35]

Other EHR-integrated applications of cognitive computing are expected to play a role in quality improvement and disease management. Again, it is already possible to tailor treatments to particular patients by comparing the outcomes of many other similar patients who were treated in various ways. When genomic science progresses further, cognitive computing will also be able to present physicians with best practice guidelines that apply to patients with a particular genetic makeup, along with other specific characteristics.

# Conclusion

Population health management has become increasingly dependent on big data because of the volume, variety, and velocity of information that healthcare organizations must manage to ensure that everybody receives appropriate care. But though many organizations are still struggling in this stage, it is only the first step on the road to a vastly more capable way to apply big data in health care.

Cognitive computing can use NLP to extract insights from the unstructured data that holds most of the relevant information about patients. It can rapidly search the medical literature and correlate what it finds with clinical and other kinds of data on a patient. It can also aggregate and analyze an extensive assortment of data, including imaging, monitoring, and genomic information as well as data on the behavioral and social determinants of health.

Cognitive computing marries data-driven analytics — using clinical, administrative, claims, and other data — with knowledge-driven analytics, which are applied to medical studies and clinical guidelines. In this dynamic process, the artificial intelligence of cognitive computing constantly learns and improves from the feedback it receives in the real world.

By identifying health problems that are missing from clinical data, providing clinical decision support, and predicting the health status of individual patients, among other tasks, cognitive computing can become a dependable and essential assistant to physicians and to organizations engaged in population health management. But it will never replace clinicians. As one paper stated:

> The collaboration between human and machine that is inherent in a cognitive system supports a best practices approach that enables healthcare organizations to gain more value from data and solve complex problems.[36]

Returning to the analogy of the three-legged stool, the population health management of the future will include two legs that some organizations are already using:

- Data aggregation, normalization, and analysis based on a flexible, scalable data lake approach
- PHM tools that automate care coordination, care management, and patient engagement

The third leg of the stool is cognitive computing, which can provide much more advanced and timely insights, using a far wider range of data than the analytic tools that are now prevalent in PHM.

Together, these three legs can support vastly improved health care at a lower cost and a better patient experience, thus meeting the criteria of the Triple Aim.

# CONCLUSION

In the decade that followed the managed care assault of the 1990s, health care largely slid back into its traditional, volume-based approach to care delivery. But today, everything is changing at warp speed to accommodate the rapid growth of value-based reimbursement. Healthcare systems that fail to keep up will eventually go out of business or be absorbed by nimbler, more efficient organizations.

Health care is a huge industry, and a vast divide separates the leaders of the second managed care revolution from those who are struggling to figure it out. In the latter camp are the majority of healthcare organizations, which still don't entirely understand population health management or the health IT applications designed to support it.

External forces are beginning to change this situation, however. As discussed in Chapter 12, Medicare penalties for excessive readmissions are pushing hospitals to work closer with discharged patients and with the patients' physicians and post–acute-care providers. Healthcare systems are also starting to collect data and analyze it in ways they never have done before. It's likely that as these organizations start focusing on other areas of quality improvement, they will use analytic and automation tools to scale their efforts to the whole patient population.

The growing competition among vendors of PHM software, as well as EHR vendors that are moving into this space, should also lead to greater efforts to educate providers about population health management. Some of these companies already offer consulting services and educational tools to help providers get to first base.

After healthcare organizations have grasped the basics of PHM and how to make their data actionable, they will be ready to reengineer themselves. First they will build care teams that enable clinicians to operate at the upper limit of their expertise. Then they will apply analytic and automation applications to facilitate care management, increase efficiency, and scale PHM to the entire population. Some organizations will also adopt a Lean approach to improve their work processes. Part of Lean thinking is to use information technology to automate as many routine tasks as possible.

Meanwhile, the current trend of telehealth and remote patient monitoring will continue to grow. Technology-enabled care delivery will evolve to the point where much that is now done in physician offices, hospitals, and outpatient settings can be done at home. Patients will use mobile apps to communicate with their providers wherever they are, to keep them apprised of changes in their health condition, and to improve their own health behavior so that they can maintain their health. Health risk assessments, functional status surveys, and other types of patient-generated data will also become commonplace. Sophisticated algorithms will filter all this information so that providers see only the data they need to respond to.

Healthcare organizations will also increasingly use a wide range of non-healthcare data to address the social determinants of health. Combined with the integration of behavioral health into mainstream medicine, the IT-supported ability to pinpoint and take action on certain SDH factors will make a huge difference in population health. But that will happen only if healthcare organizations form service delivery teams that include social service professionals and other non-clinical experts.

Finally, cognitive computing has the potential to revolutionize medicine and create the next generation of population health management. The ability of cognitive computing systems to convert unstructured data into structured data and to understand medical concepts in the literature, using natural language processing, will allow providers to combine data-driven and knowledge-driven decision support. At the same time, cognitive computing holds the key to combining clinical knowledge with new insights from genomic research, advanced image and textual processing, and data on the social determinants of health. Cognitive computing will provide new medical insights and build the capability to deliver truly personalized health care.

In the end, population health management depends on using sophisticated information technology to support both patient engagement and medical decision-making. Data is "oxygen," and the successful organizations will be those that have the best data and know how to use it to create the best outcomes.

# ENDNOTES

## Introduction

1. Sean P. Keehan, Gigi A. Cuckler, Andrea M. Sisko, Andrew J. Madison, Sheila D. Smith, Devin A. Stone, John A. Poisal, Christian J. Wolfe and Joseph M. Lizonitz, "National Health Expenditure Projections, 2014-24: Spending Growth Faster Than Recent Trends," *Health Affairs,* 34, no. 8 (2015): 1407–1417.

2. Institute of Medicine, *Crossing the Quality Chasm: A New Health System for the 21st Century.* Washington, DC: National Academy Press, 2014, 3–4.

3. Centers for Medicare and Medicaid Services (CMS), Medicare Shared Savings Program, http://www.cms.gov/Medicare/Medicare-Fee-for-Service-Payment/sharedsavingsprogram/index.html?redirect=/.

4. CMS, "Fact Sheet: Finalized Changes to the Medicare Shared Savings Program Regulations," June 4, 2015, https://www.cms.gov/Medicare/Medicare-Fee-for-Service-Payment/sharedsavingsprogram/Downloads/2015-06-04-Fact-Sheet-MSSP-ACO-Final-Rule-.pdf.

5. CMS, "Next Generation Accountable Care Organization Model," press release, Jan. 11, 2016, accessed at https://www.cms.gov/Newsroom/MediaReleaseDatabase/Fact-sheets/2016-Fact-sheets-items/2016-01-11.html.

6. CMS, "Hospital Value-Based Purchasing," accessed at http://www.cms.gov/Medicare/Quality-Initiatives-Patient-Assessment-Instruments/hospital-value-based-purchasing/index.html?redirect=/hospital-value-based-purchasing.

7. Ken Terry, "VBMs: Coming Soon to Either Increase or Lower Your Income," *Medscape,* Feb. 6, 2014, accessed at http://www.medscape.com/viewarticle/820050_1.

8. Sylvia M. Burwell, "Setting Value-Based Payment Goals — HHS Efforts to Improve U.S. Health Care," *New England Journal of Medicine,* Jan. 26, 2015, doi: 10.1056/NEJMp1500445.

9. Miranda A. Franco, Holland & Knight, "MACRA, the Sustainable Growth Rate (SGR) Reform Bill, Signed Into Law," April 30, 2015, http://www.hklaw.com/Publications/MACRA-the-Sustainable-Growth-Rate-SGR-Reform-Bill-Signed-into-Law-04-30-2015.

10. Joseph R. Swedish, "Opening Keynote Address at the Business Health Agenda 2014," March 5, 2014, accessed at `http://www.wellpoint.com/prodcontrib/groups/wellpoint/documents/wlp_assets/pw_e213326.pdf`.

11. Emily Berry, "United to attach performance conditions to more doctors' pay," *American Medical News*, Feb. 29, 2012, accessed at `http://www.amednews.com/article/20120229/business/302299997/8`.

12. Aetna Accountable Care Solutions, `http://www.aetnaacs.com`.

13. Stephen M. Shortell, Carrie H. Colla, Valerie A. Lewis, Elliott Fisher, Eric Kessell, Patricia Ramsay, "Accountable Care Organizations: The National Landscape," *Journal of Health Politics, Policy and Law*, Vol. 40, No. 4, August 2015.

14. James A. Wiley, Diane R. Rittenhouse, Stephen M. Shortell, Lawrence P. Casalino, Patricia P. Ramsay, Salma Bibi, Andrew M. Ryan, Kennon R. Copeland, and Jeffrey A. Alexander, "Managing Chronic Illness: Physician Practices Increased the Use of Care Management and Medical Home Processes," *Health Affairs*, 34, no. 1 (2015): 78–86.

15. Christine A. Sinsky, Rachel Willard-Grace, Andrew M. Schutzbank, Thomas A. Sinsky, David Margolius, and Thomas Bodenheimer, "In Search of Joy in Practice: A Report of 23 High-Functioning Primary Care Practices," *Annals of Family Medicine* 1 (2013): 272–278.

16. National Committee on Quality Assurance (NCQA), "NCA Medical Homes Pass 10,000 Mark," news release, May 7, 2015, `http://www.ncqa.org/newsroom/news-archive/2015-news-archive/news-release-may-7-2015.aspx`.

17. Thomas H. Lee and Toby Cosgrove, "Engaging Doctors in the Health Care Revolution," *Harvard Business Review*, June 2014, accessed at `http://hbr.org/2014/06/engaging-doctors-in-the-health-care-revolution/ar/1`.

18. Trust for America's Health, "F as in Fat: How Obesity Threatens America's Future," August 2013, accessed at `http://healthyamericans.org/report/108`.

19. CMS, "Stage 1 vs. Stage 2 Comparison Table for Eligible Professionals," August 2012, accessed at `https://www.cms.gov/Regulations-and-Guidance/Legislation/EHRIncentivePrograms/Downloads/Stage1vsStage2CompTablesforEP.pdf`.

20. Federal Register, "Medicare and Medicaid Programs; Electronic Health Record Incentive Program — Stage 3 and Modifications to Meaningful Use in 2015-2017," accessed at `https://www.federalregister.gov/articles/2015/10/16/2015-25595/medicare-and-medicaid-programs-electronic-health-record-incentive-program-stage-3-and-modifications`.

21. Phytel, Phytel Outreach™, accessed at `http://www3.phytel.com/solutions/population-health-management-systems/proactive-patient-outreach.aspx`.

22. Foreman KF, Stockl KM, Le LB, et al. Impact of a Text Messaging Pilot Program on Patient Medication Adherence. *Clinical Therapeutics.* Accepted 12 April 2012. Published online: 03 May 2012 (doi:10.1016/j.clinthera.2012.04.007). `http://www.clinicaltherapeutics.com/article/S0149-2918(12)00265-2/abstract`.

23. Anna-Lisa Silvestre, Valerie M. Sue and Jill Y. Allen, "If You Build It, Will They Come? The Kaiser Permanente Model of Online Health Care." *Health Affairs,* March/April 2009, vol. 28 no. 2: 334–344, accessed at `http://content.healthaffairs.org/content/28/2/334.abstract?sid=e9b8b36d-7acc-495f-b207-0a0e76b917aa`.

24. Ken Terry, "Strategy: How Mobility, Apps and BYOD Will Transform Health Care," July 1, 2012, accessed at `http://reports.informationweek.com/abstract/105/8914/Healthcare/strategy-how-mobility-apps-and-byod-will-transform-health-care.html`.

25. Institute for Health Technology Transformation, "Lean IT: Making Health Care More Efficient," Sept. 20, 2013, accessed at `http://ihealthtran.com/wordpress/2013/09/iht`$^2$`-report-lean-it-making-healthcare-more-efficient`.

26. Surescripts, "Medication History Ambulatory," accessed at `http://surescripts.com/products-and-services/medication-network-services/medication-history-ambulatory`.

27. Andy Slavitt and Karen DeSalvo, "EHR Incentive Programs: Where We Go Next," CMS Blog, Jan. 19, 2016, accessed at `http://blog.cms.gov/2016/01/19/ehr-incentive-programs-where-we-go-next/`.

## Chapter 1

1. Katherine Grace Carman, Christine Eibner, Susan M. Paddock, "Trends in Health Insurance Enrollment, 2013-15," Health Affairs, v. 34, no. 6, June 2015, p. 1044–1048.

2. Robert L. Phillips, Jr., and Andrew W. Bazemore, "Primary Care and Why It Matters for U.S. Health System Reform," *Health Affairs,* May 2010, 806–810.

3. Institute of Medicine, "Crossing the Quality Chasm: A New Health System for the 21st Century." Washington, DC: National Academy Press, 2001, 3–4.

4. Elizabeth A. McGlynn, Steven M. Asch, John Adams, Joan Keesey, Jennifer Hicks, Alison DeCristofaro, and Eve A. Kerr, "The Quality of Health Care Delivered to Adults in the United States," *New England Journal of Medicine* 348 (2003): 2635–2645.

5. Cristina Boccuti and Giselle Casillas, "Aiming for Fewer Hospital U-turns: The Medicare Hospital Readmission Reduction Program," Kaiser Family Foundation Issue Brief, Jan. 29, 2015, `http://kff.org/medicare/issue-brief/aiming-for-fewer-hospital-u-turns-the-medicare-hospital-readmission-reduction-program/`.

6. Héctor Bueno, MD, PhD; Joseph S. Ross, MD, MHS; Yun Wang, PhD; Jersey Chen, MD, MPH; María T. Vidán, MD, PhD; Sharon-Lise T. Normand, PhD; Jeptha P. Curtis, MD; Elizabeth E. Drye, MD, SM; Judith H. Lichtman, PhD; Patricia S. Keenan, PhD; Mikhail Kosiborod, MD; and Harlan M. Krumholz, MD, SM, "Trends in Length of Stay and Short-Term Outcomes Among Medicare Patients Hospitalized for Heart Failure, 1993–2006," *Journal of the American Medical Association* 303, no. 21 (2010): 2141–2147.

7. Donald M. Berwick, Thomas W. Nolan, and John Whittington, "The Triple Aim: Care, Health and Cost," *Health Affairs,* May/June 2008, 759–769.

8. Gulshan Sharma, MD, MPH; Kathlyn E. Fletcher, MD, MA; Dong Zhang, PhD; Yong-Fang Kuo, PhD; Jean L. Freeman, PhD; and James S. Goodwin, MD, "Continuity of Outpatient and Inpatient Care by Primary Care Physicians for Hospitalized Older Adults," *Journal of the American Medical Association* 301, no. 16 (2009): 1671–1680.

9. Commonwealth Fund Issue Brief, "U.S. Health Care from a Global Perspective: Spending, Use of Services, Prices, and Health in 13

Countries," http://www.commonwealthfund.org/publications/issue-briefs/2015/oct/us-health-care-from-a-global-perspective.

10. Ibid.

11. Ken Terry, "Health Spending for Privately Insured Rises 3.4%," Medscape Medical News, Oct. 29, 2015, accessed at http://www.medscape.com/viewarticle/853482.

12. Berwick, Nolan, and Whittington, "The Triple Aim" ...

13. Ibid.

14. Nicholas Stine, MD, and David Chokshi, MD, "Defining Population Health," Human Capital Blog, RWJ Foundation, Jan.23, 2013, accessed at http://www.rwjf.org/en/blogs/human-capital-blog/2013/01/defining_population.html.

15. David M. Lawrence, "How to Forge a High-Tech Marriage Between Primary Care and Population Health," *Health Affairs*, May 2010, 1004–1009.

16. David M. Lawrence, *From Chaos to Care: The Promise of Team-Based Medicine* (Cambridge, MA: Da Capo Press, 2003).

17. Institute of Medicine, "Crossing the Quality Chasm," 3.

18. Ibid., 181–206.

19. Ken Terry, *Rx for Health Care Reform* (Nashville: Vanderbilt University Press, 2007), 177–178.

20. Patient-Centered Primary Care Collaborative, "Managing Populations, Maximizing Technology: Population Health Management in the Medical Neighborhood," October 2013, accessed at http://www.pcpcc.org/resource/managing-populations-maximizing-technology.

21. Chun-Ju Hsiao and Esther Hing, "Use and Characteristics of Electronic Health Record Systems Among Office-based Physician Practices: United States, 2001-2013," Centers for Disease Control and Prevention (CDC), January 2014, accessed at http://www.cdc.gov/nchs/data/databriefs/db143.htm-x2013;2013</a>.

22. Meredith B. Rosenthal, Rushika Fernandopulle, HyunSook Ryu Song, and Bruce Landon, "Paying for Quality: Providers' Incentives for Quality Improvement," *Health Affairs*, March/April 2004, 127–141.

23. Thomas Bodenheimer, Edward H. Wagner, and Kevin Grumbach, "Improving Primary Care for Patients with Chronic Illness," *JAMA* 288 (2002): 1775–1779.

24. Thomas Bodenheimer, Edward H. Wagner, and Kevin Grumbach, "Improving Primary Care for Patients with Chronic Illness: The Chronic Care Model, Part 2," *Journal of the American Medical Association* 288 (2002): 1909–1914.

25. AAFP, AAP, ACP, AOA, "Joint Principles of the Patient-Centered Medical Home," February 2007, accessed at http://www.pcpcc.net/content/joint-principles-patient-centered-medical-home.

26. Paul A. Nutting, MD, MSPH; William L. Miller, MD, MA; Benjamin F. Crabtree, PhD; Carlos Roberto Jaen, MD, PhD; Elizabeth E. Stewart, PhD; and Kurt C. Stange, MD, PhD, "Initial Lessons from the First National Demonstration Project on Practice Transformation to a Patient-Centered Medical Home," *Annals of Family Medicine* 7 (2009): 254–260.

27. Bruce E. Landon, James M. Gill, Richard C. Antonelli, and Eugene C. Rich, "Prospects for Rebuilding Primary Care Using the Patient-Centered Medical Home," *Health Affairs*, May 2010, 827–834.

28. Elliott S. Fisher, Donald M. Berwick, and Karen Davis, "Achieving Healthcare Reform: How Physicians Can Help," *New England Journal of Medicine* 360 (2009): 2495–2497.

29. Diane R. Rittenhouse, Stephen M. Shortell, and Elliott S. Fisher, "Primary Care and Accountable Care — Two Essential Elements of Delivery-System Reform," *New England Journal of Medicine* 361 (2009): 2301–2303.

30. Stephen M. Shortell, Carrie H. Colla, Valerie A. Lewis, Elliott Fisher, Eric Kessell, Patricia Ramsay, "Accountable Care Organizations: The National Landscape," *Journal of Health Politics, Policy and Law,* Vol. 40, No. 4, August 2015.

31. Jeff Goldsmith, "The ACO: Not Ready for Prime Time," Health Affairs Blog, Aug. 17, 2009, accessed at http://healthaffairs.org/blog/2009/08/17/the-accountable-care-organization-not-ready-for-prime-time.

32. Lawrence, "How to Forge a High-Tech Marriage" ...

33. Ibid.

34. Rushika Fernandopulle and Neil Patel, "How the Electronic Health Record Did Not Measure Up to the Demands of Our Medical Home Practice," *Health Affairs*, April 2010, 622–628.

## Chapter 2

1. Kaiser Family Foundation, "Summary of New Health Reform Law," accessed at `http://www.kff.org/healthreform/upload/8061.pdf`.

2. CMS, "Shared Savings Program," accessed at `http://www.cms.gov/Medicare/Medicare-Fee-for-Service-Payment/sharedsavingsprogram/index.html`.

3. Stephen M. Shortell, Carrie H. Colla, Valerie A. Lewis, Elliott Fisher, Eric Kessell, Patricia Ramsay, "Accountable Care Organizations: The National Landscape," *Journal of Health Politics, Policy and Law,* Vol. 40, No. 4, August 2015, accessed at `http://jhppl.dukejournals.org/content/40/4/647.abstract`.

4. S. Lawrence Kocot, Farzad Mostashari, and Ross White, "Year One Results from Medicare Shared Savings Program: What It Means Going Forward," Brookings Institution Upfront blog, Feb. 7, 2014.

5. David Introcaso and Gregory Berger, "MSSP Year Two: Medicare ACOs Show Muted Success," Health Affairs Blog, Sept. 24, 2015, accessed at `http://healthaffairs.org/blog/2015/09/24/mssp-year-two-medicare-acos-show-muted-success/`.

6. Melanie Evans, "Two more Pioneer ACOs exit as new CMS model emerges," *Modern Healthcare,* Nov. 4, 2015, accessed at `http://www.modernhealthcare.com/article/20151104/NEWS/151109941`.

7. Valerie A. Lewis, Carrie H. Colla, William L. Schpero, Stephen M. Shortell, and Elliott S. Fisher, "ACO Contracting With Private and Public Payers: A Baseline Comparative Analysis, *American Journal of Managed Care.* 2014;20(12):1008–1014.

8. Jordan T. Cohen, "A Guide to Accountable Care Organizations, and Their Role in the Senate's Health Reform Bill," *Health Reform Watch,* March 11, 2010, accessed at `http://www.healthreformwatch.com/2010/03/11/a-guide-to-accountable-care-organizations-and-their-role-in-the-senates-health-reform-bill/`.

9. Ibid.

10. Ken Terry, "Gainsharing Is Becoming More Respectable," *BNET Healthcare,* July 28, 2009, accessed `http://www.cbsnews.com/news/gainsharing-is-becoming-more-respectable/`.

11. "Health Policy Brief: Bundled Payments for Care Improvement Initiative," *Health Affairs,* Nov. 23, 2015, accessed at http://healthaffairs. org/healthpolicybriefs/brief_pdfs/healthpolicybrief_148.pdf

12. Laurence C. Baker, M. Kate Bundorf, and Daniel P. Kessler, "Vertical Integration: Hospital Ownership of Physician Practice Is Associated With Higher Prices and Spending," *Health Affairs* 33, No. 5 (2014): 756–763.

13. David N. Gans, "Has the tide of practice acquisition ebbed?" *MGMA Connection,* January/February 2015, accessed at http://www.mgma. com/practice-resources/mgma-connection-plus/mgma- connection/2015/january-february-2015/oe-has-the-tide- of-practice-acquisition-ebbed.

14. Ibid.

15. Ibid.

16. "Online Connectivity: Linking Providers and Patients to Create a Community of Care," *Patient Safety & Quality Healthcare,* January/February 2010, accessed at http://www.psqh.com/ januaryfebruary-2010/391-online-connectivity.html.

17. Patient Protection and Affordable Care Act, H.R. 3590, Sec. 3022 (Medicare Shared Savings Program).

18. Department of Health and Human Services (HHS) press release, "New hospitals and health care providers join successful, cutting- edge federal initiative that cuts costs and puts patients at the center of their care," Jan. 11, 2016, accessed at http://www.hhs.gov/ about/news/2016/01/11/new-hospitals-and-health- care-providers-join-successful-cutting-edge-federal- initiative.html.

19. Sylvia M. Burwell, "Setting Value-Based Payment Goals—HHS Efforts to Improve U.S. Health Care," *New England Journal of Medicine,* Jan. 26, 2015, doi: 10.1056/NEJMp1500445.

20. American Academy of Family Physicians, "FAQ on MACRA and Medicare Payment Reform," accessed at http://www.aafp.org/ practice-management/payment/medicare-payment/faq.html.

21. CMS, "Medicare Shared Savings Program Accountable Care Organizations," accessed at https://data.cms.gov/ACO/ Medicare-Shared-Savings-Program-Accountable-Care-O/ ucce-hhpu.

22. Creagh Milford, Mercy Health, personal communication.

23. Ken Terry, "Global Capitation — It's Back," *Physicians Practice,* April 2009, accessed at http://www.physicianspractice.com/index/fuseaction/articles.details/articleID/1313.html.

24. Blue Cross Blue Shield of Massachusetts, "Alternative Quality Contract," accessed at http://www.bluecrossma.com/visitor/about-us/affordability-quality/aqc.html.

25. Zirui Song, Sherri Rose, Dana G. Safran, Bruce E. Landon, Matthew P. Day, and Michael E. Chernew, "Changes in Health Care Spending and Quality 4 Years into Global Payment," *New England Journal of Medicine* 371, no. 18 (Oct. 30, 2014): 1704–1714.

26. Alexander Cohen, Sarah Klein, and Douglas McCarthy, "Hill Physicians Medical Group: A Market-Driven Approach to Accountable Care for Commercially Insured Patients," *Commonwealth Fund Case Study,* Oct. 2014, http://www.commonwealthfund.org/~/media/files/publications/case-study/2014/oct/1770_cohen_hill_physicians_aco_case_study.pdf.

27. Josette N. Gbemudu, Bridget K. Larson, Aricca D. Van Citters, Sara A. Kreindler, Frances M. Wu, Eugene C. Nelson, Stephen M. Shortell, and Elliott S. Fisher, "Healthcare Partners: Building on a Foundation of Global Risk Management to Achieve Accountable Care," *Commonwealth Fund Case Study,* January 2012, accessed at http://www.commonwealthfund.org/~/media/Files/Publications/CaseStudy/2012/Jan/1572_Gbemudu_HealthCare_Partners_case study_01_17_2012.pdf.

28. Doug Desjardins, "Anthem, HealthCare Partners ACO Saves $4.7 Million," *HealthLeaders,* June 18, 2014, accessed at http://healthleadersmedia.com/content.cfm?topic=HEP&content_id=305623.

29. HealthCare Partners press release, "HealthCare Partners Saves $1.8 million in Anthem Blue Cross Enhanced Personal Health Care Program," June 1, 2015, http://www.prnewswire.com/news-releases/healthcare-partners-saves-18-million-in-anthem-blue-cross-enhanced-personal-health-care-program-300091375.html.

30. The Commonwealth Fund, "Mirror, Mirror on the Wall: How The Performance of the U.S. Health Care System Compares Internationally, 2010 Update," accessed at http://www.commonwealthfund.org/publications/fund-reports/2010/jun/mirror-mirror-update.

31. Institute of Medicine, *Crossing the Quality Chasm.* Washington, DC: National Academy Press, 2001.

32. David M. Lawrence, "How to Forge a High-Tech Marriage Between Primary Care and Population Health," *Health Affairs,* May 2010, 1004–1009.

33. David M. Lawrence, *From Chaos to Care: The Promise of Team-Based Medicine.* Cambridge, MA: Da Capo Press, 2003.

34. AAFP, AAP, ACP, AOA, "Joint Principles of the Patient-Centered Medical Home," February 2007, accessed at https://www.pcpcc.org/about/medical-home.

35. Paul A. Nutting, MD, MSPH; William L. Miller, MD, MA; Benjamin F. Crabtree, PhD; Carlos Roberto Jaen, MD, PhD; Elizabeth E. Stewart, PhD; and Kurt C. Stange, MD, PhD, "Initial Lessons from the First National Demonstration Project on Practice Transformation to a Patient-Centered Medical Home," *Annals of Family Medicine* 7 (2009): 254–260.

36. Greg Slabodkin, "HIE Among Hospitals Grows, Still Needs Improvement," *Health Data Management,* May 6, 2014, accessed at http://www.healthdatamanagement.com/news/HIE-Among-Hospitals-Needs-Improvement-47997-1.html?utm_campaign=daily-may%206%202014&utm_medium=email&utm_source=newsletter&ET=healthdatamanagement%3Ae2629612%3A3696614a%3A&st=email.

37. Julia Adler-Milstein, David W. Bates, and Ashish K. Jha, "Operational Health Information Exchanges Show Substantial Growth, But Long-Term Funding Remains a Concern," *Health Affairs* 32, no. 8 (August 2013): 1486–1492.

38. Ken Terry, "KLAS: 'Private' HIEs Leaving 'Public' HIEs in the Dust," *FierceHealthIT,* July 8, 2011, accessed at http://www.fiercehealthit.com/story/klas-private-hies-leaving-public-hies-dust/2011-07-08.

39. HIT Trends blog, April 2014, accessed at https://www.directtrust.org/directtrust-identifies-six-trends-for-electronic-health-information-exchange-and-interoperability-in-2016-2/.

40. Office of the National Coordinator for Health Information Technology (ONC), "Connecting Health and Care for the Nation: A Shared Nationwide Interoperability Roadmap, Final Version 1.0," 2.

41. Rushika Fernandopulle and Neil Patel, "How the Electronic Health Record Did Not Measure Up to the Demands of Our Medical Home Practice," *Health Affairs,* April 2010, 622–628.

# Chapter 3

1. National Committee on Quality Assurance (NCQA), "NCA Medical Homes Pass 10,000 Mark," news release, May 7, 2015, `http://www.ncqa.org/newsroom/news-archive/2015-news-archive/news-release-may-7-2015`.

2. National Committee on Quality Assurance (NCQA), "NCQA's Patient-Centered Medical Home Frequently Asked Questions," `https://www.ncqa.org/Portals/0/Programs/Recognition/FAQ on Practice Changes_10.9.12.pdf`.

3. Patient Centered Primary Care Collaborative (PCPCC), "Patient-Centered Medical Home 101: General Overview," slide presentation, 15.

4. NCQA, "NCQA Analysis Shows PCMH Initiatives Growing Across the Country," accessed at `http://www.ncqa.org/newsroom/details/ncqa-analysis-shows-pcmh-initiatives-growing-across-the-country`.

5. Centers for Medicare and Medicaid Services (CMS), "Multi-Payer Advanced Primary Care Practice," accessed at `https://innovation.cms.gov/initiatives/Multi-payer-Advanced-Primary-Care-Practice`.

6. Patient-Centered Primary Care Collaborative, "Benefits of Implementing the Primary Care Patient-Centered Medical Home: A Review of Cost & Quality Results, 2012," accessed at `http://www.pcpcc.org/sites/default/files/media/benefits_of_implementing_the_primary_care_pcmh.pdf`.

7. PCPCC, "Veterans Health Administration — Patient Aligned Care Team (PACT)," accessed at `https://www.pcpcc.org/initiative/veterans-health-administration-patient-aligned-care-team-pact`.

8. PCPCC, "Evidence of the Effectiveness of PCMH on Quality of Care and Cost," accessed at `http://www.amsa.org/AMSA/Libraries/Committee_Docs/Evidence_Supporting_the_PCMH_Model.sflb.ashx`.

9. Kevin Grumbach, Thomas Bodenheimer, and Paul Grundy, "The Outcomes of Implementing Patient-Centered Medical Home Demonstrations: A Review of the Evidence on Quality, Access and Costs from Recent Prospective Evaluation Studies," August 2009, paper prepared for PCPCC.

10. Robert J. Reid, Katie Coleman, Eric A. Johnson, Paul A. Fishman, Clarissa Hsu, Michael P. Soman, Claire E. Trescott, Michael Erikson, and Eric B. Larson, "The Group Health Medical Home at Year Two: Cost Savings, Higher Patient Satisfaction, and Less Burnout for Providers." *Health Affairs* 29, No. 5 (2010): 835–843.

11. Patient-Centered Patient Care Collaborative (PCPCC) "The Patient-Centered Medical Home's Impact on Cost and Quality: Annual Review of Evidence 2014-2015," February 2016, accessed at `https://www.pcpcc.org/download/6219/PCPCC-PCMH-evidence-report-Feb-2016-pages.pdf?redirect=node/204406`.

12. Paul Grundy, Kay R. Hagan, Jennie Chin Hansen, and Kevin Grumbach, "The Multi-Stakeholder Movement for Primary Care Renewal and Reform," *Health Affairs* 29, no. 5 (2010): 791–798.

13. Ibid.

14. Ibid.

15. Suzanna Felt-Lisk and Tricia Higgins, "Exploring the Promise of Population Health Management Programs to Improve Health," *Mathematica Policy Research Issue Brief,* August 2011, accessed at `https://www.mathematica-mpr.com/our-publications-and-findings/publications/exploring-the-promise-of-population-health-management-programs-to-improve-health`.

16. David Nash, "Healthcare Reform's Rx for Primary Care," *MedPage Today,* Aug. 18, 2010, accessed at `http://www.medpagetoday.com/Columns/21750`.

17. American Academy of Family Practice, American Academy of Pediatrics, American College of Physicians, and American Osteopathic Association, "Joint Principles of the Patient-Centered Medical Home," March 2007, accessed at `http://www.aafp.org/dam/AAFP/documents/practice_management/pcmh/initiatives/PCMHJoint.pdf`.

18. Bruce E. Landon, James M. Gill, Richard C. Antonelli, and Eugene C. Rich, "Prospects for Rebuilding Primary Care Using the Patient-Centered Medical Home," *Health Affairs* 29, no. 5 (2010): 827–834.

19. Blue Cross and Blue Shield Association, slide presentation, "The Patient-Centered Medical Home: BC/BS Pilot Initiatives," slides 22 and 24.

20. NCQA, "Physician Practice Connections," accessed at `https://www.ncqa.org/Portals/0/PCMH brochure-web.pdf`.

21. NCQA, "Physician Practice Connections — Patient-Centered Medical Home," accessed at https://www.ncqa.org/portals/0/public policy/PCMH_Policy_Fact_Sheet.pdf.

22. Margaret E. O'Kane and Patricia Barrett, "Sneak Preview: 2014 Patient-Centered Medical Home Recognition," NCQA slides, March 10, 2014, accessed at https://www.ncqa.org/Portals/0/Newsroom/2014/ PCMH 2014 Press Preview FINAL Slides.pdf.

23. Ken Terry, "Medical Specialists Encouraged to Use More IT," *InformationWeek Healthcare,* June 13, 2012, accessed at http://www.informationweek.com/healthcare/policy/medical-specialists-encouraged-to-use-mo/240001986.

24. US Agency for Healthcare Research and Quality, "Practice-Based Population Health: Information Technology to Support Transformation to Proactive Primary Care," July 2010, accessed at https://pcmh.ahrq.gov/sites/default/files/attachments/Information Technology to Support Transformation to Proactive Primary Care.pdf.

25. Diane R. Rittenhouse, Lawrence P. Casalino, Robin R. Gillies, Stephen M. Shortell, and Bernard Lau, "Measuring the Medical Home: Infrastructure in Large Groups," *Health Affairs* 27, no. 5 (2008): 1246–1258.

26. James A. Wiley, Diane R. Rittenhouse, Stephen M. Shortell, Lawrence P. Casalino, Patricia P. Ramsay, Salma Bibi, Andrew M. Ryan, Kennon R. Copeland, and Jeffrey A. Alexander, "Managing Chronic Illness: Physician Practices Increased the Use of Care Management and Medical Home Processes," *Health Affairs* 34, no. 1 (2015): 78–86.

27. Paul A. Nutting, MD, MSPH; William L. Miller, MD, MA; Benjamin F. Crabtree, PhD; Carlos Roberto Jaen, MD, PhD; Elizabeth E. Stewart, PhD; and Kurt C. Stange, MD, PhD, "Initial Lessons from the First National Demonstration Project on Practice Transformation to a Patient-Centered Medical Home," *Annals of Family Medicine* 7 (2009): 254–260.

28. Landon, Gill, Antonelli, and Rich, "Prospects for Rebuilding Primary Care" . . .

29. Phytel press release, "VHA, TransforMED and Phytel Awarded $20.75 Million Health Care Innovation Grant," June 20, 2012.

30. Katie Merrell and Robert A. Berenson, "Structured Payment for Medical Homes," *Health Affairs* 29, no. 5 (2010): 852–858.

31. Grundy, Hagan, Hansen, and Grumbach, "The Multi-Stakeholder Movement for" . . .

32. Blue Cross and Blue Shield Association, "The Patient-Centered Medical Home" . . ., slide 25.

33. PCPCC, "The Patient-Centered Medical Home's Impact on Cost and Quality: Annual Review of Evidence 2014-2015"...

34. Robert S. Nocon, Ravi Sharma, Jonathan M. Birnberg, Quyen Ngo-Metzger, Sang Mee Lee, and Marshall H. Chin, "Association Between Patient-Centered Medical Home Rating and Operating Cost at Federally Funded Health Centers," *Journal of the American Medical Association* 308, no. 1 (2012): 60–66.

35. Michael K. Magill, David Ehrenberger, Debra L. Scammon, Julie Day, Tatiana Allen, Andreu J. Reall, Rhonda W. Sides, Jaewhan Kim, "The Cost of Sustaining a Patient-Centered Medical Home: Experience From 2 States," *Annals of Family Medicine* 2015;13:429–435.

36. US Agency for Healthcare Research and Quality, "Practice-Based Population Health" . . .

37. Nutting, Miller, Crabtree, Jaen, Stewart, and Stange, "Initial Lessons from the First National Demonstration Project" . . .

38. US Agency for Healthcare Research and Quality, "Practice-Based Population Health". . .

39. Ken Terry, "Do Disease Registries=$$rewards?" *Medical Economics*, Nov. 4, 2005, accessed at http://medicaleconomics.modernmedicine.com/memag/article/articleDetail.jsp?id=190114&pageID=1&sk=&date=.

40. NCQA, "NCQA Analysis Shows PCMH Initiatives Growing Across the Country". . .

## Chapter 4

1. Eugene Kroch, R. Wesley Champion, Susan D. DeVore, Marla R. Kugel, Danielle A. Lloyd, and Lynne Rothney-Kozlak, "Measuring Progress Toward Accountable Care," 19, Premier Research Institute, Dec. 2012.

2. Wayne J. Guglielmo, "The Feds Ease Antitrust Rules — Cautiously," *Medical Economics,* June 21, 2002, accessed at http://medicaleconomics.modernmedicine.com/medical-economics/news/feds-ease-antitrust-rules-cautiously?page=full.

3. Alicia Gallegos, "Clinical Integration Model Gets FTC Green Light," *AM News,* March 11, 2013, accessed at http://www.amednews.com/article/20130311/government/130319976/6.

4. James J. Pizzo and Mark E. Grube, "Getting to There from Here: Evolving to ACOs Through Clinical Integration Programs, Including the Advocate Health Care Example as Presented by Lee B. Sacks, M.D.," Kaufman, Hall & Associates, 2011, accessed at http://www.advocatehealth.com/documents/app/ci_to_aco.pdf.

5. Premier Healthcare Alliance, presentation, "Clinically Integrated Networks: A Population Health Building Block," 2013.

6. Kroch, Champion, DeVore, Kugel, Lloyd, and Rothney-Kozlak, "Measuring Progress Toward Accountable Care," 6.

7. Institute for Health Technology Transformation, "Population Health Management: A Roadmap for Provider-Based Automation in a New Era of Health Care," 2012, accessed at http://ihealthtran.com/pdf/PHMReport.pdf.

8. Ibid.

9. Ashok Rai, Paul Prichard, Richard Hodach, and Ted Courtemanche, "Using Physician-Led Automated Communications to Improve Patient Health," *Journal of Population Health Management,* Vol. 14, 00, 2011. doi:10.1089/pop.2010.0033.

10. Centers for Medicare and Medicaid Services, "Stage 1 vs. Stage 2 Comparison Table for Eligible Professionals," August 2012, accessed at https://www.cms.gov/regulations-and-guidance/legislation/EHRIncentivePrograms/Downloads/Stage1vsStage2CompTAblesforEP.pdf.

11. Ann-Lisa Silvestre, Valerie M. Sue, and Jill Y. Allen, "If You Build It, Will They Come? The Kaiser Permanente Model of Online Health Care," *Health Affairs* 28, no. 2 (2009): 334–344.

12. Sarah O'Hara, "Next-Generation Clinical Integration: Early Findings from a New Research Initiative," Network Advantage blog, The Advisory Board Co., Jan. 30, 2012, accessed at https://www.advisory.com/research/health-care-advisory-board/blogs/network-advantage/2012/01/next-generation-clinical-integration-early-findings-from-a-new-research-initiative.

13. Mark C. Shields, Pankaj H. Patel, Martin Manning, and Lee Sacks, "A Model for Integrating Independent Physicians into Accountable Care Organizations," *Health Affairs* 30, no. 1 (2011): 161–172.

14. Annie Lowrey, "A Health Provider Strives to Keep Hospital Beds Empty," *The New York Times,* April 23, 2013, accessed at http://www.nytimes.com/2013/04/24/business/accountable-care-helping-hospitals-keep-medical-costs-down.html.

## Chapter 5

1. Centers for Medicare and Medicaid Services (CMS), "Data and Program Reports," https://www.cms.gov/Regulations-and-guidance/legislation/EHRIncentivePrograms/DataAndReports.html.

2. Kaiser Family Foundation, "Summary of the Affordable Care Act," accessed at http://kff.org/health-reform/fact-sheet/summary-of-the-affordable-care-act.

3. Centers for Medicare and Medicaid Services, "Multi-payer Primary Care Practice Demonstration Fact Sheet," accessed at http://www.cms.gov/Medicare/Demonstration-Projects/DemoProjectsEvalRpts/downloads/mapcpdemo_Factsheet.pdf.

4. Centers for Disease Control and Prevention, "Meaningful Use," accessed at http://www.cdc.gov/ehrmeaningfuluse/introduction.html.

5. CMS, "Medicare and Medicaid Health Information Technology: Title IV of the American Recovery and Reinvestment Act," fact sheet, June 16, 2009, accessed at https://www.cms.gov/Newsroom/MediaReleaseDatabase/Fact-sheets/2009-Fact-sheets-items/2009-06-16.html.

6. HHS (Department of Health and Human Services)/CMS, "Medicare and Medicaid Programs; Electronic Health Record Program; Final Rule," *Federal Register,* 42 CFR Parts 412, 413, 422, and 495.

7. HHS (Department of Health and Human Services)/CMS, "Medicare and Medicaid Programs; Electronic Health Record Program; Proposed Rule," a.k.a. "Notice of Proposed Rulemaking," *Federal Register,* 42 CFR Parts 412, 413, 422, and 495:1852.

8. CMS, "Medicare and Medicaid HER Incentive Program Basics," accessed at `https://www.cms.gov/Regulations-and-Guidance/Legislation/EHRIncentivePrograms/Basics.html`.

9. Ibid.

10. CMS, "An Introduction to Medicaid EHR Incentive Program for Eligible Professionals," accessed at `https://www.cms.gov/regulations-and-guidance/legislation/ehrincentiveprograms/downloads/ehr_medicaid_guide_remediated_2012.pdf`.

11. CMS, "Fact Sheet: Electronic Health Record Incentive Program and Health IT Certification Program Final Rule," Oct. 6, 2015, `https://www.cms.gov/Newsroom/MediaReleaseDatabase/Fact-sheets/2015-Fact-sheets-items/2015-10-06.html`.

12. CMS, "An Introduction to the Medicare EHR Incentive Program for Eligible Professionals," accessed at `https://www.cms.gov/regulations-and-guidance/legislation/ehrincentiveprograms/downloads/ehr_medicaid_guide_remediated_2012.pdf`.

13. CMS press release, "CMS Rule to Help Providers Make Use of Certified EHR Technology," May 20, 2014, accessed at `http://www.cms.gov/Newsroom/MediaReleaseDatabase/Press-releases/2014-Press-releases-items/2014-05-20.html`.

14. Ken Terry, "Final Rules for Meaningful Use Announced," *Medscape Medical News,* Oct. 7, 2015, `http://www.medscape.com/viewarticle/852258`.

15. HHS/CMS, "Medicare and Medicaid Programs; Electronic Health Record Program; Final Rule," *Federal Register,* 42 CFR Parts 412, 413, 422, and 495.

16. CMS press release, "CMS Rule to Help Providers" . . .

17. Terry, "Final Rules for Meaningful Use Announced" . . .

18. Ibid.

19. HHS/CMS, "Medicare and Medicaid Programs; Electronic Health Record Incentive Program — Stage 3 and Modifications to Meaningful Use in 2015 Through 2017; Final rule," *Federal Register,* 42. CFR Parts 412 and 495, Oct. 16, 2015, 62876–62888.

20. Ibid.

21. Ibid.

22. Ibid.

23. Ibid., 62876–79.

24. Ibid.

25. Mary Jo Deering, "ONC Issue Brief: Patient-Generated Health Data and Health IT," Dec. 20, 2013, accessed at http://www.healthit.gov/sites/default/files/pghd_brief_final122013.pdf.

26. Ibid.

27. William Van Doomik, "Meaningful Use of Patient-Generated Data in EHRs," blog of American Health Information Management Association, accessed at http://library.ahima.org/xpedio/groups/public/documents/ahima/bok1_050394.hcsp?dDocName=bok1_050394.

28. HHS/CMS, "Medicare and Medicaid Programs; Electronic Health Record Incentive Program — Stage 3 and Modifications to Meaningful Use in 2015 Through 2017," 62876–79.

29. Ibid., 62885-62888.

30. Terry, "KLAS: 'Private' HIEs leaving 'public' HIEs in the dust," *FierceHealthIT,* July 8, 2011, accessed at http://www.fiercehealthit.com/story/klas-private-hies-leaving-public-hies-dust/2011-07-08.

31. Greg Slabodkin,"HIE Among Hospitals Grows, Still Needs Improvement," *Health Data Management,* May 6, 2014, accessed at http://www.healthdatamanagement.com/news/HIE-Among-Hospitals-Needs-Improvement-47997-1.html.

32. The Office of the National Coordinator for Health Information Technology (ONC), "Dr. Ted Wymyslo Discusses How Health Information Exchange Supports Meaningful Use," accessed at http://www.healthit.gov/providers-professionals/dr-ted-wymyslo-discusses-how-health-information-exchange-supports-meaningful.

33. DirectTrust home page, http://www.directtrust.org.

34. HIMSS, "HIE and Meaningful Use Stage 2 Matrix," accessed at http://s3.amazonaws.com/rdcms-himss/files/production/public/HIMSSorg/Content/files/MU2_HIE_Matrix_FINAL.pdf.

35. American Academy of Family Physicians (AAFP), "FAQ on MACRA and Medicare Payment Reform," accessed at http://www.aafp.org/practice-management/payment/medicare-payment/faq.html.

36. Andy Slavitt and Karen DeSalvo, "EHR Incentive Programs: Where We Go Next," CMS Blog, Jan. 19, 2016, accessed at https://blog.cms.gov/2016/01/19/ehr-incentive-programs-where-we-go-next/.

37. iHealthBeat, "Concern Grows About Doctor Offices Opting Out of Meaningful Use," Dec. 23, 2013, accessed at `http://regional extensioncenter.blogspot.com/2014/01/meaningful-use-stage-2-now-fully.html`.

38. Mark Hagland, "Dr. Halamka's Dramatic MU Prediction in Boston," *Healthcare Informatics,* May 13, 2014, accessed at `http://www.healthcare-informatics.com/blogs/mark-hagland/dr-halamka-s-dramatic-mu-prediction-boston`.

# Chapter 6

1. Jacquelyn S. Hunt, Richard F. Gibson, John Whittington, Kitty Powell, Brad Wozney, and Susan Knudson, "Guide for Developing an Information Technology Investment Road Map for Population Health Management," *Population Health Management,* Vol. 18, No. 3, 2015.

2. Ibid.

3. Ken Terry, "Hospitals in Early Stage of Analytics Usage," *InformationWeek Healthcare,* Sept. 11, 2013, accessed at `http://www.informationweek.com/healthcare/clinical-information-systems/hospitals-in-early-stage-of-analytics-usage/d/d-id/1111502?.`

4. Terry, "Is Healthcare Big Data Ready for Prime Time?" *Information Week Healthcare,* Feb. 12, 2013, accessed at `http://www.informationweek.com/big-data/big-data-analytics/is-healthcare-big-data-ready-for-prime-time/d/d-id/1108628.`

5. IBM, "The Four V's of Big Data," `http://www.ibmbigdatahub.com/infographic/four-vs-big-data.`

6. Institute for Health Technology Transformation, "Population Health Management: A Roadmap for Provider-Based Automation in a New Era of Health Care," accessed at `http://ihealthtran.com/pdf/PHMReport.pdf.`

7. IMS Health, press release, "Patient Options Expand as Mobile Healthcare Apps Address Wellness and Chronic Disease Treatment Needs," Sept. 17, 2015, accessed at `http://www.businesswire.com/news/home/20150917005044/en/IMS-Health-Study-Patient-Options-Expand-Mobile#.VfrhjevxtNx.`

8. CMS, "Medicare and Medicaid Programs; Electronic Health Records Incentive Program — Stage 3 and Modifications to Meaningful Use in 2015 Through 2017," *Federal Register,* 80 FR 62761, Oct. 16, 2015, accessed at https://www.federalregister.gov/ articles/2015/10/16/2015-25595/medicare-and-medicaid-programs-electronic-health-record-incentive-program-stage-3-and-modifications.

9. Terry, "Remote patient monitoring: Fulfilling its promise," Medical Economics, Sept. 3, 2015, accessed at http://medicaleconomics. modernmedicine.com/medical-economics/news/remote-patient-monitoring-fulfilling-its-promise?page=0,0.

10. Colorado Beacon Consortium, "Predict, Prioritize, Prevent: Nine things practices should know about risk stratification and panel management," *Issue Brief,* Vol. 2, Issue 2, 2013, accessed at https:// www.rmhpcommunity.org/sites/default/files/resource/ Vol.%202%20Issue%202%20Predict,%20Prioritize,%20 Prevent.pdf.

11. Valerie A. Lewis, Asha Belle McClurg, Jeremy Smith, Elliott S. Fisher, and Julie P.W. Bynum, "Attributing Patients to Accountable Care Organizations: Performance Year Approach Aligns Stakeholders' Interests," *Health Affairs* (Millwood). 2013 March ; 32(3): 587–595.

12. John Morrissey, "Whose Patient Is This, Anyway?" Hospitals & Health Networks, March 10, 2015, accessed at http://www.hhnmag.com/ articles/3650-whose-patient-is-this-anyway.

13. S. Lawrence Kocot, Ross White, and Mark McClellan, "The Revised Medicare ACO Program: More Options. . .And More Work Ahead," Health Affairs Blog, June 16, 2015, accessed at http:// healthaffairs.org/blog/2015/06/16/the-revised-medicare-aco-program-more-options-and-more-work-ahead/.

14. Office of the National Coordinator for Health IT, "Patient Identification and Matching Final Report," Feb. 7, 2014, 8, accessed at http:// www.healthit.gov/sites/default/files/patient_ identification_matching_final_report.pdf.

15. Mike Millard, "IBM unveils new Watson-based analytics," *Healthcare IT News,* Oct. 25, 2011, accessed at http://www.healthcareitnews. com/news/ibm-unveils-new-watson-based-analytics-capabilities.

16. Adam Wright, Justine Pang, Joshua C. Feblowitz, Francine L. Maloney, Allison R. Wilcox, Karen Sax McLoughlin, Harley Ramelson, Louise Schneider, and David W. Bates, "Improving completeness of electronic problem lists through clinical decision support," *Journal of the American Medical Informatics Association* (2012). doi:10.1136/amiajnl-2011-000521.

17. Amanda Parsons, Colleen McCullough, Jason Wang, and Sarah Shih, "Validity of electronic health record-derived quality measurement for performance monitoring," *Journal of the American Medical Informatics Association* (2012). doi:10.1136/amiajnl-2011-000557.

18. Terry, "Natural Language Processing Takes Center Stage in EHRs," *InformationWeek Healthcare,* March 2, 2012, http://www.informationweek.com/healthcare/electronic-health-records/natural-language-processing-takes-center-stage-in-ehrs/d/d-id/1103163

19. JH Garvin, SL DuVall, BR South, BE Bray, D Bolton, J Heavirland, S Pickard, P Heidenreich, S Shen, C Weir, M Samore, and MK Goldstein, "Automated extraction of ejection fraction for quality measurement using regular expressions in Unstructured Information Management Architecture (UIMA) for heart failure," *Journal of the American Medical Informatics* (2012) Sep-Oct; 19(5):859–66. doi: 10.1136/amiajnl-2011-000535. Epub 2012 Mar 21.

20. Deloitte, "Health system analytics: The missing key to unlock value-based care," 2015, accessed at http://www2.deloitte.com/content/dam/Deloitte/us/Documents/life-sciences-health-care/us-dchs-provider-analytics-report.pdf.

21. "5 Ways Data Lakes Improve Healthcare Processes, Outcomes," *Health Data Management,* Sept. 21, 2015, accessed at http://www.healthdatamanagement.com/gallery/5-ways-data-lakes-improve-healthcare-processes-outcomes-51260-1.html?utm_medium=email&ET=healthdatamanagement:e5183565:3696614a:&utm_source=newsletter&utm_campaign=daily-sep%2021%202015&st=email.

22. Institute for Health Technology Transformation, "Analytics: The Nervous System of IT-Enabled Health Care," 2013, accessed at http://ihealthtran.com/pdf/iHT2analyticsreport.pdf?__hstc=57681909.7cf2a0ced0bf7ad78b32fc255efe31ef.1398355507700.1406819504247.1407377571536.4&__hssc=57681909.2.1407377571536&__hsfp=3901677858.

23. Ibid.

24. American Diabetes Association, "Statistics About Diabetes," http://
www.diabetes.org/diabetes-basics/statistics.

25. Anil Jain, MD, IBM Watson Health, personal communication.

26. The Dartmouth Atlas of Health Care, http://www.dartmouthatlas.
org.

27. "Analytics: The Nervous System of IT-Enabled Health Care."

28. Christopher Jones, *Geographical Information Systems and Computer Cartography.* New York: Routledge, 2013, xiii.

29. Penn Medicine, "Genetic Variation Determines Protein's Response to Anti-diabetic Drug," July 2, 2015, accessed at http://www.uphs.
upenn.edu/news/News_Releases/2015/07/lazar.

# Chapter 7

1. Marc L. Berk and Alan C. Monheit, "The Concentration of Health Care Expenditures, Revisited," *Health Affairs* 20, no. 2 (March/April 2001).

2. Agency for Healthcare Research and Quality, "The High Concentration of U.S. Health Care Expenditures," *Research in Action,* Issue 19, June 2006.

3. Ken Terry, "More Hospitals Buy Clinical Data Warehousing Apps," *InformationWeek Healthcare,* Jan. 21, 2014, http://www.
informationweek.com/healthcare/clinical-information-
systems/more-hospitals-buy-clinical-data-warehousing-
apps/d/d-id/1113500.

4. *iHealthBeat,* "Survey: Many Providers Use EHRs for Data Analytics Capabilities," May 27, 2015, http://www.healthleadersmedia.
com/technology/survey-many-providers-use-ehrs-data-
analytics-capabilities.

5. Centers for Medicare and Medicaid Services (CMS), "Accountable Care Organization 2015 Program Analysis Quality Performance," Jan. 9, 2015, accessed at https://www.cms.gov/medicare/medicare-fee-
for-service-payment/sharedsavingsprogram/downloads/
ry2015-narrative-specifications.pdf.

6. CMS, "Value-Based Payment Modifier," accessed at https://www.
cms.gov/medicare/medicare-fee-for-service-payment/
physicianfeedbackprogram/valuebasedpaymentmodifier.
html.

7. E. Ben-Chetri, C. Chen-Shuali, E. Zimran, G. Munter, and G. Nesher, "A Simplified Scoring Tool for Prediction of Readmission in Elderly Patients Hospitalized in Internal Medicine Departments," *Israeli Medical Association Journal,* 14, no. 12 (Dec. 2012): 752–6.

8. J. Donze, D. Aujesky, D. Williams, and J. L. Schnipper, "Potentially Avoidable 30-Day Hospital Readmissions in Medical Patients: Derivation and Validation of a Prediction Model," *JAMA Internal Medicine* 173, no. 8 (April 22, 2013): 632–8, doi:10.1001/jamainternmed.2013.3023.

9. Ken Terry, "Futuristic Clinical Decision Support Tool Catches On," *InformationWeek Healthcare,* Jan. 27, 2012, accessed at http://www. informationweek.com/healthcare/clinical-systems/ futuristic-clinical-decision-support-too/232500603.

10. J. Frank Wharam and Jonathan P. Weiner, "The Promise and Peril of Healthcare Forecasting," *American Journal of Managed Care* 18, no. 3 (2012):e82–e85, 2.

11. Centers for Disease Control and Prevention, "The Power to Prevent, the Call to Control: At a Glance 2009," accessed at http://www.cdc.gov/ nccdphp/publications/AAG/pdf/chronic.pdf.

12. James D. Reschovsky, Jack Hadley, and Ellyn R. Boukus, "Following the Money: Factors Associated with the Cost of Treating High-Cost Medicare Beneficiaries," *Health Services Research Journal* 46, no. 4 (Aug. 2011): 997–1021. Accessed at http://www.hschange.com/ CONTENT/1185/1185.pdf.

13. Ken Terry, "ACOs Need Claims Data for Analytics, Expert Says," *InformationWeek Healthcare,* Sept. 16, 2013, accessed at http:// www.informationweek.com/healthcare/electronic- medical-records/acos-need-claims-data-for-analytics- expe/240161353.

14. Colorado Beacon Consortium, *"Predict, Prioritize, Prevent: Nine Things Practices Should Know About Risk Stratification and Panel Management,"* Issue Brief, Vol. 2, Issue 2, accessed at https://www.rmhpcommunity.org/ sites/default/files/resource/Vol. 2 Issue 2 Predict, Prioritize, Prevent.pdf.

15. Ian Duncan, *Healthcare Risk Adjustment and Predictive Modeling* (Winstead, CT: ACTEX Publications, 2011).

16. Framingham Heart Study website, "Cardiovascular Disease (10 year risk)," http://www.framinghamheartstudy.org/risk- functions/cardiovascular-disease/.

17. Centers for Medicare and Medicaid Services, "Chronic Conditions Among Medicare Beneficiaries: 2012 Chartbook," accessed at https://www.cms.gov/research-statistics-data-and-systems/statistics-trends-and-reports/chronic-conditions/downloads/2012chartbook.pdf.

18. Colorado Beacon Consortium, Issue Brief, Vol. 2, Issue 2, p. 2.

19. Johns Hopkins University, "The Johns Hopkins ACG System: Performance Assessment," accessed at http://acg.jhsph.org/index.php?option=com_content&view=article&id=88&Itemid=116.

20. Personal communication with Ron Russell, Verisk.

21. Personal communication with Anil Jain, IBM Watson Health.

22. Colorado Beacon Consortium, Issue Brief, Vol. 2, Issue 2 . . .

23. Terry, "ACOs Need Claims Data for Analytics, Expert Says" . . .

24. HIMSS Analytics, "Clinical Analytics in the World of Meaningful Use" . . .

25. Institute for Health Technology Transformation, "Analytics: The Nervous System of IT-Enabled Healthcare," 2013, accessed at https://fshrmps.org/docs/iHT2analyticsreport.pdf.

26. Ian MacDowell, *Measuring Health: A Guide to Rating Scales and Questionnaires,* Third Edition (Oxford: Oxford University Press, 2006), accessed at http://www.a4ebm.org/sites/default/files/Measuring Health.pdf.

27. Institute of Medicine, "Capturing Social and Behavioral Domains and Measures in Electronic Health Records: Phase 2," Nov. 13, 2014, http://iom.nationalacademies.org/Reports/2014/EHRdomains2.aspx.

# Chapter 8

1. Beth Kutscher, "Hospitals, systems see operating margins shrink as expenses climb," *Modern Healthcare,* Aug. 13, 2014, http://www.modernhealthcare.com/article/20140813/NEWS/308139963.

2. Kutscher, "Not-for-profit hospital financial metrics improve, at least for now," *Modern Healthcare,* Sept. 11, 2015, http://www.modernhealthcare.com/article/20150911/NEWS/150919970.

3. Timothy Jost, "CBO Lowers Marketplace Enrollment Projections, Increases Medicaid Growth Projections," Health Affairs Blog,

Jan. 26, 2016 (updated), http://healthaffairs.org/blog/2016/01/26/cbo-lowers-marketplace-enrollment-projections-increases-medicaid-growth-projections/.

4. Kaiser Family Foundation, "Status of State Action on the Medicaid Expansion Decision," accessed at http://kff.org/health-reform/state-indicator/state-activity-around-expanding-medicaid-under-the-affordable-care-act.

5. Reed Abelson, "Health Insurance Deductibles Outpacing Wage Increases, Study Finds," *The New York Times,* Sept. 22, 2015, accessed at http://www.nytimes.com/2015/09/23/business/health-insurance-deductibles-outpacing-wage-increases-study-finds.html.

6. Lindsey Dunn, "Narrow Networks Put Hospitals on the Offensive," *Becker's Hospital Review,* Jan. 31, 2014, accessed at http://www.beckershospitalreview.com/healthcare-blog/narrow-networks-put-hospitals-on-the-offensive.html.

7. American Hospital Association (AHA), "Underpayment by Medicare and Medicaid Fact Sheet, 2015," accessed at http://www.aha.org/content/15/medicaremedicaidunderpmt.pdf.

8. AHA, "Uncompensated Hospital Care Cost Fact Sheet," January 2016, accessed at http://www.aha.org/content/15/uncompensatedcarefactsheet.pdf.

9. Leemore Dafny, "Hospital Industry Consolidation — Still More to Come?" *New England Journal of Medicine* 370 (2014): 198–199.

10. Jeffrey Young, "Health Insurance Mega-Mergers Attract Powerful Enemy," *Huffington Post,* Nov. 11, 2015, accessed at http://www.huffingtonpost.com/entry/health-insurance-mega-mergers-attract-powerful-enemy_5643a001e4b0603773477931.

11. William E. Encinosa and Jaeyong Bae, "Will Meaningful Use Electronic Medical Records Reduce Hospital Costs?" *American Journal of Managed Care* 19 (11) spec. no. 10 (Nov. 22, 2013): eS19–eSP25, accessed at http://www.ajmc.com/publications/issue/2013/2013-11-vol19-sp/Will-Meaningful-Use-Electronic-Medical-Records-Reduce-Hospital-Costs.

12. American Medical Association, letter to Department of Health and Human Services, Feb. 12, 2014, accessed at http://www.ama-assn.org/resources/doc/washington/icd-10-letter-to-cms-12feb2014.pdf.

13. Centers for Medicare and Medicaid Services, "Readmissions Reduction Program," accessed at http://www.cms.gov/Medicare/ Medicare-Fee-for-Service-Payment/AcuteInpatientPPS/ Readmissions-Reduction-Program.html.

14. Maureen McKinney, "Medicare Payments Cut for More Than 1,400 Hospitals Under Value-Based Purchasing Program," *Modern Healthcare,* Nov. 15, 2013, accessed at http://www.modernhealthcare.com/ article/20131115/NEWS/311159950.

15. CMS, "Value-Based Payment Modifier," accessed at https://www. cms.gov/medicare/medicare-fee-for-service-payment/ physicianfeedbackprogram/valuebasedpaymentmodifier. html.

16. American Academy of Family Physicians, "FAQ on MACRA and Medicare Payment Reform, accessed at http://www.aafp.org/ practice-management/payment/medicare-payment/faq.html.

17. Ken Terry, "Pay for Performance Doesn't Make Docs Jump and Shout," *CBS Money Watch,* March 11, 2009, accessed at http://www.cbsnews. com/news/pay-for-performance-doesnt-make-docs-jump- and-shout/.

18. NCQA slide presentation, "Sneak Preview: 2014 Patient-Centered Medical Home Recognition," March 10, 2014, accessed at https:// www.ncqa.org/Portals/0/Newsroom/2014/PCMH 2014 Press Preview FINAL Slides.pdf.

19. Stephen M. Shortell, Carrie H. Colla, Valerie A. Lewis, Elliott Fisher, Eric Kessell, Patricia Ramsay, "Accountable Care Organizations: The National Landscape," *Journal of Health Politics, Policy and Law,* Vol. 40, No. 4, August 2015.

20. American College of Physicians, "Detailed Summary — Medicare Shared Savings/Accountable Care Organization (ACO) Program," accessed at https://www.acponline.org/system/files/documents/ running_practice/delivery_and_payment_models/aco/aco_ detailed_sum.pdf.

21. CMS, "Bundled Payments for Care Improvement (BPCI) Initiative: General Information," accessed at http://innovation.cms.gov/ initiatives/bundled-payments.

22. Institute for Health Technology Transformation, "Episode Analytics: Essential Tools for New Healthcare Models," accessed at http://www. ihealthtran.com/episode_analytics.html.

23. Julia Adler-Milstein, "A Survey Analysis Suggests That Electronic Health Records Will Yield Revenue Gains for Some Practices and Losses for Many," *Health Affairs* 32, no. 3 (March 2013): 562–570, accessed at `http://content.healthaffairs.org/content/32/3/562.abstract`.

24. Robert H. Miller, Christopher West, Tiffany Martin Brown, Ida Sim, and Chris Ganchoff, "The Value of Electronic Health Records in Solo or Small Group Practices," *Health Affairs* 24, no. 5 (Sept. 2005): 1127–1137, accessed at `http://content.healthaffairs.org/content/24/5/1127.abstract`.

25. C. M. Cusack, A. D. Knudsen, J. L. Kronstadt, R. F. Singer, and A. L. Brown, "Practice-Based Population Health: Information Technology to Support Transformation to Proactive Primary Care," *Agency for Healthcare Research and Quality*, July 2010.

26. HIMSS press release, "HIMSS Introduces Health IT Value Suite to Realize the Value of Health IT," July 16, 2013, accessed at `http://www.himss.org/News/NewsDetail.aspx?ItemNumber=21536`.

27. Michael K. Magill, David Ehrenberger, Debra L. Scammon, Julie Day, Tatiana Allen, Andreu J. Reall, Rhonda W. Sides, and Jaewhan Kim, "The Cost of Sustaining a Patient-Centered Medical Home: Experience From 2 States," *The Annals of Family Medicine* 2015;13:429–435.

28. Mitesh S. Patel, Martin J. Arron, Thomas A. Sinsky, Eric H. Green, David W. Baker, Judith L. Bowen, and Susan Day, "Estimating the Staffing Infrastructure for a Patient-Centered Medical Home," *American Journal of Managed Care* 1, no. 19 (June 21, 2013): N6, accessed at `http://www.ajmc.com/journals/issue/2013/2013-1-vol19-n6/estimating-the-staffing-infrastructure-for-a-patient-centered-medical-home/`.

29. Patient-Centered Primary Care Collaborative (PCPCC), "The Patient-Centered Medical Home's Impact on Cost and Quality: Annual Review of Evidence 2014-2015," February 2016, accessed at `https://www.pcpcc.org/resource/patient-centered-medical-homes-impact-cost-and-quality-2014-2015`.

30. Ibid.

31. Department of Health and Human Services press release, "Medicare's Delivery System Reform Initiatives Achieve Significant Savings and Quality Improvements — Off to a Strong Start," Jan. 30, 2014, accessed at `http://www.hhs.gov/news/press/2014pres/01/20140130a.html`.

32. David Introcaso and Gregory Berger, "MSSP Year Two: Medicare ACOs Show Muted Success," Health Affairs Blog, Sept. 24, 2015, accessed at http://healthaffairs.org/blog/2015/09/24/mssp-year-two-medicare-acos-show-muted-success/.

33. Ashok Rai, Paul Prichard, Richard Hodach, and Ted Courtemanche, "Using Physician-Led Automated Communications to Improve Patient Health," *Population Health Management* 14, no. 4 (Aug. 2011): 175–180.

34. http://www.ibm.com/smarterplanet/us/en/ibmwatson/health/resources/bon-secours-virginia-medical-group

35. Ibid.

36. Robert Fortini, chief clinical officer, Bon Secours Virginia Medical Group, personal communication.

37. VHA press release, "VHA, TransforMED and Phytel Awarded $20.75 Million Health Care Innovation Challenge Grant," June 20, 2012, accessed at https://www.vha.com/AboutVHA/PressRoom/PressReleases/Pages/VHATransforMEDPhytelChallengegrant.aspx.

38. CMS Readmissions Reduction Program, fact sheet, accessed at http://www.cms.gov/Medicare/Medicare-Fee-for-Service-Payment/AcuteInpatientPPS/Readmissions-Reduction-Program.html.

39. CMS, HCAHPS fact sheet, accessed at http://www.hcahpsonline.org/files/HCAHPS Fact Sheet May 2012.pdf.

40. Jordan Rau, "Methodology: How Value Based Purchasing Payments Are Calculated," *Kaiser Health News,* Nov. 14, 2013, accessed at http://khn.org/news/value-based-purchasing-medicare-methodology.

41. http://www3.phytel.com/resources/case-studies/riverside-health-system

## Chapter 9

1. Karen Davis, Cathy Schoen, and Kristof Stremikis, "Mirror, Mirror on the Wall: How the Performance of the U.S. Health Care System Compares Internationally, 2010 Update," *The Commonwealth Fund,* June 23, 2010, accessed at http://www.commonwealthfund.org/Publications/Fund-Reports/2010/Jun/Mirror-Mirror-Update.aspx.

2. The Commonwealth Fund, Dartmouth Institute for Clinical Policy and Practice, and Patient Centered Primary Care Collaborative, "Better to Best: Value-Driving Elements of the Patient Centered Medical Home and Accountable Care Organizations," March 2011, 8, accessed at `http://www.pcpcc.org/sites/default/files/media/better_best_guide_full_2011.pdf`.

3. L. Casalino, R. R. Gillies, S. M. Shortell, J. A. Schmittdiel, T. Bodenheimer, J. C. Robinson, T. Rundall, N. Oswald, H. Schauffler, and M. C. Wang, "External Incentives, Information Technology, and Organized Processes to Improve Health Care Quality for Patients with Chronic Diseases," *Journal of the American Medical Association* 289, no. 4 (Jan. 22–29, 2003): 434–441.

4. Patient-Centered Primary Care Collaborative webinar, "Focusing Care Coordination," Mary Kay Owens.

5. Ann S. O'Malley and Peter J. Cunningham, "Patient Experiences with Coordination of Care: The Benefit of Continuity and Primary Care Physician as Referral Source," *Journal of General Internal Medicine* 24, no. 2 (2009): 170–177.

6. Emily Carrier, Tracy Yee, and Rachel A. Holzwart, "Coordination Between Emergency and Primary Care Physicians," NIHCR Research Brief No. 3, Feb. 2011, accessed at `http://www.nihcr.org/ED-Coordination.html`.

7. Hoangmai H. Pham, Joy M. Grossman, Genna R. Cohen, and Thomas Bodenheimer, "Hospitalists and Care Transitions: The Divorce of Inpatient and Outpatient Care," *Health Affairs* 27, no. 5 (Sept./Oct. 2008): 1315–1327.

8. Ann S. O'Malley and James D. Reschovsky, "Referral and Consultation Communication Between Primary Care Doctors and Specialist Physicians: Finding Common Ground," *Archives of Internal Medicine* 2011;171(1):56–65.

9. Michael Trisolini, Jyoti Aggarwal, Musetta Leung, Gregory Pope, and John Kautter, "The Medicare Physician Group Practice Demonstration: Lessons Learned on Improving Quality and Efficiency in Health Care," *The Commonwealth Fund*, February 2008, 40.

10. Richard J. Baron and Emily Desnouee, "The Struggle to Support Patients' Effort to Change Their Unhealthy Behavior," *Health Affairs* 29 (May 2010): 953–955.

11. O'Malley, "Tapping the Unmet Potential of Health Information Technology," *New England Journal of Medicine,* March 23, 2011.

12. Daniel Fields, Elizabeth Leshen, and Kevita Patel, "Driving Quality Gains and Cost Savings Through Adoption of Medical Homes," *Health Affairs* 29 (May 2010): 819–826.

13. O'Malley, "Tapping the Unmet Potential of Health Information Technology" . . .

14. AHRQ, "National Healthcare Disparities Report, 2013: Chapter 7. Care Coordination" accessed at http://www.ahrq.gov/research/findings/nhqrdr/nhdr13/chap7.html.

15. Ibid.

16. CMS fact sheet, Medicare Physician Group Practice Demonstration, December 2010, accessed at http://www.cms.gov/DemoProjectsEvalRpts/downloads/PGP_Fact_Sheet.pdf.

17. RTI International, Geisinger Clinic Physician Group Practice Demonstration: Final Site Report, July 2006.

18. National Committee on Quality Assurance (NCQA), "NCA Medical Homes Pass 10,000 Mark," news release, May 7, 2015, http://www.ncqa.org/newsroom/news-archive/2015-news-archive/news-release-may-7-2015.

19. Patient-Centered Primary Care Collaborative, "Core Value, Community Connections: Care Coordination in the Medical Home," accessed at http://www.pcpcc.org/sites/default/files/media/carecoordination_pcpcc.pdf.

20. Richard J. Baron and Emily Desnouee, "The Struggle to Support Patients' Effort to Change Their Unhealthy Behavior," *Health Affairs* 29 (May 2010): 953–955.

21. Ashok Rai, Paul Prichard, Richard Hodach, and Ted Courtemanche, "Using Physician-Led Automated Communications to Improve Patient Health," *Population Health Management* 14 (2011), accessed at http://info.phytel.com/rs/phytel/images/JournalPopulationHealth_UsingPhysician-LedAutomatedCommunications.pdf.

22. NCQA, "Standards and Guidelines for NCQA's Patient-Centered Medical Home (PCMH) 2014," accessed at http://www.acofp.org/acofpimis/Acofporg/Apps/2014_PCMH_Finals/Tools/1_PCMH_Recognition_2014_Front_Matter.pdf.

23. CMS, "CY 2015 Revisions to Payment Policies Under the Physician Fee Schedule," proposed rule, July 11, 2014, accessed at `https://www.federalregister.gov/articles/2014/07/11/2014-15948/medicare-program-revisions-to-payment-policies-under-the-physician-fee-schedule-clinical-laboratory`.

24. Robert Pear, "Medicare to Start Paying Doctors Who Coordinate Needs of Chronically Ill Patients," *The New York Times,* Aug. 16, 2014, accessed at `http://www.nytimes.com/2014/08/17/us/medicare-to-start-paying-doctors-who-coordinate-needs-of-chronically-ill-patients.html?_r=0`.

25. The Commonwealth Fund, Dartmouth Institute for Clinical Policy and Practice, and Patient-Centered Primary Care Collaborative, "Better to Best" . . . 20.

26. Ibid., 28.

27. Casalino, Gillies, Shortell, Schmittdiel, Bodenheimer, Robinson, Rundall, Oswald, Schauffler, and Wang, "External Incentives, Information Technology, and Organized Processes" . . .

28. Trisolini, Aggarwal, Leung, Pope, and Kautter, "The Medicare Physician Group Practice Demonstration" . . .

29. Phytel case studies, accessed at `http://resources.phytel.com/case-study`.

30. Ibid.

31. PCPCC, "Managing Populations, Maximizing Technology: Population Health Management in the Medical Neighborhood," October 2013, accessed at `https://www.pcpcc.org/resource/managing-populations-maximizing-technology`.

32. Office of the National Coordinator for Health Information Technology, "Tulsa Beacon Community," case study, accessed at `https://www.healthit.gov/sites/default/files/beacon-factsheet-tulsa.pdf`.

33. Donald M. Berwick, Thomas W. Nolan, and John Whittington, "The Triple Aim: Care, Health and Cost," *Health Affairs* 27 (May/June 2008), 759–769.

34. The Commonwealth Fund, Dartmouth Institute for Clinical Policy and Practice, and Patient Centered Primary Care Collaborative, "Better to Best" . . . 20–26.

## Chapter 10

1. Debora Goetz Goldberg, Tishra Beeson, Anton J. Kuzel, Linda E. Love, and Mary C. Carver, "Team-Based Care: A Critical Element of Primary Care Practice Transformation," *Population Health Management* 16 (2013): 150–156.

2. Richard J. Baron and Emily Desnouee, "The Struggle to Support Patients' Effort to Change Their Unhealthy Behavior," *Health Affairs* 29 (May 2010): 953–955.

3. Thomas Bodenheimer, Amireh Ghorob, Rachel Willard-Grace, and Kevin Grumbach, "The 10 Building Blocks of High-Performing Primary Care," *The Annals of Family Medicine* 12, no. 2 (March/April 2014): 166–171.

4. AAFP press release, "Six National Family Medicine Organizations Release 'Joint Principles: Integrating Behavioral Health Care Into the Patient-Centered Medical Home,'" March 11, 2014, accessed at http://www.aafp.org/media-center/releases-statements/all/2014/joint-principles-pcmh.html.

5. Mitesh S. Patel, Martin J. Aaron, Thomas A. Sinsky, Eric H. Green, David W. Baker, Judith L. Bowen, and Susan Day, "Estimating the Staffing Infrastructure for a Patient-Centered Medical Home," *American Journal of Managed Care* 19, no. 6 (2013): 509–516.

6. Anthem Blue Cross and Blue Shield of Colorado, press release, "More than One-Third of Colorado's Primary Care Providers Working Under New Payment and Care Coordination Arrangement with Anthem," March 12, 2014, accessed at http://www.businesswire.com/news/home/20140312006098/en/One-Third-Colorado's-Primary-Care-Providers-Working-Payment-.Uz8d5BbiQwi.

7. Ken Terry, "Physician Payment Reform: What It Could Mean to Doctors — Part 1: Accountable Care Organizations," *Medscape,* Aug. 10, 2010, accessed at http://www.medscape.com/viewarticle/726537.

8. Institute for Health Technology Transformation, "Lean Health IT: The Next Step for Clinical and Business Intelligence," accessed at http://ihealthtran.com/iHT2LeanHealthIT.pdf?submissionGuid= 082415b0-a22c-41fa-a683-c3fa0c0ee170.

9. Terry Young, Sally Brailsford, Con Connell, Ruth Davies, Paul Harper, and Jonathan H. Klein, "Using Industrial Processes to Improve Patient Care," *The BMJ,* 328 (2004): 162–4. Accessed at http://www.ncbi.nlm.nih.gov/pmc/articles/PMC314521/pdf/bmj32800162.pdf.

10. Steven J. Spear, "Fixing Health Care from the Inside, Today," *Harvard Business Review,* September 2005.

11. Paul A. Nutting, Benjamin F. Crabtree, William L. Miller, Kurt C. Stange, Elizabeth Stewart, and Carlos Jaén, "Transforming Physician Practices to Patient-Centered Medical Homes: Lessons From the National Demonstration Project," *Health Affairs* 30 (March 2011): 446.

12. Ibid.

13. Jerry Green and Amy Valentini, "A Guide to Lean Healthcare Workflows," *IBM Redbook,* August 2015, accessed at `http://www3.phytel.com/docs/default-source/resources/a-guide-to-lean-healthcare-workflows.pdf?sfvrsn=2`.

14. Institute for Health Technology Transformation, "Lean Health IT" . . .

15. Ibid.

16. Ken Terry, "Re-Engineer Your Practice — Starting Today," *Medical Economics,* Jan. 24, 2000, accessed at `http://medicaleconomics.modernmedicine.com/medical-economics/content/re-engineer-your-practice-starting-today`.

17. Institute for Health Technology Transformation, "Lean Health IT" . . .

18. Ibid.

19. Virginia Mason Institute website, "About" section, accessed at `https://www.virginiamasoninstitute.org/about/`.

20. Maryjoan D. Ladden, Thomas Bodenheimer, Nancy W. Fishman, Margaret Flinter, Clarissa Hsu, Michael Parchman, and Edward H. Wagner, "The Emerging Primary Care Workforce: Preliminary Observations from the Primary Care Team: Learning from Effective Ambulatory Practices Project," *Academic Medicine* 88, no. 12 (Dec. 2013): 1830–1834.

21. Christine A. Sinsky, Rachel Willard-Grace, Andrew M. Schutzbank, Thomas A. Sinsky, David Margolius, and Thomas Bodenheimer, "In Search of Joy in Practice: A Report of 23 High-Functioning Primary Care Practices," *Annals of Family Medicine* 1 (2013): 272–278.

22. Goldberg, Beeson, Kuzel, Love, and Carver, "Team-Based Care" . . .

23. Ibid.

24. Patient-Centered Primary Care Collaborative, "Managing Populations, Maximizing Technology: Population Health Management in the Medical Neighborhood," October 2013, accessed at `https://www.pcpcc.org/resource/managing-populations-maximizing-technology`.

25. Sinsky, Willard-Grace, Schutzbank, Sinsky, Margolius, and Thomas Bodenheimer, "In Search of Joy in Practice". . .

26. Ibid.

27. Institute for Health Technology Transformation, "Lean Health IT" . . .

28. Green and Valentini, "A Guide to Lean Healthcare Workflows". . .

29. Institute for Health Technology Transformation, "Lean Health IT" . . .

30. HIMSS press release, "HIMSS Introduces Health IT Value Suite to Realize the Value of Health IT," July 16, 2013, accessed at `http://www.himss.org/News/NewsDetail.aspx?ItemNumber=21536`.

31. `http://www.ibm.com/smarterplanet/us/en/ibmwatson/health/resources`.

32. Patient-Centered Primary Care Collaborative, "Managing Populations, Maximizing Technology: Population Health Management in the Medical Neighborhood" . . . .

33. Ashok Rai, Paul Prichard, Richard Hodach, and Ted Courtemanche, "Using Physician-Led Automated Communications to Improve Patient Health," *Journal of Population Health Management,* vol. 14, 2011, doi:10.1089/pop.2010.0033.

## Chapter 11

1. Anand K. Parekh, "Winning Their Trust," *New England Journal of Medicine* 364 (June 16, 2011): e51.

2. Thomas Pearson, "The Prevention of Cardiovascular Disease: Have We Really Made Progress?" *Health Affairs* 26, no. 1 (2007): 49–60.

3. Niteesh K. Choudhry, MD, PhD; Jerry Avorn, MD; Robert J. Glynn, ScD, PhD; Elliott M. Antman, MD; Sebastian Schneeweiss, MD, ScD; Michele Toscano, MS; Lonny Reisman, MD; Joaquim Fernandes, MS; Claire Spettell, PhD; Joy L. Lee, MS; Raisa Levin, MS; Troyen Brennan, MD, JD, MPH; and William H. Shrank, MD, "Full Coverage for Preventive Medications after Myocardial Infarction," *New England Journal of Medicine* (Nov. 14, 2011), doi:10.1056/NEJMsa1107913.

4. Lee Goldman, MD, and Arnold M. Epstein, MD, "Improving Adherence — Money Isn't the Only Thing," *New England Journal of Medicine* (Nov. 14, 2011), doi:10.1056/NEJMe1111558.

5. Ifrad Islam, "Trouble Ahead for High Deductible Health Plans?" Health Affairs Blog, Oct. 7, 2015, accessed at `http://healthaffairs.org/blog/2015/10/07/trouble-ahead-for-high-deductible-health-plans/`.

6. Pearson, "The Prevention of Cardiovascular Disease" . . .

7. David M. Lawrence, "How to Forge a High-Tech Marriage Between Primary Care and Population Health," *Health Affairs* 29, May 2010: 1004–1009.

8. Parekh, "Winning Their Trust" . . .

9. Annette M. O'Connor, John E. Wennberg, France Legare, Hilary A. Llewellyn-Thomas, Benjamin W. Moulton, Karen R. Sepucha, Andrea Sodano, and Jaime S. King, "Toward the 'Tipping Point': Decision Aids and Informed Patient Choice," *Health Affairs* 26, no. 3 (2007): 716–725.

10. Dorcas Mansell, MD, MPH; Roy M. Poses, MD; Lewis Kazis, ScD; and Corey A. Duefield, MPH, "Clinical Factors That Influence Patients' Desire for Participation in Decisions About Illness," *Archives of Internal Medicine* 160 (2000): 2991–2996.

11. American Academy of Family Physicians, American Academy of Pediatrics, American College of Physicians, and American Osteopathic Association, "Joint Principles of the Patient-Centered Medical Home," accessed at http://www.pcpcc.net/content/joint-principles-patient-centered-medical-home.

12. J. H. Hibbard, "Moving Toward a More Patient-Centered Health Care Delivery System," *Health Affairs,* October 2004, doi: 10.1377/hlthaff. var.133.

13. Ibid.

14. Center for Advancing Health, "A New Definition of Patient Engagement: What Is Patient Engagement and Why Is It Important?" (2010). Accessed at http://www.cfah.org/pdfs/CFAH_Engagement_Behavior_Framework_current.pdf.

15. Judith H. Hibbard, Eldon R. Mahoney, Ronald Stock, and Martin Tusler, "Do Increases in Patient Activation Result in Improved Self-Management Behaviors?" *Health Services Research* 42, no. 4 (August 2007): 1443–1463.

16. Ibid.

17. J. O. Prochaska, John Norcross, and Carlo DiClemente, *Changing for Good* (New York: HarperCollins, 1995, 2002).

18. Karen Glanz, Barbara K. Rimer, and K.J. Viswanath, *Health Behavior and Health Education,* 3rd Edition (San Francisco: Jossey-Bass Inc., 2002).

19. Ibid.

20. Martha Hostetter and Sarah Klein, "In Focus: Using Behavioral Economics to Advance Population Health and Improve the Quality of Health Care Services," Commonwealth Fund Quality Matters series, June/July 2013, accessed at http://www.commonwealthfund.org/publications/newsletters/quality-matters/2013/june-july/in-focus.

21. Peter J. Cunningham, Judith Hibbard, and Claire B. Gibbons, "Raising Low 'Patient Activation' Rates Among Hispanic Immigrants May Equal Expanded Coverage in Reducing Access Disparities," *Health Affairs* 30, no. 10 (2011): 1888–1894.

22. Institute of Medicine, *Health Literacy: A Prescription to End Confusion* (Washington, DC: National Academy Press, 2004).

23. Ian Duncan, *Healthcare Risk Adjustment and Predictive Modeling* (Winstead, CT: ACTEX Publications, 2011).

24. Ashok Rai, Paul Prichard, Richard Hodach, and Ted Courtemanche, "Using Physician-Led Automated Communications to Improve Patient Health," *Journal of Population Health Management,* vol. 14, 2011, doi:10.1089/pop.2010.0033.

25. Peter Boland, Phil Polakoff, and Ted Schwab, "Accountable Care Organizations Hold Promise, But Will They Achieve Cost and Quality Targets?" *Managed Care,* October 2010, accessed at http://www.managedcaremag.com/archives/1010/1010.ACOs.html.

26. Steven M. Schwartz, Brian Day, Kevin Wildenhaus, Anna Silberman, Chun Wang, and Jordan Silberman, "The Impact of an Online Disease Management Program on Medical Costs Among Health Plan Members," *American Journal of Health Promotion* 25, no. 2 (2010): 126–133.

27. Lindsay E. Sears, Sangeeta Agrawal, James A. Sidney, Patricia H. Castle, Elizabeth Y. Rula, Carter R. Coberley, Dan Witters, James E. Pope, and James K. Harter, "The Well-Being 5: Development and Validation of a Diagnostic Instrument to Improve Population Well-Being," *Population Health Management* 2014;17:357–365, accessed at http://www.ncbi.nlm.nih.gov/pmc/articles/PMC4273178/pdf/pop.2013.0119.pdf.

28. Hibbard, "Moving Toward a More Patient-Centered System" . . .

29. Susannah Fox and Maeve Duggan, "Health Online 2013," Pew Research Center, Jan. 15, 2013, accessed at http://www.pewinternet.org/files/old-media//Files/Reports/PIP_HealthOnline.pdf.

30. Emmi Solutions website, http://www.emmisolutions.com/resources/whitepapers-and-ebooks.

31. S. Greenfield, S. H. Kaplan, J. E. Ware Jr., E. M. Yano, and H. J. Frank, "Patients' Participation in Medical Care: Effects on Blood Sugar Control and Quality of Life in Diabetics," *Journal of General Internal Medicine* 3 (1988): 448–457.

32. C. M. Renders, G. D. Valk, S. J. Griffin, E. H. Wagner, J. T. Eijk Van, and W. J. Assendelft, "Interventions to Improve the Management of Diabetes in Primary Care, Outpatient, and Community Settings: A Systematic Review," *Diabetes Care* 24 (2001): 1821–1833.

33. Thomas Reinke, "Want to Change Patients' Behavior? Look to the Internet," *Managed Care,* July 2009, accessed at http://www.managedcaremag.com/archives/0907/0907.engagement.html.

34. HealthMedia website, http://www.healthmedia.com.

35. Ken Terry, "Monitor Patients Online?" *Medical Economics,* July 23, 2001, accessed at http://www.modernmedicine.com/modernmedicine/article/articleDetail.jsp?id=118617.

36. Pershing Yoakley & Associates, "Providing and Billing Medicare for Chronic Care Management: 2015 Medicare Physician Fee Schedule Final Rule," November 2014, accessed at http://www.hscrc.state.md.us/documents/md-maphs/wg-meet/cc/2015-01-23/2-Chronic-Care-Whitepaper-PYA.pdf.

37. E. A. Balas, S. Krishna, R. A. Kretschmer, T. R. Cheek, D. F. Lobach, and S. A. Boren, "Computerized Knowledge Management in Diabetes Care," *Medical Care* 42 (2004): 610–621.

38. M. C. Gibbons, R. F. Wilson, L. Samal, C. U. Lehmann, K. Dickersin, P. Lehmann, H. Aboumatar, J. Finkelstein, E. Shelton, R. Sharma, and E. B. Bass, *Impact of Consumer Health Informatics Applications, Evidence Report/Technology Assessment No. 188.* (Prepared by Johns Hopkins University Evidence-Based Practice Center under contract No. HHSA 290-2007-10061-I.) AHRQ Publication No. 09(10)-E019. Rockville, MD: Agency for Healthcare Research and Quality, October 2009.

39. Ken Terry, "VA Telehealth Lauded as Model Healthcare Program," *InformationWeek Healthcare,* Jan. 24, 2012, accessed at http://www.informationweek.com/mobile/va-telehealth-lauded-as-model-healthcare-program/d/d-id/1102433.

40. Jared Rhoads and Clive Flashman, "Teleservices for Better Health: Expanding the Horizon of Patient Engagement," CSC Global Institute

for Emerging Healthcare Practices, accessed at `http://assets1.csc.com/health_services/downloads/CSC_TeleServices_for_Better_Health_Expanding_the_Horizon_of_Patient_Engagement.pdf`.

41. Jonah Comstock, "Telemonitoring reduces readmissions 44 percent in 4-year, 500-patient study," *MobiHealthNews,* Oct. 3, 2014, `http://mobihealthnews.com/37076/telemonitoring-reduces-readmissions-44-percent-in-4-year-500-patient-study/`.

42. Monica Anderson, "The Demographics of Device Ownership," *Pew Research Internet Project,* Oct. 29, 2015, accessed at `http://www.pewinternet.org/2015/10/29/the-demographics-of-device-ownership/?beta=true&utm_expid=53098246-2.Lly4CFSVQG2lphsg-KopIg.1&utm_referrer=https%3A%2F%2Fwww.google.com%2F`.

43. Ken Terry, "Mobile Apps: Proposed FDA Rule Will Disrupt Industry," *InformationWeek,* July 21, 2011, accessed at `http://www.informationweek.com/news/healthcare/policy/231002336`.

44. Ken Terry, "Apple FaceTime May Be HIPAA Secure," *InformationWeek,* Oct. 21, 2011, accessed at `http://www.informationweek.com/news/healthcare/mobile-wireless/231900634`.

45. Charlene C. Quinn, Michelle D. Shardell, Michael L. Terrin, Erik A. Barr, Shoshana H. Ballew, and Ann L. Gruber-Baldini, "Cluster-Randomized Trial of a Mobile Phone Personalized Behavioral Intervention for Blood Glucose Control," *Diabetes Care* 34, no. 9 (Sept. 2011): 1934–1942.

46. Jae-Hyoung Cho, Hye-Chung Lee, Dong-Jun Lim, Hyuk-Sang Kwon, and Kun-Ho Yoon, "Mobile Communication Using a Mobile Phone with a Glucometer for Glucose Control in Type 2 Patients with Diabetes: As Effective as an Internet-based Glucose Monitoring System," *Journal of Telemedicine and Telecare* 15, no. 2 (March 2009): 77–82.

47. Anna-Lisa Silvestre, Valerie M. Sue, and Jill Y. Allen, "If You Build It, Will They Come? The Kaiser Permanente Model of Online Care," *Health Affairs* 28, no. 2 (2009): 334–344, doi:10.1377/hlthaff.28.2.334.

48. Paul C. Tang and David Lansky, "The Missing Link: Bridging the Provider-Patient Information Gap," *Health Affairs,* 24, no. 5 (2005): 1290–1295, doi:10.1377/hlthaff.24.5.1290.

49. David W. Bates and Asaf Bitton, "The Future of Health Information Technology in the Patient-Centered Medical Home," *Health Affairs* 29, no. 4 (2010): 614–621, doi:10.1377/hlthaff.2010.0007.

50. Don Detmer, Meryl Bloomrosen, Brian Raymond, and Paul Tang, "Integrated Personal Health Records: Transformative Tools for Consumer-Centric Care," *BMC Medical Informatics and Decision Making* 8 (2008): 45, doi:10.1186/1472-6947-8-45.

51. Brian S. McGowan, Molly Wasko, Bryan Steven Vartabedian, Robert S. Miller, Desirae D. Freiherr, and Maziar Abdolrasulnia, "Understanding the Factors That Influence the Adoption and Meaningful Use of Social Media by Physicians to Share Medical Information," *Journal of Medical Internet Research*, 14, no. 5 (2012): e117.

52. Pamela Lewis Dolan, "Nearly All Doctors Are Now on Social Media," *American Medical News*, Sept. 26, 2011, accessed at http://www.ama-assn.org/amednews/2011/09/26/bil20926.htm.

53. Ken Terry, "Doctors, Patients Not Using the Same Social Spaces," *InformationWeek*, Sept. 30, 2011, accessed at http://www.informationweek.com/news/healthcare/patient/231602459.

# Chapter 12

1. Stephen F. Jencks, Mark V. Williams, and Eric A. Coleman, "Rehospitalizations Among Patients in the Medicare Fee-for-Service Program," *New England Journal of Medicine* 360 (2009): 1418–1428.

2. "Julia James, Health Policy Brief: Medicare Hospital Readmissions Reduction Program," *Health Affairs*, Nov. 12, 2013, accessed at http://healthaffairs.org/healthpolicybriefs/brief_pdfs/healthpolicybrief_102.pdf.

3. Stephanie Reardon, "Preventable Readmissions Cost CMS $17 billion," RevCycle Intelligence, Jan. 13, 2015, accessed at http://revcycleintelligence.com/news/preventable-readmissions-cost-cms-17-billion.

4. Suni Kripalani, Amy T. Jackson, Jeffrey L. Schnipper, and Eric A. Coleman, "Promoting Effective Transitions of Care at Hospital Discharge," *Journal of Hospital Medicine* 2 (2007): 314–323.

5. Jencks, Williams, and Coleman, "Rehospitalizations Among Patients" . . .

6. CMS, "Readmissions Reduction Program," accessed at http://www.cms.gov/Medicare/Medicare-Fee-for-Service-Payment/AcuteInpatientPPS/Readmissions-Reduction-Program.html.

7. "Health Policy Brief: Medicare Hospital Readmissions Reduction Program" . . .

8. CMS Innovation Center, fact sheet, "New HHS Data Shows Major Strides Made in Patient Safety, Leading to Improved Care and Savings," May 7, 2014, accessed at https://innovation.cms.gov/Files/reports/patient-safety-results.pdf.

9. Ken Terry, "Patient Safety Front and Center," *Hospitals & Health Networks,* July 2011.

10. CMS, "Bundled Payments for Care Improvement Initiative Fact Sheet," Jan. 30, 2014, accessed at https://www.cms.gov/Newsroom/MediaReleaseDatabase/Fact-sheets/2014-Fact-sheets-items/2014-01-30-2.html.

11. Rich Daly and Jessica Zigmond, "CMS Issues Proposed ACO Regulation," *Modern Healthcare,* March 31, 2011.

12. Kripalani, Jackson, Schnipper, and Coleman, "Promoting Effective Transitions of Care" . . .

13. Ibid.

14. Susan Baird Kanaan, "Homeward Bound: Nine Patient-Centered Programs Cut Readmissions," California Healthcare Foundation report, September 2009.

15. Gail Neilsen and Peg Bradke, presentation at Institute for Healthcare Improvement conference, July 13, 2011.

16. Edwin D. Boudreaux, Sunday Clark, and Carlos A. Camargo, "Telephone Follow-up after the Emergency Department Visit: Experience with Acute Asthma," *Annals of Emergency Medicine,* June 2000;35:555-563.

17. Kripalani, Jackson, Schnipper, and Coleman, "Promoting Effective Transitions of Care" . . .

18. Ibid.

19. Kripalani S., LeFevre F., Phillips CO, Williams MV, Basaviah P, and Baker DW, "Deficits in Communication and Information Transfer Between Hospital-Based and Primary Care Physicians: Implications for Patient Safety and Continuity of Care," *Journal of the American Medical Association* 297, no. 8 (2007): 831–841.

20. Roy CL, Poon EG, Karson AS, Ladak-Merchant Z, Johnson RE, Maviglia SM, and Gandhi TK, "Patient Safety Concerns Arising from Test Results That Return after Hospital Discharge," *Annals of Internal Medicine* 143, no. 2 (2005): 121–128.

21. Kripalani, Jackson, Schnipper, and Coleman, "Promoting Effective Transitions of Care" . . .

22. Ibid.

23. Society of Hospital Medicine website, Project BOOST, accessed at `http://www.hospitalmedicine.org/AM/Template.cfm?Section=Home&TEMPLATE=/CM/HTMLDisplay.cfm&CONTENTID=27659`.

24. Physician Consortium for Performance Improvement, "Care Transitions Performance Measurement Set," June 2009.

25. Transitions of Care Consensus Policy Statement, American College of Physicians–Society of General Internal Medicine–Society of Hospital Medicine–American Geriatrics Society–American College of Emergency Physicians–Society of Academic Emergency Medicine, *Journal of General Internal Medicine* 24, no. 8 (Aug. 2009): 971–976.

26. Phytel presentation, "IHI and PCMH Perspectives."

27. Peg Bradke and Gail Nielsen, "Getting Started," presentation at Institute of Healthcare Improvement seminar, "Reducing Avoidable Readmissions by Improving Transitions of Care," July 13, 2011.

28. Kanaan, "Homeward Bound," op. cit.

29. Eric A. Coleman, Carla Parry, Sandra Chalmers, and Sung-Joon Min, "The Care Transitions Intervention: Results of a Randomized Controlled Trial," *Archives of Internal Medicine* 166, no. 17 (2006): 1822–1828.

30. Ibid.

31. Eric A. Coleman, Jodi D. Smith, Janet C. Frank, Sung-Joon Min, Carla Parry, and Andrew M. Kramer, "Preparing Patients and Caregivers to Participate in Care Delivered Across Settings: The Care Transitions Intervention," *Journal of the American Geriatric Society* 52 (2004): 1817–1825.

32. Paula Span, "Clearing the Path Home," New York Times, Aug. 11, 2014, accessed at `http://newoldage.blogs.nytimes.com/2014/08/11/clearing-the-path-home/?_r=2`.

33. Ibid.

34. Naylor MD, Brooten DA, Campbell RL, et al., "Advanced Practice Nurse Directed Transitional Care Reduced Readmission or Death in Elderly Patients Admitted to Hospital with Heart Failure," *Journal of the American Geriatric Society*, 2004; 52: 675–84.

35. Vicky Dudas, Thomas Bookwalter, Kathleen M. Keer, and Stephen Z. Pantilat, "The Impact of Follow-Up Telephone Calls to Patients after Hospitalization," *American Journal of Medicine*, 111, no. 9, supplement 2: 26–30.

36. *Journal of Emergency Medicine,* 6 (1988).

37. Nielsen and Bradke presentation, op. cit.

38. Kripalani, Jackson, Schnipper, and Coleman, "Promoting Effective Transitions of Care" . . .

39. Emmi website, http://www.emmisolutions.com.

40. Mari Edlin, "Digital Health Coaching Brings Care Management to Everyday Life," *Managed Healthcare Executive,* Jan. 1, 2011.

41. Office of the National Coordinator for Health Information Technology, "Improving Hospital Transitions and Care Coordination Using Automated Admission, Discharge and Transfer Alerts," May 2013, accessed at https://www.healthit.gov/sites/default/files/onc-beacon-lg1-adt-alerts-for-toc-and-care-coord.pdf.

42. Physician Consortium for Performance Improvement, "Care Transitions Performance Measurement Set" . . .

43. Kripalani, Jackson, Schnipper, and Coleman, "Promoting Effective Transitions of Care" . . .

44. Physician Consortium for Performance Improvement, "Care Transitions Performance Measurement Set" . . .

45. Kathleen Louden, "Creating a Better Discharge Summary: Is Standardization the Answer?" *American College of Physicians Hospitalist,* March 2009.

46. Janice Simmons, "Direct Project Gets Widespread Industry Support," Fierce EMR, March 24, 2011, accessed at http://www.fiercehealthcare.com/ehr/direct-project-gets-widespread-industry-support.

47. CMS, "Comments of CMS Acting Administrator Andy Slavitt at the J.P. Morgan Annual Health Care Conference, Jan. 11, 2016," the CMS Blog, Jan. 12, accessed at https://blog.cms.gov/2016/01/12/comments-of-cms-acting-administrator-andy-slavitt-at-the-j-p-morgan-annual-health-care-conference-jan-11-2016/.

48. Ken Terry, "Senate HELP Committee Launches Draft Health IT Bill," *Medscape Medical News,* Jan. 22, 2016, accessed at http://www.medscape.com/viewarticle/857635.

49. Terry, "True Interoperability Is Still Far Off," *iHealthBeat,* Jan. 6, 2016, accessed at http://www.medscape.com/viewarticle/857635.

50. Terry, "FHIR blazes new (and needed) path in healthcare," CIO.com, Feb. 23, 2016, accessed at `http://www.cio.com/article/3036753/health/fhir-blazes-new-and-needed-path-in-healthcare.html`.

## Chapter 13

1. Edward Blatt, Eloise O'Riordan, Ljubisav Matejevic, and Martin Duggan, "Addressing Social Determinants and Their Impact on Health Care," IBM Cúram Research Institute, February 2013, accessed at `http://public.dhe.ibm.com/common/ssi/ecm/zz/en/zzw03212usen/ZZW03212USEN.PDF`.

2. Michael L. Barnett, John Hsu, and J. Michael McWilliams, "Patient Characteristics and Differences in Hospital Admission Rates," *Journal of the American Medical Association: Internal Medicine,* published online Sept. 14, 2015. doi:10.1001/jamainternmed.2015.4660. Accessed at `http://archinte.jamanetwork.com/article.aspx?articleid=2434813`.

3. Institute for Alternative Futures, "Community Health Centers Leveraging the Social Determinants of Health" 2012, accessed at `http://www.altfutures.org/pubs/leveragingSDH/IAF-CHCsLeveragingSDH.pdf`.

4. Ibid.

5. Institute of Medicine, "Capturing Social and Behavioral Domains and Measures in Electronic Health Records: Phase 2," Nov. 13, 2014, `http://iom.nationalacademies.org/Reports/2014/EHRdomains2.aspx`.

6. Ibid.

7. Ronald Bayer and Sandro Galea, "Public Health in the Precision-Medicine Era," *New England Journal of Medicine,* 2015;373:499–501.

8. California Healthline, "Report: Demographic Disparities in California Greatly Affect Health," Aug. 28, 2015, accessed at `http://www.californiahealthline.org/articles/2015/8/28/report-demographic-disparities-in-calif-greatly-affect-health`.

9. Sara N. Bleich, Jessica Jones-Smith, Julia A. Wolfson, Xiazhou Zhu, and Mary Story, "The Complex Relationship Between Diet and Health," *Health Affairs,* 34, no. 11 (2015): 1813–1820.

10. Ibid.

11. Joel Goh, Jeffrey Pfeffer, and Stefanos Zenios, "Exposure to Harmful Workplace Practices Could Account for Inequality in Life Spans Across Different Demographic Groups," *Health Affairs,* 34, no. 10 (2015): 1761–1768.

12. Robert Wood Johnson Foundation, "Health Care's Blind Side: The Overlooked Connection Between Social Needs and Good Health," accessed at `http://www.rwjf.org/content/dam/farm/reports/surveys_and_polls/2011/rwjf71795`.

13. Commonwealth Fund Brief, "Models of Care for High-Need, High-Cost Patients: An Evidence Synthesis," posted online Oct. 29, 2015, at `http://www.commonwealthfund.org/publications/issue-briefs/2015/oct/care-high-need-high-cost-patients?omnicid=EALERT914438&mid=%25%25emailaddr%25%25`.

14. Laura McGovern, George Miller, and Paul Hughes-Cromwick, "Health Policy Brief: The Relative Contribution of Multiple Determinants to Health Outcomes," *Health Affairs,* Aug. 21, 2014, accessed at `http://www.healthaffairs.org/healthpolicybriefs/brief.php?brief_id=123`.

15. "Community Health Centers Leveraging the Social Determinants of Health: Case Studies," accessed at `http://www.altfutures.org/pubs/leveragingSDH/IAF-CHCsLeveragingSDH.pdf`.

16. Ibid.

17. Ibid.

18. Melinda K. Abrams and Eric C. Schneider, MD, "Fostering a High-Performance Health System That Services Our Nation's Sickest and Frailest," The Commonwealth Fund blog, Oct. 29, 2015, accessed at `http://www.commonwealthfund.org/publications/blog/2015/oct/fostering-a-high-performance-health-system-sickest-and-frailest?omnicid=EALERT914438&mid=%25%25emailaddr%25%25`.

19. David R. Williams, Manuela V. Costa, and Selina A. Mohammed, "Moving Upstream: How Interventions that Address the Social Determinants of Health Can Improve Health and Reduce Disparities," *Journal of Public Health Management and Practice,* Nov. 2008; 14(Suppl): S8-17.

20. Ibid.

21. Arvin Garg, Brian Jack, and Barry Zuckerman, "Addressing the Social Determinants of Health Within the Patient-Centered Medical Home:

Lessons from Pediatrics," *Journal of the American Medical Association,* April 25, 2013, E1-E2.

22. National Committee for Quality Assurance, "PCMH 2014 Standards and Guidelines," accessed at http://hccn.ccalac.org/Resources/ Documents/PCMH Recognition 2014_Standards and Guidelines.pdf.

23. New York State Department of Health, "Medicaid Health Homes," accessed at https://www.health.ny.gov/health_care/ medicaid/program/medicaid:health_homes/.

24. New York State Department of Health, "Delivery System Reform Incentive Payment (DSRIP) Program," accessed at http://www. health.ny.gov/health_care/medicaid/redesign/dsrip/.

25. Craig Jones, Karl Finison, Katharine McGraves-Lloyd, Timothy Tremblay, Mary Kate Mohlman, Beth Tanzman, Miki Hazard, Steven Maier, and Jenney Samuelson, "Vermont's Community-Oriented All-Payer Medical Home Model Reduces Expenditures and Utilization While Delivering High-Quality Care," *Population Health Management,* 2015. doi:10.1089/ pop.2015.0055. Accessed at http://online.liebertpub.com/doi/ pdfplus/10.1089/pop.2015.0055.

26. Montefiore seminar at HIMSS annual meeting, April 2015.

27. Atul Gawande, "The Hot Spotters," *The New Yorker,* Jan. 24, 2011, accessed at http://www.newyorker.com/magazine/2011/01/24/the- hot-spotters.

28. Sarah Klein and Martha Hostetter, "In Focus: Integrating Behavioral Health and Primary Care," Commonwealth Fund, Quality Matters Archive, Aug./Sept. 2014, accessed at http://www. commonwealthfund.org/publications/newsletters/quality- matters/2014/august-september/in-focus.

29. Ibid.

30. Patient-Centered Primary Care Collaborative (PCPCC), "Why Behavioral Health Needs to Be Integrated into the Patient-Centered Medical Home," presentation slides, https://www.pcpcc.org/resource/ behavioral-health-integration-pcmh.

31. Ibid.

32. Chris Collins, Denise Levis Hewson, Richard Munger, and Torlen Wade, "Evolving Models of Behavioral Health Integration in Primary Care," Millbank Memorial Fund, 2010, accessed at http://www.milbank.org/ uploads/documents/10430EvolvingCare/EvolvingCare.pdf.

33. "Why Behavioral Health Needs to Be Integrated into the Patient-Centered Medical Home."

34. "In Focus: Integrating Behavioral Health and Primary Care."

35. Ibid.

36. Ibid.

37. SAMHSA-HRSA Center for Integrated Health Systems, "Integrating Behavioral Health into Primary Care," accessed at `http://www.integration.samhsa.gov/integrated-care-models/behavioral-health-in-primary-care`.

38. AHRQ, "The Academy for Integrating Behavioral Health and Primary Care," website, `http://integrationacademy.ahrq.gov`.

39. NCQA, "New NCQA Patient-Centered Medical Home Standards Raise the Bar," press release, March 24, 2014, accessed at `http://www.ncqa.org/newsroom/news-archive/2014-news-archive/news-release-march-24-2014`.

40. "Why Behavioral Health Needs to Be Integrated into the Patient-Centered Medical Home."

41. Ibid.

42. "Evolving Models of Behavioral Health Integration in Primary Care."

43. Engel, G. "The Need for a New Medical Model: A Challenge for Biomedicine," *Science* 196 (4286):129–36. doi:10.1126/science.847460. Accessed at http://dx.doi.org/doi:10.1126/science.847460.

44. "Fostering a High-Performance Health System That Services Our Nation's Sickest and Frailest."

45. "Capturing Social and Behavioral Domains and Measures in Electronic Health Records: Phase 2."

46. Cúram Software Ltd. website, `http://www-01.ibm.com/software/info/curam`.

## Chapter 14

1. Donald M. Berwick, Thomas W. Nolan, and John Whittington, "The Triple Aim: Care, Health and Cost," *Health Affairs*, May/June 2008, 759-769.

2. F. and K. Verspoor, "Big Data in Medicine Is Driving Big Changes," *Yearbook of Medical Informatics*, 2014;9(1):14–20.

3. Martin S. Kohn, Jimeng Sun, Sarah Knoop, Amnon Shabo, Boaz Carmeli, and Daby Sow, IBM Research, "Health Analytics and the Transformation of Health Care," unpublished working paper.

4. John Markoff, "Computer Wins on 'Jeopardy!': Trivial, It's Not," *The New York Times,* Feb. 16, 2011, accessed at `http://www.nytimes.com/2011/02/17/science/17jeopardy-watson.html?pagewanted=all&_r=0`

5. Judith Hurwitz, Marcia Kaufman, and Adrian Bowles, *Cognitive Computing and Big Data Analytics,* Chapter 11: "Building a Cognitive Healthcare Application," 184. Indianapolis: John Wiley & Sons, Inc., 2015.

6. Leonard D'Avolio, "6 Questions to Guide Natural Language Processing Strategy," *InformationWeek,* Feb. 12, 2013, accessed at `http://www.informationweek.com/big-data/big-data-analytics/6-questions-to-guide-natural-language-processing-strategy/d/d-id/1108629`.

7. Ibid.

8. Michael Weiner, IBM Watson, personal communication.

9. Eduardo Blanco and Dan Moldovan, "Some Issues on Detecting Negation from Text," Proceedings of the 24th International Florida Artificial Intelligence Research Society Conference, accessed at `https://www.google.com/url?sa=t&rct=j&q=&esrc=s&source=web&cd=1&ved=0CCMQFjAAahUKEwjK78yZ7s7IAhVJ2GMKHb5vAyg&url=https%3A%2F%2Fwww.aaai.org%2Focs%2Findex.php%2FFLAIRS%2FFLAIRS11%2Fpaper%2Fdownload%2F2629%2F3031&usg=AFQjCNH87t7WKBvZnCs-78aOT4F75s_ZlQ&sig2=t6yZYnOWRz80akyIEGKnfw`.

10. Susan Feldman and Judy Hanover, "Unlocking the Power of Unstructured Data," IDC Health Insights white paper, June 2012, accessed at `http://public.dhe.ibm.com/software/data/sw-library/ecm-programs/IDC_UnlockingThePower.pdf`.

11. Ibid.

12. IBM press release, "Doctors' Notes Turn into EMR Insights with Natural Language Processing Software," Feb. 19, 2014, accessed at `http://www-03.ibm.com/press/us/en/pressrelease/43232.wss`.

13. Weiner and IBM press release, "IBM Predictive Analytics to Detect Patients at Risk for Heart Failure," Feb. 19, 2014, accessed at `http://www-03.ibm.com/press/us/en/pressrelease/43231.wss`

14. "Building a Cognitive Healthcare Application," 193 . . .

15. "Health Analytics and the Transformation of Health Care" . . .

16. Bruce Upbin, "IBM Watson Hits Daily Double Fighting Cancer with Memorial Sloan Kettering," *Forbes,* March 22, 2012, accessed at `http://www.forbes.com/sites/bruceupbin/2012/03/22/ibm-watson-hits-daily-double-fighting-cancer-with-memorial-sloan-kettering.`

17. MD Anderson Cancer Center press release, "MD Anderson Taps IBM Watson to Power 'Moon Shots' Mission," Oct. 18, 2013, accessed at `http://www.mdanderson.org/newsroom/news-releases/2013/ibm-watson-to-power-moon-shots-.html.`

18. Ken Terry, "IBM's Watson Hits Medical School," *InformationWeek Healthcare,* Nov. 2, 2012, accessed at `http://www.informationweek.com/healthcare/clinical-information-systems/ibms-watson-hits-medical-school/d/d-id/1107199.`

19. Terry, "Big data makes a difference at Penn Medicine," Oct. 8, 2015, CIO.com, accessed at `http://www.cio.com/article/2990428/healthcare/big-data-makes-a-difference-at-penn-medicine.html.`

20. Kathy McGroddy, IBM Watson, personal communication.

21. "Health Analytics and the Transformation of Health Care," and Weiner, personal communication . . .

22. "Health Analytics and the Transformation of Health Care" . . .

23. "Building a Cognitive Healthcare Application," 177 . . .

24. "Health Analytics and the Transformation of Health Care" . . .

25. Terry, "Remote patient monitoring: fulfilling its promise," *Medical Economics,* Sept. 3, 2015, accessed at `http://medicaleconomics.modernmedicine.com/medical-economics/news/remote-patient-monitoring-fulfilling-its-promise.`

26. Ibid.

27. Ibid.

28. Edward Blatt, Eloise O'Riordan, Ljubisav Matejevic, and Martin Duggan, IBM Cúram Research Institute, "Addressing Social Determinants and Their Impact on Health Care," February 2013, accessed at `https://www.google.com/url?sa=t&rct=j&q=&esrc=s&source=web&cd=1&ved=0CB4QFjAAahUKEwjNmML4gs_IAhVP8GMKHSxrC8w&url=https%3A%2F%2Fwww.longwoods.com%2Farticles%2Fimages%2FSocialHealth_IBM.pdf&usg=AFQjCNGjb4ID69_p2-c4aoT3dH1ZCwax5Q&sig2=TbT_BGRwSVWm1sBWyV1j8A.`

29. Ibid.

30. Greg Goth, "GIS, Boots on Ground Prove Powerful Healthcare Combination," Health Data Management, July 21, 2015, accessed at `http://www.healthdatamanagement.com/news/GIS-Boots-on-Ground-Prove-Powerful-Healthcare-Combination-50918-1.html?portal=community-health`.

31. "Building a Cognitive Healthcare Application," 187–188 . . .

32. McGroddy, personal communication.

33. IBM press release, "IBM Watson Health Cloud Capabilities Expand," Sept. 10, 2015, accessed at `https://www-03.ibm.com/press/us/en/pressrelease/47624.wss`.

34. Terry, "EHR Interoperability With Long-Term Care Providers Wanted, but Who Will Pay?" *iHealthBeat,* July 30, 2015, accessed at `http://www.ihealthbeat.org/insight/2015/ehr-interoperability-with-longterm-care-providers-wanted-but-who-will-pay`.

35. Jane E. Brody, "The Road to Cancer Treatment Through Clinical Trials," *The New York Times,* March 23, 2015, accessed at `http://well.blogs.nytimes.com/2015/03/23/the-road-to-cancer-treatment-through-clinical-trials`.

36. "Building a Cognitive Healthcare Application," 179 . . .

Made in the USA
Middletown, DE
23 May 2017